SANDSTONE

Climbing in South East England

Written and Photographed by
DAVID ATCHISON-JONES

There are no mountains unfortunately in the South East of England. The North Downs chalk ridge that forms the white cliffs of Dover, is linked with the South Downs ridge that gives the magnificent cliffs at Beachy Head. This band of chalk formed a basin where sand built up, which in turn eventually solidified to produce the sandstone rock in this central Weald area. Sandstone is a quite a variable rock, especially in terms of granularity, texture, hardness, and consequently shape. In the south east, the granularity is medium, unlike the coarse gritstone of the peak district or a brand new climbing wall hold. This means it offers only a mid level of friction, which in many ways is perfect for the soft skin of your hands. However, this much lower level of friction for the feet, requires a much higher level of footwork skill than you would need at a normal indoor climbing wall - expect a tough initiation.

The compression of the sandstone is also only moderate, which means that singular grains of sand can easily be broken off. A kick with the edge of a hard sole, will simply break grains of sand from the surface. However, a soft step with a precisely placed climbing shoe - will leave all of the surface grains intact. Invariably, there will always be grains of loose sand on the surface of the rock, either knocked off by a previous climber, or washed down by the rain etc. These grains of sand act as ball bearings on the surface of the rock. If the grains are few, they will be squeezed into the rubber of a climbing sole and it will grip well. If there are many, then the whole sole will simply rest on them - and simply slide when your weight is applied. As they slide, your foot slips (aagh!) and they grind into other grains embedded in the surface, breaking them off too. Not only do you slip off, but you actually grind through the surface of the rock causing erosion. Blowing off the loose grains does work, but they rebound and sting your eyes. The old hands at climbing on this type of rock will carry a loose rag in a pocket, simply to delicately swish off loose sand before using a hold - no wonder 'their feet stick so well' and they climb so damn well. (**Even a toothbrush will wear away the softer parts of the rock.**)

Medium granularity in sandstone does not often allow a good chemical reaction to take place during compression, and hence there are virtually no solid quartz sheets formed in the rock - the plus side is that it's impossible to polish. (At Fontainebleau, the fine grainularity polishes the underlying solid quartz.) Consequently, any proud face holds will always be brittle and liable to snap off. Additionally, the rock is much weaker when wet, so using anything other than big flat holds in damp conditions is simply going to destroy the rock superfast. Weathering on the surface of the sandstone produces a hard crust (but still very soft). If this is broken you will see very light soft rock underneath - avoid these holds please. (They will usually be treated with resin paint to harden up quickly - see www.jingowobbly.com/climbing/sandstone for more info on erosion and what you can do to help). The softness of the rock is such that top roping or bouldering is the norm on all of the outcrops in this book. Erosion is a big factor with this fragile rock - see page 6. With many thousands of visitors each year, climbers are simply asked to minimise erosion wherever possible. Lowering off a climb is felt unnecessary erosion, so you are asked to walk down. Abseiling can be accommodated at high ropes courses and outdoor walls in the SE, so this also would cause unnecessary erosion.

Using this guidebook should be straightforward. Each outcrop is marked with tabs down the side of the book, and begins with a general intro, maps, approach and layout details. All outcrops go from left to right into areas (bottom tab bars with sub sectors). Each sector is given access/erosion consideration details - with arrows to indicate the easiest way to set up the belay. Each page is laid out as a little competition, with the routes numbered in order of difficulty. Stars for climbs are simply personal preference, and additional (font grades in colour) will help subdivide the more broad based UK trad grades. The jingo and wobbly symbols illustrate particularly hard moves, and the reach hand will be a useful warning to the shorter climber. The inside back cover has a full index of symbols that appear in the book. Dates and names for first solo ascents (Solo) and top rope ascents (TR) are given where known. Tick boxes are included for you to keep a personal record of routes done.

HARRISON'S ROCKS*** 👟 9-20 min 🚼12m

This is the major outcrop in the area and is popular for all levels of climbers.
West facing, protected from north winds, cold in a.m. sunny in p.m.
Quite good for bouldering, but a lot stays damp - needs a dry period.
Big crag - make sure to meet at a particular area-sector. Ok-ish for picnics.

UK 2a-4c	87	font 2a-3c
UK 5a-5b	74	font 4a-4c
UK 5c-6a	157	font 5a-5c+
UK 6b	82	font 6a-6c+
UK 6c-7a	12	font 7a-8c

HARRISON'S ROCKS

BOWLES ROCKS*** 👟 1-5 min 🚼12m

Very popular crag, easy routes can be very busy.
South facing and a real sun trap. Cold east winds tend to howl through.
Very nice for bouldering at every level, lots of good traverses.
A very easy area to meet up with friends. Superb for picnics.

UK 2a-4c	57	font 2a-3c
UK 5a-5b	32	font 4a-4c
UK 5c-6a	40	font 5a-5c+
UK 6b	45	font 6a-6c+
UK 6c-7a	11	font 7a-8c

BOWLES ROCKS

HIGH ROCKS*** 👟 1-5 min 🚼13m

Big crag with the best routes in the hard grades - hefty entrance fee.
Some sunny areas, but a lot is north west facing, chilly until late on.
A top quality bouldering area for top quality boulderers.
Very picturesque to laze around in the sun and enjoy.

UK 2a-4c	44	font 2a-3c
UK 5a-5b	57	font 4a-4c
UK 5c-6a	104	font 5a-5c+
UK 6b	91	font 6a-6c+
UK 6c-7a	63	font 7a-8c

HIGH ROCKS

HIGH ROCKS ANNEXE* 👟 2-3 min 🚼8m

Small outcrop of nice rock, very quiet and out of the way.
South facing but enshrouded by Yew tree canopy, stays very shady.
Some bouldering but bad ground slip - best to avoid.
Naff for picnics but nice setting.

UK 2a-4c	21	font 2a-3c
UK 5a-5b	16	font 4a-4c
UK 5c-6a	10	font 5a-5c+
UK 6b	4	font 6a-6c+
UK 6c-7a	3	font 7a-8c

HIGH ROCKS ANNEXE

HAPPY VALLEY* 👟 2 min 🚼7m

Some small bouldering and top roping, soft rock, generally fun.
West facing boulders, top roping on a shady pinnacle
West facing bouldering in the easier grades.
Nice place to visit for an evening session.

UK 2a-4c	24	font 2a-3c
UK 5a-5b	5	font 4a-4c
UK 5c-6a	10	font 5a-5c+
UK 6b	3	font 6a-6c+
UK 6c-7a	0	font 7a-8c

HAPPY VALLEY

BULLS HOLLOW* 👟 2-4 min 🚼12m

Dingy old sandstone quarry, very quiet with it's fair share of insects.
North East facing, some morning sun, needs a good dry spell.
Neaby Toad Rock gives over 100 boulder problems on sandy rock.
Quarry is turgid, but Toad Rock is superb for picnics - busy with folk.

UK 2a-4c	26	font 2a-3c
UK 5a-5b	13	font 4a-4c
UK 5c-6a	25	font 5a-5c+
UK 6b	3	font 6a-6c+
UK 6c-7a	1	font 7a-8c

BULLS HOLLOW

ERIDGE GREEN ROCKS** 👟 1-10 min 🚼12m

A long twisting and rambling outcrop, quiet and away from it all.
East facing - sunny in the early morning, lovely shade in afternoon.
A good selection of hard bouldering - soft sandy rock breaking up.
Nice for picnic. Perfect on sunny days with wind, suffers from biting insects.

UK 2a-4c	30	font 2a-3c
UK 5a-5b	34	font 4a-4c
UK 5c-6a	69	font 5a-5c+
UK 6b	37	font 6a-6c+
UK 6c-7a	15	font 7a-8c

ERIDGE GREEN

UNDER ROCKS* 👟 10 min 🚼9m

A very quiet and out of the way place, limited routes and quality.
South facing but in the trees and very shady, best in spring.
No worthwhile bouldering, some sectors very sandy.
Very quiet for picnic, awkward walk in.

UK 2a-4c	7	font 2a-3c
UK 5a-5b	6	font 4a-4c
UK 5c-6a	23	font 5a-5c+
UK 6b	6	font 6a-6c+
UK 6c-7a	0	font 7a-8c

UNDER ROCKS

STONE FARM ROCKS*** 👟 2-5 min 🚼7m

A series of buttress high on a ridge, nice views and relaxed atmosphere.
South facing and catches the wind, dries quickly.
Popular for bouldering in all grades.
Superb for picnics with lovely views.

UK 2a-4c	44	font 2a-3c
UK 5a-5b	27	font 4a-4c
UK 5c-6a	35	font 5a-5c+
UK 6b	15	font 6a-6c+
UK 6c-7a	5	font 7a-8c

STONE FARM

👟 Walk in time; 1st-last sector   🚼 Child friendly & approx height ⬍

This is not an instruction book of how to be safe whilst climbing - see opposite the Jingo Wobbly - Learning to Climb on Indoor Walls - this covers both indoor and outdoor climbing techniques. These tips should help those new to the style of climbing found on this soft sandstone.

BOULDERING:

Your feet will not grip to anything if they are covered in sand or anything on the sole. Ideally clean your shoes before stepping onto a clean carpet at the base of a problem. A piece of DPM (damp proof membrane) underneath stops moisture soaking through. Position your crash pad a bit further out - which is therefore easy and comfortable to land on. Loose sand is the boulderers enemy, but so is soft rock. A big loose rag is ideal for swishing off the surface loose sand (and cleaning your shoes). In many parts - brushing even with a soft brush will erode the rock, always think and inspect first. (Note: See **www.jingowobbly.com** for up to date erosion notes, resins & chemicals to harden the rock)

TOP ROPING:

Make sure that you ask other local climbers what are the best local techniques for climbing and setting up a belay. Generally, the rock is very soft and will be cut through by a moving rope. All belay ropes and slings must therefore be static and not stretch. However, even knots tighten up - which means the belay will move a small amount. Your knot will grind into the rock and destroy the sheath of the rope - protect both your rope and the rock with a piece of small carpet. Having a small piece of DPM underneath (secured by prussik tie when needed), allows the belay knot to move over the rock without wear. Always make sure the belay karabiner/s are free hanging where possible. If this is some way down the climb, then place an additional quickdraw to clip as you lead the top part of the climb. Always therefore use a dynamic rope for climbing.

My essential standard equipment for a day climbing:

Carpet with DPM under, cotton pof & beer towel.
Dynamic 30 metre climbing rope. (Same rope as I use to lead on an indoor climbing wall.)
4 non stretch slings 1.2m - or combination for 5m.
3 screwgate krabs, 1 quickdraw.
10m short static rope &15m long static rope (belays).
Knot and edge protector.
Crash Pad & picnic, (Harrison's - a big umbrella for those heavy showers, there aren't many big overhangs).

JINGO WOBBLY ▲ LEARNING SERIES

CLIMBING DYNO-MITE
LEARNING to CLIMB on INDOOR WALLS

Plus development skills for outdoor Bouldering and Sport Climbing.

Bouldering technique

Alpine safety

Indoor Wall skills

Sport power and endurance

DAVID ATCHISON-JONES

CLIMBING DYNOMITE

If you are new to any sort of climbing or bouldering, this is the perfect book to accelerate your learning progress. All the tips and tricks for sandstone and granite bouldering are explained.

This book shows you all of the different techniques for both indoor and outdoor bouldering. All examples are illustrated by some of the greatest names in bouldering.

You will instantly improve by reading and understanding all the tips and tricks.

All the ropework that you need for holiday sport climbing is covered in detail, from starting out - up to multi pitch techniques. All essential when visiting the European super climbing spots.

BOREAL

www.jingowobbly.com

BEAL

HARRISON'S ROCKS

BOWLES ROCKS

HIGH ROCKS

HIGH ROCKS ANNEXE

HAPPY VALLEY

BULLS HOLLOW

ERIDGE GREEN

UNDER ROCKS

STONE FARM

Harrison's Rocks is the largest outcrop in the South East, and certainly is the most popular due to the extensive range of routes in the mid grades. It's mostly vertical with rounded holds, making even the easiest climbs pretty mean and tough. It keeps morning shade for most of the crag, and is often chilly till after lunch on all but the southern most sections. If you are approaching for the first time, I would advise you to approach via the low track, then keep on the lower footpath at the base of the woods until you reach an area that you want to climb, then strike up on one of the small trails direct to your chosen sector. The path that runs along the foot of the rock is very up and down, and often is busy with people belaying etc. There is only a limited amount of bouldering at Harrison's, even so it is worth bringing a bouldering mat if you want to boulder. There are not really any big overhangs - so if it looks like a big downpour may happen - take a brolly or cag. The high track through the woods is quickest to reach the far end, but confusing if you don't know where the descent gullies are. There are some lovely picnic spots above the rocks which get a good amount of sunshine, and are usually quiet. There are many insitu belay bolts on top, but you will often need to use trees for top rope belay points, so bringing a length of static rope in addition to 4 long slings is worthwhile. The rocks usually remain damp and green in the winter months.

Location: Harrison's Rocks **SAT NAV info**
P1 - Parking Grid reference: **TQ 534 364**
P1 - Postcode **TN3 9NJ**
Rocks (Niblick) Grid reference: **TQ 532 355**

Please use the main car park for Harrison's Rocks at P1 - Bring £1 coins for small parking donation. From Groombridge at the roundabout on the B2110, go SSE along Station Road - soon passing village shops on your right. Pass The Junction pub on your right, and go over the railway bridge. In 200 metres, fork R at a blind turn. In 80 metres turn right on a small road that leads down to a large parking area with toilets in the centre. Various paths lead to the outcrop. The mid forest track is drier underfoot - best after a rainy period. By Train-Eridge: Go along Forge Road to a level crossing at Forge Farm, then use low path.

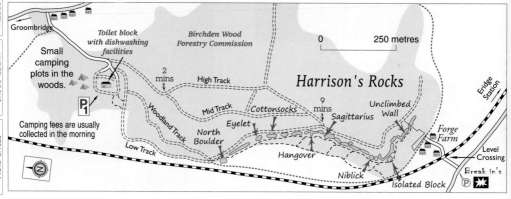

| North Boulder | Eyelet | Dinosauros | Bow Window | Pig Tail Slab | Sewer | Vice | Isolated Boulder | Crucifix |
| Teddy Bear | Cottonsocks | Hangover | Sagittarius | Circle | Niblick | Sunshine | Spider Wall | Unclimbed Wall |

HARRISON'S ROCKS

BOWLES ROCKS

HIGH ROCKS

HIGH ROCKS ANNEXE

HAPPY VALLEY

BULLS HOLLOW

ERIDGE GREEN

UNDER ROCKS

STONE FARM

1b
- [ ] Boxing Day Cracker (f 2a) p67
- [ ] Fingernail Crack (f 2a) p28
- [ ] Isometric Chimney (f 2a) p102
- [ ] Snake's Crawl (f 2a) p49

2a
- [ ] Cracking Up (f 2a) p72
- [ ] Easy Cleft Left (f 2a) p98
- [ ] Scout Chimneys (f 2a) p93
- [ ] Junend Arete (f 3a) p47
- [ ] Way Down (2a) p40
- [ ] Dark Chimney (f 2a) p38
- [ ] Tame Corner (f 2a) p68
- [ ] Giant's Staircase (f 2a) p40
- [ ] Big Cave Left (f 2a) p87
- [ ] Passage Chimney (f 2a) p62
- [ ] Don (f 2a) p20

2b
- [ ] Little Cave (f 2a) p49
- [ ] Arrow Crack (f 2a) p40
- [ ] Tame Variant (f 2b) p68
- [ ] OK Coral (f 2b) p14
- [ ] Big Cave Right (f 2b) p87
- [ ] Boulder Bridge Route (f 2b) p84
- [ ] Noisome Cleft No.l (f 2a) p60
- [ ] Flotsam (f 2b) p67
- [ ] Small Chimney (f 2b) p53
- [ ] Open Chimney (f 2b) p24
- [ ] The Fonz (2b) p47

3a
- [ ] Windowside Spout (f 3a) p38
- [ ] Charon's Chimney (f 3a) p98
- [ ] Awkward Cleft Right (f 3a) p98
- [ ] Longbow Chimney (f 2b) p40
- [ ] Back Passage (f 2a) p93
- [ ] Sinner's Wall (f 2a) p49
- [ ] Tight Chimney (f 2b) p20
- [ ] Horizontal Birch (f 2a) p46
- [ ] A Small bit of Black (f 2a) p26
- [ ] Beech Corner (f 2a) p33

3b
- [ ] Dave (f 2b) p20
- [ ] Noisome Cleft No.2 (f 2b) p60
- [ ] Happy Days (f 3a) p47
- [ ] Smooth Chimney (f 2c) p79
- [ ] Kukri Wall (f 3a) p19
- [ ] Pickled Pogo Stick (f 2b) p72
- [ ] Wellington's Chimney (f 3a) p65
- [ ] Jetsam (f 3a) p67
- [ ] The Green Cleft (f 3b) p60

3c
- [ ] Snout Crack (f 3a) p33
- [ ] Birch Tree Crack (f 3a) p97

4a
- [ ] Pig Tail Slab (3a) p47
- [ ] Left Edge (f 3a) p47
- [ ] Bow Window (f 3a) p38
- [ ] Cottonsocks Traverse (f 3a) p24
- [ ] Corridor Route (f 3a) p72

- [ ] Right Hand Crack (f 3a) p26
- [ ] Steph (f 3a) p27
- [ ] Root Route 1 (f 3b) p24
- [ ] Trees are Green (f 3a) p18
- [ ] Crack and Cave (f 3a) p90
- [ ] Sashcord Crack (f 3a) p40
- [ ] Trigger (f 3a) p14
- [ ] Fallen Block Mantle (f 3a) p48
- [ ] Right Circle (f 3a) p50
- [ ] Ejector (f 3a) p23

4b
- [ ] Rum and Ribena (f 3b) p92
- [ ] Thingy (f 3b) p90
- [ ] Moonlight Arête (f 3b) p59
- [ ] Flying Scotsman (3b) p49
- [ ] The Sandpipe (f 3b) p56
- [ ] Birch Tree Wall (f 3c) p97
- [ ] Breakknife Buttress (f 3b) p19
- [ ] The Vice (f 3b) p71
- [ ] Eyelet (f 3b) p20
- [ ] Downfall (f 3b) p46
- [ ] Gilbert's Gamble (f 3b) p23
- [ ] Toeing the Line (f 3b) p68
- [ ] Long Crack (f 3b) p44
- [ ] Sabre Crack (f 3b) p66
- [ ] Saint Gotthard (f 3b) p55
- [ ] Tight Chimney Slab (f 3b) p23
- [ ] Awkward Crack (f 3b) p34

4c
- [ ] Big Crack (f 3c) p40
- [ ] Starlight (f 3c) p59
- [ ] The Sewer (f 3c) p56
- [ ] Kukri Wall Direct (f 3c) p19
- [ ] Deadwood Crack (f 3c) p68
- [ ] Coffin Corner (f 3c) p53
- [ ] Sunshine Crack (f 3c) p76
- [ ] Slab Direct (f 3c) p34
- [ ] Isolated Buttress Climb (f 3c) p82
- [ ] Greasy Crack (f 3c) p47
- [ ] Wanderfall (f 3c) p97
- [ ] Hell Wall (f 4a) p98

5a
- [ ] Root Route I.5 (f 4a) p24
- [ ] Penknife (f 4a) p19
- [ ] Grant's Crack (f 4a) p90
- [ ] Little Cousin (f 4a) p92
- [ ] Two Toed Sloth (f 4a) p79
- [ ] Fallen Block Wall (f 4a) p48
- [ ] Pelmet (f 4a) p38
- [ ] Long Layback (f 4a) p37
- [ ] Groovy Graeme (f 4a) p14
- [ ] Giant's Ear (f 4a) p47
- [ ] Dark Chimney Buttress (f 4a) p38
- [ ] Senarra (f 4a) p98
- [ ] Garden Slab Right (f 4a) p93
- [ ] Wander at Leisure (f 4a) p97
- [ ] Garden Slab Left (f 4a) p93
- [ ] Weeping Slab (f 4a) p27
- [ ] Sun Ray (f 4a) p102

- [ ] Zig Zag (f 4a) p103
- [ ] Signalbox Arete (f 4a) p49
- [ ] Sagittarius (f 4a) p43

5b
- [ ] Big Toe Wall (5b) p47
- [ ] Half Crown Corner (f 4b) p94
- [ ] Rhapsody-Satsuma (f 4b) p72
- [ ] Ringlet (f 4b) p20
- [ ] Right Under-Nose (f 4b) p87
- [ ] Unclimbed Wall (f 4b) p101
- [ ] Caroline (f 4b) p66
- [ ] Fallen Block Elim (f 4b) p48
- [ ] Forester's Wall (f 4b) p62
- [ ] Pipe Cleaner (f 4b) p56
- [ ] Baldrick's Boulderdash (f 4b) p87
- [ ] Jagger (f 4b) p86
- [ ] Casement Wall (f 4b) p38
- [ ] Slab Crack (f 4b) p34
- [ ] Very Sinfull (f 4b) p49
- [ ] Goats Head Soup (f 4b) p53
- [ ] Sinners Slimebag (f 4b) p50
- [ ] Boulder Route (f 4b) p86
- [ ] Whatsaname (f 4b) p90
- [ ] Thingamywobs (f 4b) p90
- [ ] Rum and Coke (f 4b) p92
- [ ] Cunning Stunts (f 4b) p92
- [ ] Cabbage Patch Blues (f 4b) p92
- [ ] Tiptoe thru the Tulips (f 4b) p93
- [ ] Big Cave Wall (f 4b) p89
- [ ] Letterbox (f 4b) p14
- [ ] Birchden Wall (f 4c) p82
- [ ] Stupid Effort (f 4b) p44
- [ ] Saint's Wall (f 4b) p50
- [ ] Rough Boy (f 4c) p87
- [ ] Birch Nose (f 4c) p72
- [ ] Don Juander (f 4c) p97
- [ ] Niblick (f 4c) p65
- [ ] Knight's Gambit (f 4c) p74
- [ ] Belts and Braces (f 4c) p67
- [ ] Long Stretch (f 4c) p53
- [ ] Small Wall (f 4c) p53
- [ ] Flower Power Jules (f 4c) p66
- [ ] Far Left (f 4c) p101
- [ ] Squank (f 4c) p61
- [ ] Tubesnake Boogie (f 4c) p61
- [ ] Noisome Wall (f 4c) p60
- [ ] Usurper (f 4c) p18
- [ ] Set Square Arête (f 4c) p74
- [ ] Ragtime (f 4c) p14
- [ ] Singlet (f 4c) p20
- [ ] Stranger than Friction (f 4c) p27
- [ ] Jungle Juice (f 4c) p24
- [ ] Dinosaurus (f 4c) p29
- [ ] Sliding Corner (f 4c) p28
- [ ] Snout (f 4c) p30
- [ ] Quarterdome (f 4c) p40
- [ ] The Stag (f 4c) p71
- [ ] Cucumber Madness (f 4c) p27

HARRISON'S ROCKS

BOWLES ROCKS

HIGH ROCKS

HIGH ROCKS ANNEXE

HAPPY VALLEY

BULLS HOLLOW

ERIDGE GREEN

UNDER ROCKS

STONE FARM

5c

- ☐ Sunset Wall (f 5a) p14
- ☐ Spout Crossing (f 5a) p38
- ☐ Elementary (f 5a) p101
- ☐ Quiver (f 5a) p43
- ☐ Edward's Wall (f 5a) p82
- ☐ Finger Stain (f 5a) p40
- ☐ West Wall (f 5a) p81
- ☐ Birchden Corner (f 5a) p82
- ☐ Spider Wall (f 5a) p89
- ☐ Wildcat Wall (f 5a) p68
- ☐ Shodan (f 5a) p94
- ☐ Carrera (f 5a) p24
- ☐ Ear-ring (f 5a) p86
- ☐ Spout Buttress (f 5a) p38
- ☐ Bulging Wall (f 5a) p102
- ☐ The Corner (f 5a) p94
- ☐ The Clamp (f 5a) p72
- ☐ Bow Window L-H (f 5a) p38
- ☐ Solstice (f 5a) p102
- ☐ Ziggy (f 5a) p14
- ☐ Araldite Wall (f 5a) p93
- ☐ Bonanza (f 5a) p62
- ☐ Smear Campaign (f 5a) p27
- ☐ Ten Foot Pole (f 5a) p61
- ☐ Blue Peter (f 5a) p33
- ☐ El Loco (f 5a) p61
- ☐ Crowborough Corner (f 5a) p84
- ☐ Pete's Reach (f 5a) p66
- ☐ Tomcat (f 5a) p30
- ☐ Bootless Buzzard (f 5a) p67
- ☐ Lady Jane (f 5a) p66
- ☐ El Loco (f 5b) p61
- ☐ Elastic (f 5b) p20
- ☐ Victoria (f 5b) p72
- ☐ Serendipity (f 5b) p26
- ☐ Reverse Traverse (f 5b) p79
- ☐ Soft Cock (f 5b) p67
- ☐ Biceps Buttress (f 5b) p93
- ☐ The Scoop (f 5b) p98
- ☐ L.H.T. (f 5b) p93
- ☐ Slimfinger Crack (f 5b) p44
- ☐ Soft Rock'er (f 5b) p79
- ☐ Bovver Boot (f 5b) p92
- ☐ Knight's Move (f 5b) p74
- ☐ Hitchcock's Horror (5b) p66
- ☐ Good Friday (f 5b) p53
- ☐ Bloody Sunday (f 5b) p50
- ☐ Plumb Line (f 5b) p86
- ☐ Bad Finger (f 5b) p86
- ☐ Dynamo (f 5b) p18
- ☐ Mighty Midge (f 5b) p49
- ☐ Original Route (f 5b) p14
- ☐ Central Groove (f 5b) p18
- ☐ Sullivan's Stake (f 5b) p23
- ☐ Little Sagittarius (f 5b) p43
- ☐ Vulture Crack (f 5b) p46
- ☐ Diversion (f 5b) p82
- ☐ Toxophilite (f 5b) p43

- ☐ Piecemeal Wall (f 5b) p79
- ☐ Sewer Wall (f 5b) p56
- ☐ Smiliodan (f 5b) p29
- ☐ Green Fingers (f 5b) p80
- ☐ North West Corner (f 5b) p81
- ☐ Mantlepiece (f 5b) p33
- ☐ Blackeye Wall (f 5b) p26
- ☐ Pince Nez Arete (5b) p65
- ☐ Slanting Crack (f 5b) p26
- ☐ Rotton Stump Wall (f 5b) p28
- ☐ Directors (f 5b) p47
- ☐ Archer's Wall (f 5b) p43
- ☐ Baskerville (f 5b) p101
- ☐ My Dear Watson (f 5b) p101
- ☐ Sticky Wicket (f 5b) p28
- ☐ Toad (f 5b) p20
- ☐ Witches Broomstick (f 5b) p103
- ☐ Venison Burger (f 5b) p71
- ☐ Rift (f 5b) p103

6a

- ☐ Mr. Splodge (f 5c) p97
- ☐ Smiliodan Direct (f 5c) p29
- ☐ Patient Parmar (f 5c) p20
- ☐ Yosemite Big W Climb (f 5c) p40
- ☐ Pan (f 5c) p82
- ☐ Last Chance (f 5c) p89
- ☐ Bow Window Dir (f 5c) p38
- ☐ Archer's Wall Direct (f 5c) p43
- ☐ Counterfeit (f 5c) p26
- ☐ Pullover (f 5c) p98
- ☐ Wailing Wall (f 5c) p84
- ☐ Marcus's Arete (f 5c) p46
- ☐ Left Circle (f 5c) p53
- ☐ Boysen's Arête (f 5c) p84
- ☐ Orangutang (f 5c) p56
- ☐ The Wallow (f 5c) p87
- ☐ Forget-me-Knot (f 5c) p89
- ☐ Edward's Effort (f 5c) p82
- ☐ Sand Piper (f 5c) p23
- ☐ Minnie the Minx (f 5c) p101
- ☐ Dinosaurus Direct (f 5c) p29
- ☐ Grist (f 5c) p43
- ☐ Toevice (f 5c) p71
- ☐ Celestial's Reach (f 5c) p34
- ☐ Indian Summer (f 5c) p62
- ☐ Roger the Dodger (f 5c) p101
- ☐ The Sting (f 5c) p46
- ☐ Awkward Crack (f 5c) p28
- ☐ Silver Star (f 6a) p14
- ☐ Luncheon Shelf (f 6a) p37
- ☐ Dodgepot (f 6a) p97
- ☐ Trip Psyco Tortoise (f 6a) p24
- ☐ Grasshopper (f 6a) p23
- ☐ Arachnophobia (f 6a) p89
- ☐ Handvice (f 6a) p71
- ☐ Blackeye Wall Direct (f 6a) p26
- ☐ Frank's Arete (f 6a) p82
- ☐ Forester's Wall Direct (f 6a) p62
- ☐ Second Chance (f 6a) p89

- ☐ The Flakes (f 6a) p37
- ☐ South West Corner (f 6a) p81
- ☐ Muscle Crack (f 6a) p94
- ☐ Root Route 2 (f 6a) p24
- ☐ Gall Stone (f 6a) p84
- ☐ Right Unclimbed (f 6a) p101
- ☐ Panther's Wall (f 6a) p30
- ☐ Madness (f 6a) p33
- ☐ Fat and Middle-Aged (f 6a) p74
- ☐ Short Hangover (f 6a) p34
- ☐ Desperate Dan (f 6a) p101
- ☐ Gardeners Q Time (f 6a) p40
- ☐ Coronation Crack (f 6a) p37
- ☐ Grant's Wall (f 6a) p90
- ☐ Photina (f 6a) p18
- ☐ Grant's Groove (f 6a) p90
- ☐ The Knam (f 6a) p76
- ☐ New Hat (f 6a) p18
- ☐ Rotton Thump Arête (f 6a) p28
- ☐ Guy's Problem (f 6a) p33
- ☐ Incisor (f 6a) p27
- ☐ Fang (f 6a) p27
- ☐ Wisdom (f 6a) p27
- ☐ Deep Thought (f 6a) p20
- ☐ Inimitability (f 6a) p33
- ☐ Bloody Fingers (f 6a) p80
- ☐ Long Hangover (f 6a) p34
- ☐ The Mank (f 6a) p76
- ☐ Skid Marx (f 6a) p98
- ☐ The Bishop & the Actress (f 6a) p49
- ☐ Battle of the Bulge (f 6a) p86
- ☐ Plagiarism (f 6a) p60
- ☐ Noisome Wall Direct (f 6a) p60
- ☐ The Sod (f 6a) p61
- ☐ Sharp Dressed Man (f 6a) p61
- ☐ Bostic (f 6a) p60
- ☐ Meat Cleaver (f 6a) p103
- ☐ Max (f 6a) p103
- ☐ In Limbo (f 6a) p50
- ☐ Stardust (f 6a) p34
- ☐ Healey Peeleys (f 6a) p53

6b

- ☐ Shytte (f 6a+) p23
- ☐ Mister Spaceman (f 6a+) p84
- ☐ Brookslight (f 6a+) p59
- ☐ Woodside Blossom (f 6a+) p68
- ☐ Neutral (f 6a+) p103
- ☐ Philippa (f 6a+) p94
- ☐ Crucifix (f 6a+) p94
- ☐ Demons of Death (f 6a+) p98
- ☐ Rowan Tree Wall (f 6a+) p55
- ☐ Flakes Direct (f 6a+) p37
- ☐ Hangover (f 6a+) p37
- ☐ Sossblitz (f 6a+) p62
- ☐ Bioplastic (f 6a+) p20
- ☐ Neighbours (f 6a+) p40
- ☐ Fowler's Wall (f 6a+) p62
- ☐ Jingo Wobbly (f 6a+) p101
- ☐ Pascale (f 6a+) p55

☐ The Nuts (f 6a+) p55
☐ Monkey's Bow (f 6a+) p59
☐ Powder Finger (f 6a+) p80
☐ Cannibals (f 6a+) p56
☐ Purple Nasty (f 6a+) p92
☐ Special Invitation (f 6a+) p18
☐ Torque Wrench (f 6b) p14
☐ Glendale Crack (f 6b) p50
☐ Wailing Wall Elim (f 6b) p84
☐ Papillon (f 6b) p14
☐ Skin Job (f 6b) p74
☐ Crusing D.J. (f 6b) p37
☐ Psycho (f 6b) p56
☐ The Republic (f 6b) p65
☐ Eric (f 6b) p79
☐ Reach for the Sky (f 6b) p74
☐ Piano (f 6b) p14
☐ Karen's Kondom (f 6b) p79
☐ Bloody Staircase (f 6b) p80
☐ Red River (f 6b) p14
☐ The Sheriff (f 6b) p14
☐ Full on Fling (f 6b) p14
☐ Black Widdowson (f 6b) p89
☐ Storming Cuvier Rempart (f 6b) p81
☐ Goats do Roam (f 6b) p54
☐ Krypton Factor (f 6b) p80
☐ Nut Tree (f 6b) p38
☐ Teddy Bear's Picnic (f 6b) p18

☐ Sandbag (f 6b) p76
☐ Violent Sprat (f 6b) p18
☐ Reve (f 6b) p14
☐ Gretta (f 6b) p50
☐ Supernatural (f 6b) p37
☐ Uncertainty (f 6b) p28
☐ Finger Popper (f 6b) p94
☐ Alligator Snatch (f 6b) p14
☐ Backbreaker (f 6b+) p14
☐ Tiptoe through Lichen (f 6b+) p90
☐ That Man's an Animal (f 6b+) p43
☐ Twiglet (f 6b+) p20
☐ Alexander Beetle (f 6b+) p82
☐ Force of Destiny (f 6b+) p37
☐ Kicks (f 6b+) p65
☐ The Bolts (f 6b+) p55
☐ Hector's House (f 6b+) p94
☐ What the Butler Saw (f 6b+) p62
☐ Stubble (f 6b+) p103
☐ Woolly Cub (f 6b+) p81
☐ Pincnib (f 6b+) p65
☐ Wellington's Boot (f 6b+) p65
☐ Jumping Jack Flash (f 6c) p46
☐ Hard Condom (f 6c) p79
☐ Magic Wall (f 6c) p94
☐ Bulging Bloddy Bonanza (f 6c) p62
☐ Woolly Jumper-dyno (f 6c) p81
☐ Powder Monkey (f 6c) p56

☐ Dr. Pepper (f 6c) p79
☐ Primate Shot (f 6c) p59
☐ Oliver James (f 6c) p59
☐ Lager Shandy (f 6c) p34
☐ Woolly Bear (f 6c) p81
☐ Blue Murder (f 6c) p33
☐ The Powerband (f 6c+) p103
☐ Strong Struggle (f 6c+) p14
☐ The Limpet (f 6c+) p37

6c
☐ Soft Rock (f 7a) p26
☐ Finger Flow (f 7a) p14
☐ Woolly Hat (f 7a) p81
☐ What Crisis (f 7a) p44
☐ In Crisis (f 7a+) p44
☐ Dennis the Menace (f 7a+) p101
☐ Flying Griffin (f 7a+) p 46
☐ A Killing Joke (f 7b) p50
☐ Tempestivity (f 7b) p60
☐ Lager Frenzy (f 7b) p34
☐ Banana Republic (f 7b) p65

7a
☐ Supply and Demand (f 7b+) p50

HARRISON'S ROCKS
BOWLES ROCKS
HIGH ROCKS
HIGH ROCKS ANNEXE
HAPPY VALLEY
BULLS HOLLOW
ERIDGE GREEN
UNDER ROCKS
STONE FARM

[UK 5c] ORIGINAL ROUTE-NORTH BOULDER (font 5b), James Emerson ▽

HARRISON'S ROCKS
BOWLES ROCKS
HIGH ROCKS
HIGH ROCKS ANNEXE
HAPPY VALLEY
BULLS HOLLOW
ERIDGE GREEN
UNDER ROCKS
STONE FARM

UK Trad   Fontainebleau colour (font grade)   Ticked

2b ① **OK Coral**✶ (f 2b)   S TR
A direct easy way up the groove.

4a ② **Trigger** (f 3a)   S TR
Top mantle is the only difficulty (morpho).

5a ③ **Groovy Graeme**✶ (f 4a)   S TR
Direct finish is fun.

5b ④ **Letterbox**✶ (f 4b)   S TR
A good hold on top.

5b ⑤ **Ragtime**✶ (f 4c)   S TR
Top mantle might thwart wall climbers.

5c ⑥ **Sunset Wall**✶ (f 5a)   S TR
A bit tricky. (Rock to the right is very sandy now.)

5c ⑦ **Ziggy**✶ (f 5a)   S TR
Tricky arête, climbed on the R + mantle.

5c ⑧ **Original Route**✶✶ (f 5b)   S TR
A powerful groove, but no finger strength needed.

6a ⑨ **Silver Star** (f 6a)   S TR
Top mantle is difficult - dodgy hold!

6b ⑩ **Torque Wrench**✶✶ (f 6b)   S TR
Steeper than it looks, wearing away - will be (f 6b) soon.

6b ⑪ **Papillon**✶ (f 6b)   S TR
Drifiting right at the top - possibly (f 6a+).

6b ⑫ **Piano**✶ (f 6b)   S TR
The short wall.

6b ⑬ **Red River**✶ (f 6b)   S TR
Pockets then crimps.

6b ⑭ **The Sheriff**✶✶ (f 6b)   S TR
Direct up the blunt nose.

UK Trad   Fontainebleau colour (font grade)   Ticked

6b ⑮ **Full on Fling**✶ (f 6b)   S TR
Right-hand finish, could be well-ard.

6b ⑯ **Reve**✶ (f 6b)   S TR
Direct finish to Papillon.

6b ⑰ **Alligator Snatch**✶ (f 6b)   S TR
Arête climbed on L, dynamic.

6b ⑱ **Back Breaker**✶ (f 6b+)   S TR
Holds wearing away.

6b ⑲ **Strong Struggle**✶✶ (f 6c+)   S TR
Edges and dynamic.

6c ⑳ **Finger Flow**✶ (f 7a)   S TR
Technical and powerful.

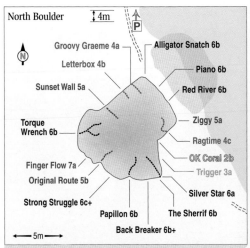

North Boulder   4m

Groovy Graeme 4a   Alligator Snatch 6b
Letterbox 4b
Sunset Wall 5a   Piano 6b
   Red River 6b
Torque
Wrench 6b   Ziggy 5a
   Ragtime 4c
Finger Flow 7a   OK Coral 2b
Original Route 5b   Trigger 3a
Strong Struggle 6c+   Silver Star 6a
Papillon 6b   The Sherrif 6b
Back Breaker 6b+

← 5m →

Access & Erosion: The rock here is wearing out - see www.jingowobbly.com for tips on chemical hardening.

Crag layout map - page 8
Graded tick list - page 10

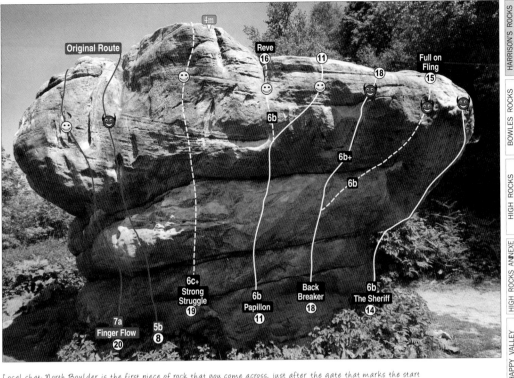

Original Route

Reve
16

11

Full on Fling
15

18

4m

6b

6b+

6b

6c+
Strong Struggle
19

6b
Papillon
11

Back Breaker
18

6b
The Sheriff
14

7a
Finger Flow
20

5b
8

HARRISON'S ROCKS

BOWLES ROCKS

HIGH ROCKS

HIGH ROCKS ANNEXE

HAPPY VALLEY

BULLS HOLLOW

ERIDGE GREEN

UNDER ROCKS

STONE FARM

Local chat: North Boulder is the first piece of rock that you come across, just after the gate that marks the start of the BMC owned area of Harrison's Rocks. You can pass it either by going through the gap, or around the sunny southern side. This type of free standing boulder is very rare in South East England since the geology of the sandstone is much more prone to leaving edges. The compactness of the sandstone is low, and as such wears away very easily. North Boulder has suffered from intense use over the past 100 years and shows it. The problems are very good, but change grade with use – so don't expect these grades to remain – even for a few months.

Access & Erosion: Please do not attempt to climb anywhere on this block in trainers, normal shoes or boots. Clean your feet well first, and step off a clean piece of carpet. Definitely use a bouldering mat to protect the ground from repeated falling off. Most descend via a jump across the back of the boulder.

6a
Silver Star
9

3a
Trigger
2

2b
OK Coral
1

4c
Ragtime
5

5a
Ziggy
7

6b
Red River
13

6b
Piano
12

6b
Alligator Snatch
17

North Boulder   Eyelet   Dinosauros   Bow Window   Pig Tail Slab   Sewer   Vice   Isolated Boulder   Crucifix
Teddy Bear   Cottonsocks   Hangover   Sagittarius   Circle   Niblick   Sunshine   Spider Wall   Unclimbed Wall

HARRISON'S ROCKS

BOWLES ROCKS

HIGH ROCKS

HIGH ROCKS ANNEXE

HAPPY VALLEY

BULLS HOLLOW

ERIDGE GREEN

UNDER ROCKS

STONE FARM

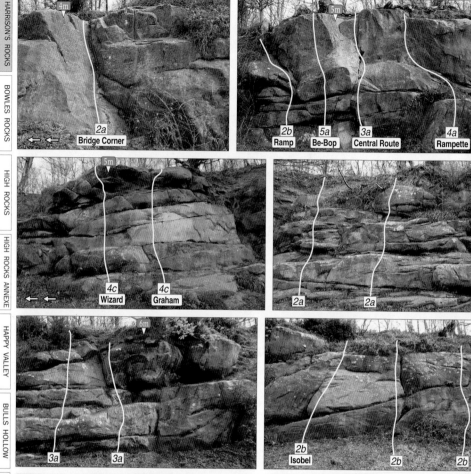

4m
2a Bridge Corner

5m
2b Ramp | 5a Be-Bop | 3a Central Route | 4a Rampette

5m
4c Wizard | 4c Graham

2a | 2a

6m
3a | 3a

2b Isobel | 2b | 2b

2b | 3b | 2b | 3a

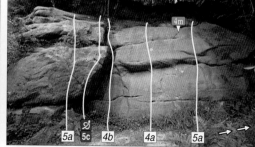

4m
5a | 5c | 4b | 4a | 5a

Local chat: Sandown Crags is the name given to the long line of small cliffs after you pass North Boulder to your left. The horizontal breaks are close together, making it ideal for small kids – who generally can't reach the holds on longer climbs. Muddy at the top, best in a dry spell. Not all the routes have names. Grades are for adults – will be a lot harder for shorties.

Access & Erosion: Most of the belay trees are some way back, you will need a short 10m static rope to extend the belay karabiner from a tree to the edge.

[UK 6b] TORQUE WRENCH (font 6b), Iain Campbell ▷

North Boulder | Eyelet | Dinosauros | Bow Window | Pig Tail Slab | Sewer | Vice | Isolated Boulder | Crucifix
Teddy Bear | Cottonsocks | Hangover | Sagittarius | Circle | Niblick | Sunshine | Spider Wall | Unclimbed Wall

HARRISON'S ROCKS

BOWLES ROCKS

HIGH ROCKS

HIGH ROCKS ANNEXE

HAPPY VALLEY

BULLS HOLLOW

ERIDGE GREEN

UNDER ROCKS

STONE FARM

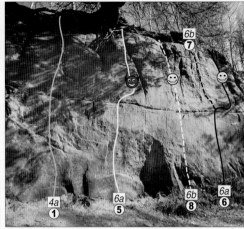

Local chat: A very flat wall, quite untypical for Southern Sandstone. Stays wet after rain and remains damp during a wet summer. In a good dry spell gives some very good short routes, slightly too high for comfortable bouldering.

Access & Erosion: Soft rock, so don't climb on this section if it is damp. Access top by going up the R side past Kukri Wall, then easily up and back along. 4 slings should be adequate - there is 2 metres of crud to exit after the rock finishes.

		UK Trad	Fontainebleau colour (font grade)	Ticked

4a **(1) Trees are Green** (f **3a**)   S   TR
And so are slabs beneath them!
Solo: 1990's   TR: 1963 Teresa Hill

5b **(2) Usurper**✰✰ (f **4c**)   S   TR
Obvious sloping crackline.
Solo: 1970's   TR:1970's Tim Daniells

5c **(3) Dynamo**✰✰ (f **5b**)   S   TR
Start with a dyno, then technical.
Solo: 1970's   TR:1970's

5c **(4) Central Groove**✰ (f **5b**)   S   TR
The often dirty groove.
Solo: 1990's   TR:1970's

6a **(5) Photina** (f **6a**)   S   TR
A mantle then awkward finger crack.
Solo: 1993 Tim Allen   TR: 1993 Robin Mazinke

6a **(6) New Hat**✰ (f **6a**)   S   TR
Mantle then move right to the groove.
    TR: 1993 Robin Mazinke

6b **(7) Special Invitation** (f **6a+**)   S   TR
A direct finish to New Hat with a mantle finish.
    TR: 2003 C. Gibson

6b **(8) Teddy Bear's Picnic**✰ (f **6b**)   S   TR
A pretty difficult mantle, then nice wall above.
Solo: 1996 John Patterson   TR: 1970's

6b **(9) The Violent Sprat** (f **6b**)   S   TR
Climbing the wall without the arête to the right.
Solo: 2006 Andy Hughes

UK Trad   Fontainebleau colour (font grade)   Ticked

| 3b | **(1) Kukri Wall** (f 3a) | S | TR |

The central cracks system.
Solo: Pre 1950's

| 4b | **(2) Breadknife Buttress** ⋅⋋ (f 3b) | S | TR |

The best route on this shady buttress - technical.
Solo: Pre 1950's

| 4c | **(3) Kukri Wall Direct** (f 3c) | S | TR |

The wall to the right - technical on small holds.
Solo: Pre 1950's

| 5a | **(4) Penknife** (f 4a) | S | TR |

A tricky lower mantleshelf.
Solo: 1995 Robin Mazinke

Local chat: A small wall set up a little bank, which gets very overgrown during summer. Keeps a good deal of heavy shade.

Access & Erosion: Go up an easy ramp to the right - a bit of a horror gully to the left. You need a short static rope to set up belays for some of these routes.

Crag layout map - page 8
Graded tick list - page 10

Teddy Bear   Cottonsocks   Hangover   Sagittarius   Circle   Niblick   Sunshine   Spider Wall   Unclimbed Wall
North Boulder   Eyelet   Dinosauros   Bow Window   Pig Tail Slab   Sewer   Vice   Isolated Boulder   Crucifix

HARRISON'S ROCKS
BOWLES ROCKS
HIGH ROCKS
HIGH ROCKS ANNEXE
HAPPY VALLEY
BULLS HOLLOW
ERIDGE GREEN
UNDER ROCKS
STONE FARM

HARRISON'S ROCKS

BOWLES ROCKS

HIGH ROCKS

HIGH ROCKS ANNEXE

HAPPY VALLEY

BULLS HOLLOW

ERIDGE GREEN

UNDER ROCKS

STONE FARM

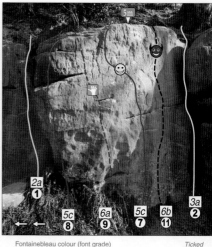

UK Trad		Fontainebleau colour (font grade)	Ticked	
2a	①	Don☆ (f 2a)	S	TR

Climb the chimney crack in the right corner.
Solo: 1960's

| 3a | ② | Tight Chimney☆ (f 2b) | S | TR |

A squeezy little number.
Solo: Pre 1950's

| 3b | ③ | Dave☆ (f 2b) | S | TR |

An awkward step up-mantleshelf.
Solo: 1960's

| 4b | ④ | Eyelet☆☆ (f 3b) | S | TR |

A steep little overhang requiring a technical finish.
Solo: Pre 1950's

| 5b | ⑤ | Ringlet☆ (f 4b) | S | TR |

The obvious rounded nose.
Solo: 1960's

| 5b | ⑥ | Singlet☆ (f 4c) | S | TR |

Don't forget to heel hook..
Solo: 1970's

UK Trad		Fontainebleau colour (font grade)	Ticked	
5c	⑦	Elastic☆☆☆ (f 5b)	S	TR

Uses the one finger pocket - be careful.
Solo: 1958 John Smoker

| 5c | ⑧ | Toad☆ (f 5b) | S | TR |

Awkward.
Solo: 1960's

| 6a | ⑨ | Patient Parmer☆☆ (f 5c) | S | TR |

Small edges and quite technical.
Solo: 1999 Chris Murray

| 6a | ⑩ | Deep Thought (f 6a) | S | TR |

Small boulder problem.
Solo: 1999 Chris Murray

| 6b | ⑪ | Bioplastic☆ (f 6a+) | S | TR |

A micro-micro eliminate.
Solo: 1981 David Atchison-Jones

| 6b | ⑫ | Twiglet☆ (f 6b+) | S | TR |

The overhang direct with a good left hand undercut.
Solo: 1994 Robin Mazinke

Local chat: The Eyelet area is a very nice little bay, set just above the main footpath along the outcrop. It's a sun trap on cold spring afternoons - but also gets a good shade canopy during mid summer. The top of Eyelet used to be easy - with tree roots to grab, alas these are now gone and many find getting over the top extremely difficult - it is not the best route to try and solo for the inexperienced. The other short routes are very much boulder problems and are quite challenging to onsight.

Top access & erosion beta: Best go to the left of the buttress for top belay access. Some bolts on top, so a couple of static slings should suffice. (No belay above route 1 - Don, you will need a short static for this belay). Really make sure to extend the belay over the edge as this area really has suffered from rope groove erosion. Don't forget to use a bouldering mat if you are not using a rope - to protect the ground below (and perhaps yourself too).

Crag layout map - page 8
Graded tick list - page 10

[UK 4b] EYELET (font 3b), Julia Black ▷

| North Boulder | Eyelet | Dinosauros | Bow Window | Pig Tail Slab | Sewer | Vice | Isolated Boulder | Crucifix |
| Teddy Bear | Cottonsocks | Hangover | Sagittarius | Circle | Niblick | Sunshine | Spider Wall | Unclimbed Wall |

UK Trad	Fontainebleau colour (font grade)	Ticked		UK Trad	Fontainebleau colour (font grade)	Ticked
3a	**(1) Tight Chimney** ☆ (f 2b)	S TR		5c	**(5) Sullivan's Stake** ☆ (f 5b)	S TR
	A squeezy little number.				Quite technical.	
	Solo: Pre 1940's				*Solo: 1970's*	
4a	**(2) Ejector** ☆☆☆ (f 3a)	S TR		6a	**(6) Sand Piper** ☆ (f 5c)	S TR
	Many try this route - and many fail, prepare to be ejected.				A technical wall climb on small holds.	
	Solo: Pre 1960's				*Solo: 1980's Frank Shannon*	
4b	**(3) Gilbert's Gamble** ☆☆ (f 3b)	S TR		6a	**(7) Grasshopper** (f 6a)	S TR
	Relies on good friction, how lucky do you feel?				A direct start to Tight Chimney Slab.	
	Solo:1960's				*Solo: 1980's*	
4b	**(4) Tight Chimney Slab** ☆ (f 3b)	S TR		6b	**(8) Shytte** (f 6a+)	🗑 S TR
	A rising line - mediocre.				It's all in the name.	
	Solo: Pre 1950's				*Solo: 1994 Chris Murray*	

Local chat: Ejector is one of the all time classic routes at Harrison's. It's easy enough to be attempted by a beginner, but technical enough to repel just about every first timer. At the top there just aren't any holds, so the aspirant gets ejected out of the groove. Those who climb well can make this problem look so easy it is ridiculous. Many of the other little climbs are fun in summer when they fully dry out.

Top access & erosion beta: Easiest to go up to the right of the buttress. There are bolts placed at the 7m high point, which need to be extended down to the top edge of Ejector. You will need a short static rope extension for most of the other routes.

BOREAL

◁ *[UK 4a] EJECTOR (font 3a), Rob Diamond*

Crag layout map - page 8
Graded tick list - page 10

North Boulder   Eyelet   Dinosauros   Bow Window   Pig Tail Slab   Sewer   Vice   Isolated Boulder   Crucifix
Teddy Bear   Cottonsocks   Hangover   Sagittarius   Circle   Niblick   Sunshine   Spider Wall   Unclimbed Wall

HARRISON'S ROCKS · BOWLES ROCKS · HIGH ROCKS · HIGH ROCKS ANNEXE · HAPPY VALLEY · BULLS HOLLOW · ERIDGE GREEN · UNDER ROCKS · STONE FARM

HARRISON'S ROCKS

BOWLES ROCKS

HIGH ROCKS

HIGH ROCKS ANNEXE

HAPPY VALLEY

BULLS HOLLOW

ERIDGE GREEN

UNDER ROCKS

STONE FARM

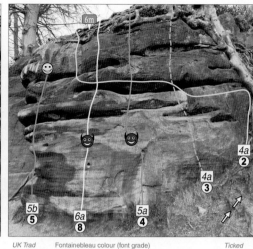

UK Trad	Fontainebleau colour (font grade)	Ticked
2b (1)	**Open Chimney**★★ (f 2b)	S TR

Climb the obvious corner.
Solo: Pre 1940's

4a (2)	**Cottonsocks Traverse**★★★ (f 3b)	S TR

An excellent way up this pretty steep wall.
Solo: Pre 1950's

4a (3)	**Root Route 1** (f 3b)	S TR

Hardly inspiring
Solo: Pre 1950's

5a (4)	**Root Route 1.5**★ (f 4a)	S TR

A steep little overhang requiring a technical finish.
Solo: 1980's

UK Trad	Fontainebleau colour (font grade)	Ticked
5b (5)	**Jungle Juice**★★ (f 4c)	S TR

Rounded and awkward on very worn rock.
Solo: 1982 David Atchison-Jones   TR: 1970's

5c (6)	**Carrera** (f 5a)	S TR

A slab that can be climbed in many different ways.
Solo: 1980's   TR: 1970's Tim Daniells

6a (7)	**Trip of the Psychedelic Tortoise** (f 6a)	S TR

Overhanging mantle - often damp.
Solo: 1990's   TR: 1985 Paul Stone

6a (8)	**Root Route 2**★ (f 6a)	S TR

Holds have worn away making the start rather difficult.
Solo: Pre 1950's

Local chat: A very popular little spot that gets very welcome shade in a hot summer. The lower part of this buttress has worn away considerably to give some pretty hard starts to the routes. Cottonsocks Traverse is the regular adventure for many, with quite a punchy move high up for beginners.

Top access & erosion beta: It is easiest to access the top to the right of the buttress. As you will see from the cement in the rope grooves, this area has suffered badly. Please make sure to extend the sling over the edge. Most climbers set up a belay off the tree roots, but be sure to back up to something substantial - a short static rope is useful.

Crag layout map - page 8
Graded tick list - page 10

[UK 5a] ROOT ROUTE 1.5 (font 4a), Lauren Ford ▷

Teddy Bear   Cottonsocks   Hangover   Sagittarius   Circle   Niblick   Sunshine   Spider Wall   Unclimbed Wall

North Boulder   Eyelet   Dinosauros   Bow Window   Pig Tail Slab   Sewer   Vice   Isolated Boulder   Crucifix

HARRISON'S ROCKS

BOWLES ROCKS

HIGH ROCKS

HIGH ROCKS ANNEXE

HAPPY VALLEY

BULLS HOLLOW

ERIDGE GREEN

UNDER ROCKS

STONE FARM

UK Trad	Fontainebleau colour (font grade)		Ticked

3a ① A Small bit of Black (f 2a)   S   TR

Not a very big route.
Solo: Pre 1960's

4a ② Right Hand Crack ☆ (f 3a)   S   TR

Technical and troublesome for beginners.
Solo: Pre 1940's

5c ③ Serendipity ☆ (f 5b)   S   TR

Climbing the wall without using the crack up right.
Solo: 1989 Matt Smith

5c ④ Blackeye Wall ☆☆ (f 5b)   S   TR

A powerful crack to layaway, then escape left nervously.
Solo: Pre 1960's

UK Trad	Fontainebleau colour (font grade)		Ticked

5c ⑤ Slanting Crack ☆☆ (f 5b)

Many different ways - all awkward.
Solo: 1970's   TR: Pre 1960's

6a ⑥ Counterfeit ☆ (f 5c)   S   TR

A crimpy little wall,, very easy to fluff.
Solo: 1970's   TR: Pre 1960's

6a ⑦ Blackeye Wall Direct ☆☆ (f 6a)   S   TR

Topping out direct is somewhat airy.
Solo: 1979 David Atchison-Jones

6c ⑧ Soft Rock ☆ (f 7a)   S   TR

The short wall, holds tend to break off.
Solo: 1990 Matt Smith

Local chat: This wall is set high above the lower path and the ground is slowly dropping away. Most problems can easily be bouldered with a pad and team of spotters. A nice selection of climbs that vary in style quite a bit. The rock isn't that strong, and in the case of Soft Rock – may not be climbable any longer. Counterfeit is wearing too.

Top access & erosion beta: Most climbers boulder these routes, but the ground has subsided a good couple of feet - please use crash pads at all times. Be very careful with placing your feet - do not scrabble with them and wear away the few hand holds that there are. Bolts at the top, 3 slings should do.

Crag layout map - page 8
Graded tick list - page 10

HARRISON'S ROCKS

BOWLES ROCKS

HIGH ROCKS

HIGH ROCKS ANNEXE

HAPPY VALLEY

BULLS HOLLOW

ERIDGE GREEN

UNDER ROCKS

STONE FARM

UK Trad		Fontainebleau colour (font grade)	Ticked	
4a	**① Steph** (f 3a)		S	TR

A crack.
Solo: 1990 Chris Tullis

| 5a | **② Weeping Slab** (f 4a) | | S | TR |

Damp.
Solo: Pre 1960's

| 5b | **③ Stranger than Friction** (f 4c) | | S | TR |

Wall climb.
Solo: 1990 Chris Tullis

| 5b | **④ Cucumber Madness** (f 4c) | | S | TR |

The left arête.
Solo: 2004 Brian Kavanagh

UK Trad		Fontainebleau colour (font grade)	Ticked	
5c	**⑤ Smear Campaign** (f 5a)		S	TR

Left end of buttress.

TR: 1990 Chris Tullis

| 6a | **⑥ Incisor** (f 6a) | | S | TR |

Left of wall.
Solo: 1980's

TR: Pre 1960's

| 6a | **⑦ Fang** (f 6a) | | S | TR |

Centre line.
Solo: 1980's

| 6a | **⑧ Wisdom** (f 6a) | | S | TR |

Right on wall.
Solo: 1980's

Local chat: This buttress is set up above the general line of the crag. It is very often wet and grimey. Best climbed in a dry early spring.

Top access & erosion beta: Easiest approach up the left side - often overgrown as these routes are less popular.

HARRISON'S ROCKS

BOWLES ROCKS

HIGH ROCKS

HIGH ROCKS ANNEXE

HAPPY VALLEY

BULLS HOLLOW

ERIDGE GREEN

UNDER ROCKS

STONE FARM

UK Trad	Fontainebleau colour (font grade)	Ticked		UK Trad	Fontainebleau colour (font grade)	Ticked

1b ① Fingernail Crack (f 2a)   S TR

A very short route.

Solo: Pre 1940's

5b ② Sliding Corner ☆ (f 4c)   S TR

Climb diagonally up to the arête to finish direct.

Solo: Pre 1960's

5c ③ Rotten Stump Wall ☆☆ (f 5b)   S TR

A very good introduction to slopers and sandstone tricks.

Solo: 1970's   TR: Pre 1960's

5c ④ Sticky Wicket ☆☆ (f 5b)   S TR

Rather greasy cracks - damn good fun when dry.

Solo: 1981 David Atchison-Jones   TR: 1970's

6a ⑤ Awkward Crack (f 5c)   S TR

A very cramped route with the back wall behind you.

Solo: 1990's

6a ⑥ Rotten Thump Arête ☆ (f 6a)   S TR

A good direct line with attitude.

Solo: 1970's

6b ⑦ Uncertainty (f 6b)   S TR

A somewhat blank wall.

Solo: 1992 John Patterson   TR: 1980's

Local chat: An easy place to simply walk on by with the routes being short, but check these out. They're surprisingly good and entertaining, tricky to read, and a very good challenge to onsight. Sector is shady and stays green during a damp summer spell - ideal in a dry spring or very hot summer.

Access & Erosion: Go up to the left of the buttress, which is one of the main ways down if approaching the outcrop from the high path. Bolt belay on top of the arête, but you will need slings and a short 10m static for many of the belays. Definitely use a crash pad if bouldering; be warned - the tops are tricky so a rope is well worth the effort.

Crag layout map - page 8
Graded tick list - page 10

UK Trad	Fontainebleau colour (font grade)	*Ticked*	*UK Trad*	Fontainebleau colour (font grade)	*Ticked*

5b	① **Dinosaurus**☆☆ (f **4c**)	S TR

Taking the centre of the high wall.
Solo: 1960's   *TR: Pre 1960's*

5c	② **Smiliodan**☆ (f **5b**)	S TR

A very nice way up this steep wall.
Solo: 1980's   *TR: 1970's*

6a	③ **Smiliodan Direct**☆☆ (f **5c**)	S TR

Taking a direct line is harder and better.
Solo: 1980's Guy McLelland

6a	④ **Dinosaurus Direct**☆ (f **5c**)	S TR

The lower arête
Solo: 1980's   *TR: 1960's Chris Bonnington*

Local chat: A small wall of superb quality sandstone. Too smooth to offer many routes, but some good ones at that. Fortunately the tree at the top is still alive and provides very good topping out holds. Ground below falls away and is not ideal for bouldering.

Access & Erosion: You can get to the top on the right via scrambling up the tree roots, but going L around the previous buttress is a lot easier. Slings - using the rather obvious tree.

First Ascent Notes: There is certainly no shortage of publications that both record and illustrate, the substantial amount of climbing that has been done in the South East of England over the past 100 years. Indeed, the photos of the past show a surprising amount of rock erosion - even back in the 1940's. They also clearly illustrate that climbing with a rather tight top rope - was pretty common. I am in no doubt however, that there were many brilliant climbers operating on the sandstone well before the 1970's, and believe that many of the climbs in this book were soloed by people who didn't make a thing of it, and therefore remain hidden from any historical record. In my experience, a great many of the finest climbers are very quiet, do their own thing, and remain pretty hidden from the public eye. On the historical front, it is well known that many authors take a rather inventive approach when writing history, including material not disproved, rather than facts well proven. I have opted for the latter approach when noting the first ascent dates and names, and when there is any chance of ambiguity - I have simply given the rough year or decade in which a route was first thought climbed.

HARRISON'S ROCKS | BOWLES ROCKS | HIGH ROCKS | HIGH ROCKS ANNEXE | HAPPY VALLEY | BULLS HOLLOW | ERIDGE GREEN | UNDER ROCKS | STONE FARM

HARRISON'S ROCKS
BOWLES ROCKS
HIGH ROCKS
HIGH ROCKS ANNEXE
HAPPY VALLEY
BULLS HOLLOW
ERIDGE GREEN
UNDER ROCKS
STONE FARM

| UK Trad | Fontainebleau colour (font grade) | Ticked | | UK Trad | Fontainebleau colour (font grade) | Ticked |

5b ① Snout✭✭ (f 4c)   S TR

The funny shaped arête - awkward.
Solo: Pre 1940's

5c ② Tomcat✭ (f 5a)   S TR

A very nice little route.
Solo: 1981 David Atchison-Jones   TR: 1975 Simon Matthews

6a ③ Panther's Wall✭✭✭ (f 6a)   S TR

Holds wearing away - grade may increase.
Solo: 1960's   TR: 1950's Trevor Panther

Local chat: Panther's Wall has been the nemesis for many a climber. Always graded at 6a, but never easy and catches most climbers out.

Access & Erosion: Access by the tree roots to the L, or walk a long way round to the L. Bolt belay on top, consider using a low belay karabiner for route of Snout. Very awkward landing and not a good bouldering spot, since the moves on Panther's Wall will spit you off in a very haphazard manner from a great height!

Crag layout map - page 8
Graded tick list - page 10

[UK 5c] TOMCAT (font 5a), Catherine Hendrie ▷

North Boulder   Eyelet   Dinosaurus   Bow Window   Pig Tail Slab   Sewer   Vice   Isolated Boulder   Crucifix
Teddy Bear   Cottonsocks   Hangover   Sagittarius   Circle   Niblick   Sunshine   Spider Wall   Unclimbed Wall

HARRISON'S ROCKS

BOWLES ROCKS

HIGH ROCKS

HIGH ROCKS ANNEXE

HAPPY VALLEY

BULLS HOLLOW

ERIDGE GREEN

UNDER ROCKS

STONE FARM

UK Trad	Fontainebleau colour (font grade)		Ticked

3a ① Beech Corner (f 2a) — S TR
The corner with a tree in the way.
Solo: Pre 1950's

3c ② Snout Crack★★★ (f 3a) — S TR
Pretty whizzo little route.
Solo: Pre 1940's

5c ③ Blue Peter★★ (f 5a) — S TR
A troublesome little number.
Solo: Pre 1950's

5c ④ Mantlepiece (f 5b) — S TR
Excellent mantleshelf practise.
Solo: 1983 Guy McLelland

6a ⑤ Madness★ (f 6a) — S TR
A much easier and more pleasant finish to Blue Murder.
Solo: 1982 David Atchison-Jones   TR: 1980 David A-Jones

6a ⑥ Guy's Problem★★ (f 6a) — S TR
Quite a powerful little number.
Solo: 1980's Guy McLelland

Local chat: A real mixed bag of allsorts in this sector. Not the most popular of bays, but still offering some good technical problems.

Access & Erosion: Go to the left and up tree roots. You will need a short static rope plus slings to set up a belay.

◁ [UK 6b] BLUE MURDER (font 6c), Jaro Lebl

UK Trad	Fontainebleau colour (font grade)		Ticked

6a ⑦ Inimitability (f 6a) — S TR
Technical.
TR: 1992 Steve Quinton

6b ⑧ Blue Murder★ (f 6c) — S TR
A steep and awkward crack.
Solo: 1980's   TR: 1970's

HARRISON'S ROCKS

BOWLES ROCKS

HIGH ROCKS

HIGH ROCKS ANNEXE

HAPPY VALLEY

BULLS HOLLOW

ERIDGE GREEN

UNDER ROCKS

STONE FARM

UK Trad	Fontainebleau colour (font grade)	Ticked

4b ① **Awkward Crack** ☆☆ (f **3b**) S TR
Name says it all, rounded holds, wide bridging helps.
Solo: Pre 1940's

4c ② **Slab Direct** ☆☆ (f **3c**) S TR
Lovely slab moves (UK 5a direct start for tiny tots).
Solo: Pre 1940's

5b ③ **Slab Crack** (f **4b**) Slime S TR
A very greasy crack - basically dire.
Solo: 1960's   TR: Pre 1940's

6a ④ **Celestial's Reach** ☆☆ (f **5c**) S TR
A surprisingly good route when clean and dry.
Solo: 1982 Dan Lewis   TR:1965 Ben Wintringham

6a ⑤ **Madness** ☆ (f **6a**) S TR
A much easier and more pleasant finish to Blue Murder.
Solo: 1982 David Atchison-Jones   TR: 1980 David A-Jones

6a ⑥ **Short Hangover** ☆☆☆ (f **6a**) Ω S TR
Very much the classic line up the north side of the
overhanging Luncheon Shelf, involving a highly awkward
mantle. Stepping into the large pocket high up is testing.
Solo: 1960's   TR: 1960's

*Local chat: The slab routes at the back used to be easier,
but the nice sharp holds have been worn away. The steep
North Wall to the right is rarely dry and forms a damp little
alcove in the rocks. This remains in the shade for most of
the year, but during a good heat wave, the wall will dry out.*

UK Trad	Fontainebleau colour (font grade)	Ticked

6a ⑦ **Long Hangover** ☆☆ (f **6a**) Ω S TR
A long traverse joining Short Hangover.
Solo: 1960's   TR: 1960's

6a ⑧ **Stardust** ☆☆ (f **6a**) S TR
Often damp and dirty, but good when dry.
                              TR: 1970 Gordon Somerville

6b ⑨ **Hangover** ☆☆☆ (f **6a+**) S TR
A fun acrobatic route that requires a leglock in the break
beneath the Luncheon Shelf, then to cut loose and swing
round. Physically easy, but complicated to onsight.
Solo: 1979 Andy Meyers   TR: 1960's

6b ⑩ **Lager Shandy** ☆☆ (f **6c**) S TR
Requiring a dyno - often damp.
                              TR: 1993 Steve Quintor

6c ⑪ **Lager Frenzy** ☆☆ (f **7b**) S TR
The steep overhanging wall was previously climbed with
pegs (Slab Bay Wall A1 - Trevor Panther 1950's). This has
left a few meagre holds to powerfully levitate between.
                              TR: 1987 Dave Turner

*Access & Erosion: Go back left along the outcrop to get
up to the top. Bolt belays on the nose and above the
slab at the back, requiring up to 4 slings. A short static
rope is needed to set up a belay for the harder routes.*

Crag layout map - page 8
Graded tick list - page 10

HARRISON'S ROCKS
BOWLES ROCKS
HIGH ROCKS
HIGH ROCKS ANNEXE
HAPPY VALLEY
BULLS HOLLOW
ERIDGE GREEN
UNDER ROCKS
STONE FARM

UK Trad   Fontainebleau colour (font grade)   *Ticked*   UK Trad   Fontainebleau colour (font grade)   *Ticked*

5a **① Long Layback**☆☆☆ (f **4a**)   S TR
This is a stiff layback on slippery holds, try very hard.
Solo: Pre 1930's   TR: 1920's

6a **② Luncheon Shelf**☆ (f **6a**)   S TR
Worn out holds are making the top more difficult.
Solo: 1970's   TR: Pre 1960's

6a **③ The Flakes**☆☆☆ (f **6a**)   S TR
A weaving line of very good holds - until, bugger I'm off!
Solo: 1970's Andy Meyers   TR: 1960's Ben Wintringham

6a **④ Coronation Crack**☆☆☆ (f **6a**)   S TR
Can be climbed with either small edges or jams, wicked.
Solo: 1970's Stevie Haston   TR: 1960's Martin Boysen

6b **⑤ Flakes Direct**☆☆☆ (f **6a+**)   S TR
A small but rather nasty little roof.
Solo: 1983 David Atchison-Jones   TR: 1976 Martin Randall

6b **⑥ Hangover**☆☆☆ (f **6a+**)   S TR
Enjoy the swing - belayer watch for flying legs etc.
Solo: 1979 Andy Meyers   TR: 1960's

6b **⑦ The Cruising DJ**☆☆ (f **6b**)   S TR
A dynamic slap for the Luncheon Shelf.
Solo: 1983 Dan Lewis   TR: 1982 David Atchison-Jones

6b **⑧ Supernatural**☆☆ (f **6b**)   S TR
Crimpy territory.
   TR: 1999 Daimon Beail

6b **⑨ Force of Destiny**☆☆☆ (f **6b+**)   S TR
A fine lower eliminate - then a tad on the steep side.
   TR: 1989 David Atchison-Jones

6b **⑩ The Limpet**☆☆ (f **6c+**)   S TR
More tiny crimps since holds have broken off.
Solo: 1992 Chris Murray   TR: 1965 Ben Wintringham

Local chat: This somewhat intimidating bay offers a whole array of superb classic routes of substantial length.

◁ [UK 6b] THE CRUISING DJ (font 6b), Ian Stronghill

Top access & erosion beta: Scamper up the bay - 50 yds to the right. Make sure to extend belay karabiner over edge. A short static rope is essential.

HARRISON'S ROCKS

BOWLES ROCKS

HIGH ROCKS

HIGH ROCKS ANNEXE

HAPPY VALLEY

BULLS HOLLOW

ERIDGE GREEN

UNDER ROCKS

STONE FARM

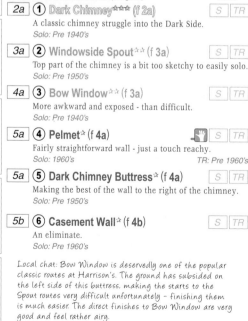

UK Trad	Fontainebleau colour (font grade)		Ticked

2a ① Dark Chimney★★★ (f 2a)   S   TR

A classic chimney struggle into the Dark Side.
Solo: Pre 1940's

3a ② Windowside Spout★★ (f 3a)   S   TR

Top part of the chimney is a bit too sketchy to easily solo.
Solo: Pre 1950's

4a ③ Bow Window★★ (f 3a)   S   TR

More awkward and exposed - than difficult.
Solo: Pre 1940's

5a ④ Pelmet★ (f 4a)   S   TR

Fairly straightforward wall - just a touch reachy.
Solo: 1960's   TR: Pre 1960's

5a ⑤ Dark Chimney Buttress★ (f 4a)   S   TR

Making the best of the wall to the right of the chimney.
Solo: Pre 1950's

5b ⑥ Casement Wall★ (f 4b)   S   TR

An eliminate.
Solo: Pre 1960's

Local chat: Bow Window is deservedly one of the popular classic routes at Harrison's. The ground has subsided on the left side of this buttress, making the starts to the Spout routes very difficult unfortunately – finishing them is much easier. The direct finishes to Bow Window are very good and feel rather airy.

UK Trad	Fontainebleau colour (font grade)		Ticked

5c ⑦ Spout Crossing★★ (f 5a)   S   TR

Getting into the groove can be problematic.
Solo: 1960's   TR: Pre 1950

5c ⑧ Spout Buttress★★ (f 5a)   S   TR

Leaving the ground is not guaranteed.
Solo: 1960's

5c ⑨ Bow Window Left Hand★★ (f 5b)   S   TR

Good climbing deviating away from the steepest part.
Solo: 1960's

6a ⑩ Bow Window Direct★★★ (f 5c)   S   TR

Going direct through the overhang is powerful.
Solo: 1960's

6b ⑪ Nut Tree★ (f 6b)   S   TR

Staying on the rounded arête.
Solo: 1985 Dan Lewis

Access & Erosion: Easiest way up in some 70 yards to the left, and then back along the top. Belay bolts for Bow Window - but still use a sling and locking karabiner. Exten[d] other belays well over the edge. A crash pad is best for the starts of the Spout area, since you are often not high enough for the rope to hold you.

Crag layout map - page 8
Graded tick list - page 10

[UK 4a] BOW WINDOW (font 3a), Meghan Read ⊳

North Boulder   Eyelet   Dinosauros   Bow Window   Pig Tail Slab   Sewer   Vice   Isolated Boulder   Crucifix
Teddy Bear   Cottonsocks   Hangover   Sagittarius   Circle   Niblick   Sunshine   Spider Wall   Unclimbed Wall

HARRISON'S ROCKS

BOWLES ROCKS

HIGH ROCKS

HIGH ROCKS ANNEXE

HAPPY VALLEY

BULLS HOLLOW

ERIDGE GREEN

UNDER ROCKS

STONE FARM

UK Trad	Fontainebleau colour (font grade)		Ticked

2a ① Way Down (f 2a) — S | TR

Not so easy with a rucksack, but a doddle anyway.
Solo: Pre 1980's

2a ② Giant's Staircase☆ (f 2a) — S | TR

Nothing too sensational.
Solo: Pre 1950's · *TR: Pre 1950's*

2b ③ Arrow Crack☆ (f 2a) — S | TR

The obvious very short right angled corner.
Solo: Pre 1950's · *TR: Pre 1950's*

3a ④ Longbow Chimney (f 2b) — Slime | S | TR

Often very damp and greasy.
Solo: Pre 1950's · *TR: Pre 1950's*

4a ⑤ Sashcord Crack☆☆☆ (f 3a) — S | TR

Good holds all the way, but pretty steep.
Solo: Pre 1960's

4c ⑥ Big Crack☆ (f 3c) — S | TR

Technical and troublesome for beginners.
Solo: 1970's

UK Trad	Fontainebleau colour (font grade)		Ticked

5b ⑦ Quarterdome☆☆☆ (f 4c) — S | TR

Short but very good - think heel hook.
Solo: 1998 Robin Mazinke · *TR: 1998 Chris Tul...*

5c ⑧ Finger Stain (f 5a) — S | TR

Technical on small edges.
Solo: 1970's

6a ⑨ Yosemite Big Wall Climb☆ (f 5c) — S | TR

Topping out direct is somewhat airy.
Solo: 1995 Robin Mazinke

6a ⑩ Gardeners Question Time (f 6a) — S | TR

The short wall.
Solo: 1987 Ben Bevan-Pritchard

6b ⑪ Neighbours☆☆ (f 6a+) — S | TR

A short and technical eliminate - good fun.
Solo: 1982 David Atchison-Jones · *TR: 1982 David A-Jone...*

Local chat: This bay was re-formed during rock stabilisation during the 1980's. Blocks were placed to make a continuous line of cliffs at the point of way down. The cleaned buttresses allowed the development and addition of some short easy climbs. Most of the routes in this sector are one move wonders – fun but not worth a detour.

Top access & erosion beta: Climbing up the way down is the usual access, but if carrying lots of gear - perhaps go to the right for 70 yds and up the to the left of Pig Tail Slabs. There are a few belay bolts on top here, but be sure to extend the belay with a sling and locking karabiner over the edge. You will need a long 15m static rope to set up belays on the right side of this sector.

Crag layout map - page 8
Graded tick list - page 10

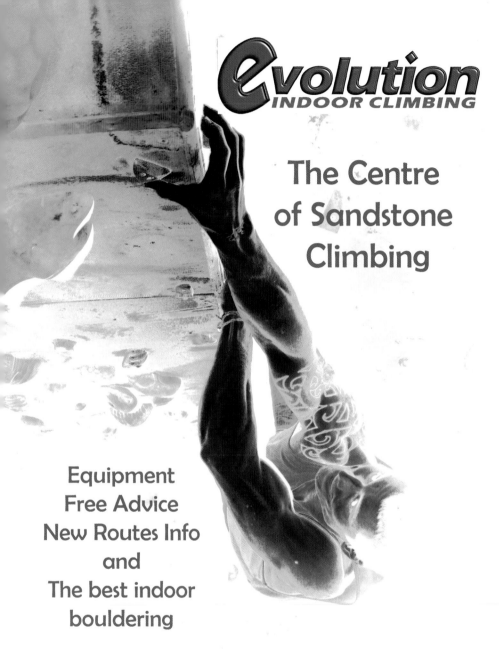

HARRISON'S ROCKS

BOWLES ROCKS

HIGH ROCKS

HIGH ROCKS ANNEXE

HAPPY VALLEY

BULLS HOLLOW

ERIDGE GREEN

UNDER ROCKS

STONE FARM

UK Trad	Fontainebleau colour (font grade)	Ticked

3a **(1) Longbow Chimney (f 2b)**   Slime | S | TR
Often very damp and greasy.
Solo: Pre 1950's   *TR: Pre 1950's*

5a **(2) Sagittarius**☆☆☆ **(f 4a)**   S | TR
A butch start - but technical and lovely thereafter.
Solo: 1970's   *TR: Pre 1960's*

5c **(3) Quiver**☆☆☆ **(f 5a)**   S | TR
A bit complicated to onsight as it is usually greasy
Solo: 1970's   *TR: Pre 1960's*

5c **(4) Little Sagittarius**☆☆ **(f 5b)**   S | TR
More technical wall stuff.
Solo: 1970's   *TR: Pre 1960's*

5c **(5) Toxophilite**☆☆☆ **(f 5b)**   S | TR
Technical wall stuff.
Solo: 1970's   *TR: Pre 1960's*

UK Trad	Fontainebleau colour (font grade)	Ticked

5c **(6) Archer's Wall**☆☆ **(f 5b)**   S | TR
Steep bastard of a bugger.
Solo: 1970's   *TR: Pre 1960's*

6a **(7) Archer's Wall Direct**☆☆☆ **(f 5c)**   S | TR
Take on the full challenge of the overhanging nose.
Solo: 1970's   *TR: Pre 1960's*

6a **(8) Grist**☆ **(f 5c)**   S | TR
Dyno up this greasy arête.
Solo: 1990's   *TR: 1970's Martin Randall*

6b **(9) That Man's an Animal**☆ **(f 6b+)**   S | TR
A technical wall that needs to be in a dry condition.
TR: 1990's

Access & Erosion: Easiest to go around the nose to the right and up the gully in 30 yards (or solo up the easy corner to the left). For the routes on the left side of the wall, you will need two static ropes to form a yoke from trees quite a way back. Bolt belays around the nose of Archer's Wall. Make sure to set up the karabiner over the edge, and protect the top edge where possible.

Local chat: This is a superb wall, just on the nice side of vertical, however - only good to rest on if you have plenty of stamina. Stays greasy after wet weather, but dries out completely in a good spell. Gets the evening sun if the trees below are pollarded. Very good routes to go on when your arms are tired from steep cranking.

◁ *[UK 5c] QUIVER (font 5a), Rachel Hoyland*

BEAL LA PASSION VERTICALE

Crag layout map - page 8
Graded tick list - page 10

Teddy Bear   Cottonsocks   Hangover   **Sagittarius**   Circle   Niblick   Sunshine   Spider Wall   Unclimbed Wall
North Boulder   Eyelet   Dinosauros   Bow Window   Pig Tail Slab   Sewer   Vice   Isolated Boulder   Crucifix

HARRISON'S ROCKS - Sagittarius (Crisis)

HARRISON'S ROCKS

BOWLES ROCKS

HIGH ROCKS

HIGH ROCKS ANNEXE

HAPPY VALLEY

BULLS HOLLOW

ERIDGE GREEN

UNDER ROCKS

STONE FARM

UK Trad	Fontainebleau colour (font grade)	Ticked		UK Trad	Fontainebleau colour (font grade)	Ticked

4b (1) Long Crack✩✩✩ (f **3b**) S TR
A struggle for most aspirants - face either way.
Solo: Pre 1930's   *TR: 1920's*

5b (2) Stupid Effort✩✩✩ (f **4b**) S TR
Technical mixture of power and flexibility required.
Solo: Pre 1960's Johnnie Lees

5c (3) Slimfinger Crack✩✩✩ (f **5b**) S TR
Starting is easy, but getting into the crack is diabolical.
Solo: 1940's Tony Moulam   *TR: Pre 1950's*

Local chat: The Crisis bay is one of the more intimidating parts of Harrison's. Most of the routes seem tough for their grade, and on average get the better of most aspirant's first efforts. Even though many of the routes here have been soloed, the landings are nasty and you are best recommended to use a rope!

Access & Erosion: Go to the right of the wall and up the gully to the right of the wedged block. Belay bolts at the top - static slings should suffice. Short static rope to extend belay for Archer's Wall DIrect.

6a (4) Archer's Wall Direct✩✩✩ (f **5c**) S TR
Take on the full challenge of the overhanging nose.
Solo: 1970's

? (5) River Dance (f **?**) S TR
An unrepeated line, leaving long crack after 10 feet.
TR: 1996 Barry Franklin

6c (6) What Crisis✩✩ (f **7a**) S TR
Some climbers make this look easy - most don't.
Solo: 1993 Chris Murray   *TR: 1985 Guy McLelland*

6c (7) In Crisis✩✩ (f **7a+**) S TR
A better finish than the very easy direct line.
TR: 2009 Barnaby Ventham (Probably done before)

> Crag layout map - page 8
> Graded tick list - page 10

BOREAL

[UK 5b] STUPID EFFORT (font 4b), Steve Glennie ▷

| Teddy Bear | Cottonsocks | Hangover | *Sagittarius* | Circle | Niblick | Sunshine | Spider Wall | Unclimbed Wall |
| North Boulder | Eyelet | Dinosauros | Bow Window | Pig Tail Slab | Sewer | Vice | Isolated Boulder | Crucifix |

HARRISON'S ROCKS

BOWLES ROCKS

HIGH ROCKS

HIGH ROCKS ANNEXE

HAPPY VALLEY

BULLS HOLLOW

ERIDGE GREEN

UNDER ROCKS

STONE FARM

UK Trad	Fontainebleau colour (font grade)	Ticked
3a	**(1) Horizontal Birch** (f 2a)	S TR

A substantial lack of a Birch Tree!
Solo: Pre 1930's

| **4b** | **(2) Downfall** ☆ (f 3b) | S TR |

Climb lower wall, then the upper pocketed wall.
Solo: Pre 1950's · *TR: Pre 1950's*

| **5c** | **(3) Slimfinger Crack** ☆☆☆ (f 5b) | S TR |

Starting is easy, but getting into the crack is diabollical.
Solo: 1940's Tony Moulam · *TR: Pre 1950's*

| **5c** | **(4) Vulture Crack** ☆☆☆ (f 5b) | S TR |

Technical wall stuff.
Solo: 1970's Laurie Holliwell · *TR: Pre 1950's*

UK Trad	Fontainebleau colour (font grade)	Ticked
6a	**(5) Marcus's Arete** ☆ (f 5c)	S TR

Almost a boulder problem.
Solo: 1996 Pete Atkinson · *TR: 1996 Pete Church*

| **6a** | **(6) The Sting** ☆ (f 5c) | S TR |

Much easier when the holds are dry.
Solo: 1982 Dan Wajzner · *TR: 1976 Martin Randall*

| **6b** | **(7) Jumping Jack Flash** ☆ (f 6c) | S TR |

Dyno up with a funky mantle to finish.
TR: 1990 Paul Widdowson

| **6c** | **(8) Flying Griffin** ☆ (f 7a+) | S TR |

A fun eliminate dyno up the wall without the crack.
TR: 2000's

Local chat: A short low wall offering fun routes. Set in the shade, these are ideal on a hot summers day – fun ticks without great exertion. Note There are woodland plans to clear a lot of tree cover, so this area may well dry out and be very good indeed.

Access & Erosion: Go up the gully to the right of Downfall. A long static is needed for some of the belay set ups.

Crag layout map - page 8
Graded tick list - page 10

Teddy Bear   Cottonsocks   Hangover   *Sagittarius*   Circle   Niblick   Sunshine   *Spider Wall*   *Unclimbed Wall*
North Boulder   Eyelet   Dinosauros   Bow Window   Pig Tail Slab   Sewer   Vice   Isolated Boulder   Crucifix

UK Trad		Fontainebleau colour (font grade)		Ticked		UK Trad		Fontainebleau colour (font grade)			Ticked
2a	①	**Junend Arete**✶ (f 2a)		S	TR	4c	⑥	**Greasy Crack**✶ († 3c)		C	TR

2a ① Junend Arete✶ (f 2a)
Technically climb the left side of the arête.
Solo: Pre 1950's   *TR: Pre 1950's*

2b ② The Fonz✶ (f 2b)
Short but fun.
Solo: Pre 1960's

3b ③ Happy Days✶ (f 3a)
Fun wall with a mantle to finish.
Solo: Pre 1960's

4a ④ Pig Tail Slab✶ (f 3a)
A fun short slab route.
Solo: Pre 1950's   *TR: Pre 1950's*

4a ⑤ Left Edge✶ (f 3a)
Another short route.
Solo: Pre 1950's   *TR: Pre 1950's*

4c ⑥ Greasy Crack✶ († 3c)
Enjoyable if dry.
Solo: 1950's   *TR: Pre 1950's*

5a ⑦ Giant's Ear✶✶ (f 4a)
Skill, balance and dry conditions required.
Solo: Pre 1950's   *TR: Pre 1950's*

5b ⑧ Big Toe Wall✶✶ (f 5b)
A mantle on this slab requires deft skill.
Solo: 1980's

5c ⑨ Directors (f 5b)
A manky slab, getting harder as the rock falls apart.
TR: 1990's Robin mazinke

Local chat: These small slabs have been popular with complete beginners, but have worn very badly over the years and are somewhat harder than in the previous guidebook. The higher tier gives high quality moves - but the routes are very short indeed.. The base of the higher tier is above the footpath and out of the main thoroughfare, can be a quiet little spot.

Access & Erosion: Go up the ramps to the left. You will need a long static (15m) for setting up a belay on the slab routes in the centre. The top wall has belay bolts, but often stays damp which results in a weak rock structure. Please avoid climbing in these conditions to preserve the rock.

HARRISON'S ROCKS | BOWLES ROCKS | HIGH ROCKS | HIGH ROCKS ANNEXE | HAPPY VALLEY | BULLS HOLLOW | ERIDGE GREEN | UNDER ROCKS | STONE FARM

HARRISON'S ROCKS

BOWLES ROCKS

HIGH ROCKS

HIGH ROCKS ANNEXE

HAPPY VALLEY

BULLS HOLLOW

ERIDGE GREEN

UNDER ROCKS

STONE FARM

UK Trad	Fontainebleau colour (font grade)		Ticked			UK Trad	Fontainebleau colour (font grade)		Ticked	

4a **①** **Fallen Block Mantleshelf**☆☆☆ (f **3a**) S TR

No prizes for guessing the technique required.
Solo: Pre 1950's   *TR: Pre 1950's*

5a **②** **Fallen Block Wall**☆☆ (f **4a**) S TR

Follow the easiest line.
Solo: Pre 1950's   *TR: Pre 1950's*

5b **③** **Fallen Block Eliminate** (f **4b**) S TR

Direct and short.
Solo: Pre 1960's

Local chat: An area prone to overgrowth and green unpleasantness - may change with clearance. When dry - the routes are short & fun.

JULIE TULLIS CAMPSITE - at Harrison's Rocks car park

North Boulder	Eyelet	Dinosauros	Bow Window	Pig Tail Slab	Sewer	Vice	Isolated Boulder	Crucifix
Teddy Bear	Cottonsocks	Hangover	Sagittarius	Circle	Niblick	Sunshine	Spider Wall	Unclimbed Wall

Right-side tabs: HARRISON'S ROCKS · BOWLES ROCKS · HIGH ROCKS · HIGH ROCKS ANNEXE · HAPPY VALLEY · BULLS HOLLOW · ERIDGE GREEN · UNDER ROCKS · STONE FARM

1K Trad	Fontainebleau colour (font grade)		Ticked	UK Trad	Fontainebleau colour (font grade)		Ticked

1b (1) Snake's Crawl☆ (f 2a) — S TR

A weird route, either inside or outside.

Solo: Pre 1950's   *TR: Pre 1950's*

2b (2) Little Cave (f 2a) — S TR

A caving experience.

Solo: Pre 1950's   *TR: Pre 1950's*

3a (3) Sinner's Wall (f 2a) — Slime S TR

A wandering and greasy experience.

Solo: Pre 1950's   *TR: Pre 1950's*

4b (4) Flying Scotsman ☆☆ (f 3b) — S TR

The easiest and best line up this part.

Solo: Pre 1960's

Local chat: This is an area that stays damp and horrible if the trees are not trimmed in front of the crag. In the past with clearance etc. the buttress cleans up very well and dry to offer a lovely selection of middle grade routes.

5a (5) Signalbox Arête ☆☆ (f 4a) — S TR

A surprisingly good little route.

Solo: 1950's   *TR: Pre 1950's*

5b (6) Very Sinfull (f 4b) — Grim Slime S TR

Greasy and ghastly direct start to Sinner's Wall.

Solo: Pre 1960's

5c (7) Mighty Midge ☆☆☆ (f 5b) — S TR

Good steep climbing - but short.

TR: 2000 Carrie Atchison-Jones

6a (8) The Bishop and the Actress (f 6a) — Slime S TR

The steep and greasy twin crackline.

TR: 1994 Robin mazinke

Access & Erosion: Way up to the left, just slings needed for the easier routes. The rock on this section has been damp for many years - give it time to dry out before climbing on it please.

CAMPING

There is a basic site at Harrison's run by the BMC, with small individual plots. There are toilets, and sinks with hot & cold water for washing up. Usually there is a camp fire on weekend evenings and plenty of climbers around.

Note: There are also commercial campsites locally (which are certainly not cheap); Manor Court Farm to the north of Groombridge, Camping & Caravanning club site at Crowborough, and at Hook Farm near Forest Row - all have websites.

Crag layout map - page 8
Graded tick list - page 10

North Boulder	Eyelet	Dinosauros	Bow Window	Pig Tail Slab	Sewer	Vice	Isolated Boulder	Crucifix
Teddy Bear	Cottonsocks	Hangover	Sagittarius	Circle	Niblick	Sunshine	Spider Wall	Unclimbed Wall

HARRISON'S ROCKS

BOWLES ROCKS

HIGH ROCKS

HIGH ROCKS ANNEXE

HAPPY VALLEY

BULLS HOLLOW

ERIDGE GREEN

UNDER ROCKS

STONE FARM

UK Trad	Fontainebleau colour (font grade)		Ticked
4a	**① Right Circle**☆☆ (f **3a**)		S · TR

A classic corner - beefy to start.
Solo: Pre 1940's

| **5b** | **② Sinners Slimebag** (f **4b**) | | S · TR |

The greasy crack leading to a sapling - may dry out.
Solo: Pre 1950's   TR: Pre 1950's

| **5b** | **③ Saint's Wall**☆☆ (f **4b**) | | S · TR |

A dyno for the ledge solves everything.
Solo: Pre 1930's

| **5c** | **④ Bloody Sunday**☆☆ (f **5b**) | | S · TR |

Following the centre of the wall.
Solo: 1970's

| **6a** | **⑤ Left Circle**☆☆ (f **5c**) | | 〰 S · TR |

Only for those with strong fingers.
Solo: 1980's   TR: 1950's (5b with high ground).

UK Trad	Fontainebleau colour (font grade)		Ticked
6a	**⑥ In Limbo**☆ (f **6a**)		S · TR

Quite technical.
Solo: 1990's   TR: 1990 Mike Vetterlei

| **6b** | **⑦ Glendale Crack**☆☆ (f **6b**) | | S · TR |

Fingerlocks and lock offs - powerful.
Solo: 1975 Stevie Haston   Peg route:1960'

| **6b** | **⑧ Gretta**☆☆ (f **6b**) | | S · TR |

Going L is an option - but not an easy one.
Solo: 1984 David Atchison-Jones   TR: 1984 Jerry Pee

| **6c** | **⑨ A Killing Joke**☆ (f **7b**) | | 〰 S · TR |

The very crimpy arête, holds snap and grade changes.
Solo: 1993 Dan Wajzner

| **7a** | **⑩ Supply and Demand** ✍☆ (f **7b+**) | | 〰 S · TR |

Sit start to A Killing Joke from the right on more crimps.
Solo: 2002 Ian Stronghill

Local chat: Quite a mixed area. Plenty of good holds higher up. However, with the ground subsiding over the years - most of the starts are fiendishly hard – unfortunate since the top parts are way easy by comparison.

Access & Erosion: Easiest way up to the left, 4 slings should be adequate for this sector.

BOREAL

[UK 6a] LEFT CIRCLE (font 5c), David Atchison-Jones (photo Rob Foster) ⊳

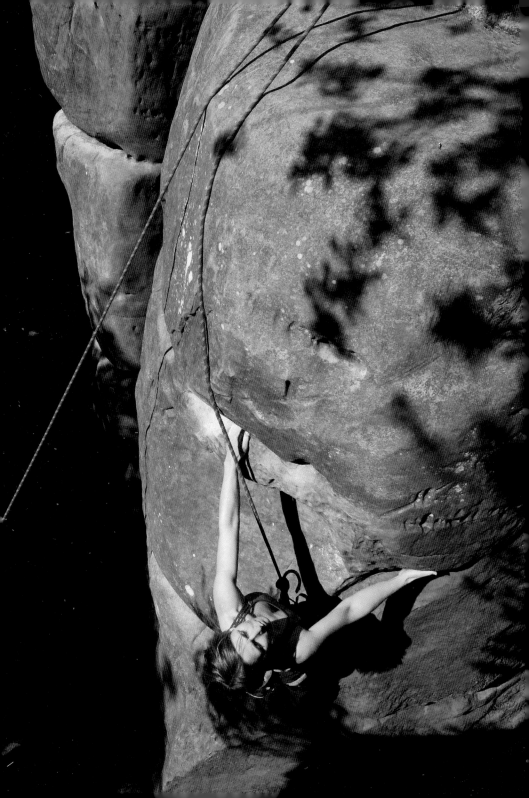

7m

HARRISON'S ROCKS

BOWLES ROCKS

HIGH ROCKS

HIGH ROCKS ANNEXE

HAPPY VALLEY

BULLS HOLLOW

ERIDGE GREEN

UNDER ROCKS

STONE FARM

UK Trad	Fontainebleau colour (font grade)	Ticked	UK Trad	Fontainebleau colour (font grade)	Ticked

2b (1) Small Chimney ✭✭ (f 2b)   S TR
Small - but a good fun outing.
Solo: Pre 1940's

4a (2) Right Circle ✭✭ (f 3a)   S TR
A classic corner - beefy to start.
Solo: Pre 1940's

4c (3) Coffin Corner ✭ (f 3c)   S TR
Start in the corner but finish up the wall.
Solo: Pre 1960's

5b (4) Goat's Head Soup ✭✭ (f 4b)   S TR
Not obvious - sustained with reasonable holds.
Solo: 1980's   TR: 1980's

5b (5) Long Stretch ✭ (f 4c)   S TR
Very apt route name.
Solo: Pre 1960's

Local chat: A good small buttress with a nice selection of short routes. The rock is quite soft here so grades may well change either way. Set back behind the gully in the centre is a fun boulder problem called Goats do Roam - a very low crawl-mantle out of a cave - Font 6a and a bit.

5b (6) Small Wall ✭✭ (f 4c)   S TR
A small wall but with big moves.
Solo: Pre 1950's   TR: Pre 1950's

5c (7) Good Friday (f 5b)   S TR
An excellent small arête - no pushover.
Solo: 1960's   TR: Pre 1960's

6a (8) Left Circle ✭✭ (f 5c)   S TR
Only for those with strong fingers.
Solo:1980's   TR: 1950's at 5b with high ground.

6a (9) Healey Peelys ✭ (f 6a)   S TR
Very fingery wall start.
Solo: 1982 Joe Healey

6c (10) A Killing Joke ✭ (f 7b)   S TR
The very crimpy arête, holds snap and grade changes.
Solo: 1993 Dan Wajzner

7a (11) Supply and Demand ☹ ✭ (f 7b+)   S TR
Sit start to A Killing Joke from the right on more crimps.
Solo: 2002 Ian Stronghill

Top access & erosion beta: You can access the top via the gully in the centre, but this can be damp and yukky. Going to the right and up through a secret passage in the rocks is fun. Bolt belay for Small Chimney, but you will need 2 static ropes for the other routes - complicated belay set ups.

◁ [UK 5b] GOATS HEAD SOUP (font 4b), Catherine Hendrie

Crag layout map - page 8
Graded tick list - page 10

HARRISON'S ROCKS

BOWLES ROCKS

HIGH ROCKS

HIGH ROCKS ANNEXE

HAPPY VALLEY

BULLS HOLLOW

ERIDGE GREEN

UNDER ROCKS

STONE FARM

Tick   Fontainebleau bouldering grades

S **(1) Montana** (f **2a**) Straightforward slab.

S **(2) Verbier** (f **2b**) Warm up mantle.

S **(3) Monch** (f **2c**) Climb with arête on your right.

S **(4) Leukwarm** (f **3a**) Good easy mantle.

S **(5) Sass Fee** (f **3a**) Another easy mantle.

S **(6) Hard Furka** (f **3c**) Climb with arête on your left.

S **(7) Grimey Grimsel** (f **4a**) Often green unfortunately.

S **(8) Lugano** ☠ (f **4a**) Tricky semi highball on arête.

S **(9) Como** (f **4a**) Steady wall.

S **(10) Lecco** (f **4a**) Have a spotter.

S **(11) The Horn** (f **4b**) Climb with arête on your left.

S **(12) Eigerrrr** (f **4b**) Obvious crackline.

S **(13) Billy Bong** ☠ (f **4c**) Big drop!

S **(14) Maggiore** ☠ (f **5a**) Arête with mantle.

S **(15) Young Frau** (f **5b**) Slap up.

S **(16) Domodossola** ☠ (f **5c**) A demanding wall.

S **(17) Arco** (f **6a**) Only one move.

S **(18) Goats Do Roam** ⚖ (f **6b**) An infuriating mantle.

Local chat: This is a hidden little bouldering area set up above the rocks. Unfortunately it stays greasy and damp quite often, but in a hot spell it stays thankfully cool - its lovely for mid grade bouldering. Worth doing as a circuit of 18 problems. Goats Do Roam (after the wine), is a classic.

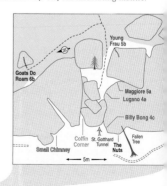

HARRISON'S ROCKS

BOWLES ROCKS

HIGH ROCKS

HIGH ROCKS ANNEXE

HAPPY VALLEY

BULLS HOLLOW

ERIDGE GREEN

UNDER ROCKS

STONE FARM

UK Trad	Fontainebleau colour (font grade)	Ticked

4b ① **Saint Gotthard**✮✮✮ (f **3b**) S TR
A wandering line but sensible when you are climbing.
Solo: Pre 1940's

6b ② **Rowan Tree Wall**✮✮ (f **6a+**) S TR
Too wet to ascend usually.
Solo: 1970's

6b ③ **Pascale**✮✮ (f **6a+**) S TR
A fine wall when it dries out.
TR: 1994 John Patterson

UK Trad	Fontainebleau colour (font grade)	Ticked

6b ④ **The Nuts**✮✮✮ (f **6a+**) S TR
Very technical - with some sketchy slopers too.
Solo: 1982 David Atchison-Jones   TR: 1965 Trevor Panther

6b ⑤ **The Bolts**✮ (f **6b+**) S TR
A rather steep prow with a difficult top out.
Solo: 1998 John Patterson   TR: 1990's

Local chat: This is a persistently wet and damp area. From time to time – when the trees in front of the rocks are cut back, this area does dry out to give some excellent routes.

Access & Erosion: There is a hidden route to the top of the crag here via the Saint Gotthard Tunnel - a passage between the jammed blocks. This leads up to a small bouldering area called The Simplon Boulder Park - another damp area that only dries out in a hot summer spell. There are bolts on top of route 4 - The Nuts, so 3 slings should be fine. For route 5 The Bolts, there are no close belay options - you will need a long static rope, (or bouncy ankles).

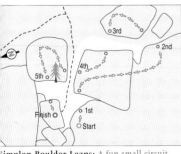

Simplon Boulder Leaps: A fun small circuit of leaps. 1st - is a warm up, 2nd is fun, 3rd is a good distance, 4th is a whopper going down, and 5th is possibly suicidal to stay on the block.

> **Crag layout map - page 8**
> **Graded tick list - page 10**

North Boulder   Eyelet   Dinosauros   Bow Window   Pig Tail Slab   *Sewer*   Vice   Isolated Boulder   Crucifix
Teddy Bear   Cottonsocks   Hangover   Sagittarius   Circle   Niblick   Sunshine   Spider Wall   Unclimbed Wall

HARRISON'S ROCKS

BOWLES ROCKS

HIGH ROCKS

HIGH ROCKS ANNEXE

HAPPY VALLEY

BULLS HOLLOW

ERIDGE GREEN

UNDER ROCKS

STONE FARM

UK Trad	Fontainebleau colour (font grade)	Ticked

4b **(1)** **The Sandpipe**☆☆ (f 3b)   Slime S TR
A damp start up the Sewer then take the left corner.
Solo: Pre 1930's

4c **(2)** **The Sewer**☆☆ (f 3c)   Slime S TR
A damp awkward start - then taking the right corner.
Solo: Pre 1930's

5b **(3)** **Pipe Cleaner** (f 4b)   S TR
Often greasy.
Solo: 1990 Tim Skinner

5c **(4)** **Sewer Wall**☆☆ (f 5b)   S TR
Awkward off-width, and slimely at the best of times.
Solo: Pre1950's

Local chat: This area is called The Sewer, named after
the natural drainage funnel in the centre of the cliff.
Wet it may be, but at least it doesn't smell. Don't rush
into ticking these routes until they dry out fully – yes it
does happen from time to time, and then it is very good
indeed. Rather too high for bouldering.

UK Trad	Fontainebleau colour (font grade)	Ticked

6a **(5)** **Orangutang**☆☆☆ (f 5c)   S TR
Much easier when you know how!
Solo: 1970's   TR: 1967 Greg Morga

6b **(6)** **Cannibals**☆☆ (f 6a+)   S TR
Climbs the high arête.
    TR: 1991 A Powe

6b **(7)** **Psycho**☆☆☆ (f 6b)   S TR
Avoid the holds at the start of Orangutang and dyno via
slopers all the way to the break.
    TR: 2000 David Atchison-Jone

6b **(8)** **Powder Monkey**☆☆ (f 6c)   Slime S TR
Pretty full on all the way - needs a long dry spell.
    TR: 1990 Paul Widdowso

*Top access & Erosion beta: Go to the left and access
the top via the St. Gotthard Tunnel route. You will
definitely need a short 10m static rope to reach the
solid tree belays quite a way back. Make sure to protect
the rounded top of the cliff with sling protectors.*

Crag layout map - page 8
Graded tick list - page 10

[UK 6b] PSYCHO (font 6b), Jérôme Curoy ▷

HARRISON'S ROCKS
BOWLES ROCKS
HIGH ROCKS
HIGH ROCKS ANNEXE
HAPPY VALLEY
BULLS HOLLOW
ERIDGE GREEN
UNDER ROCKS
STONE FARM

UK Trad	Fontainebleau colour (font grade)		Ticked
4b	**① Moonlight Arête**☆☆☆ (f **3b**)		S TR

The classic line up the front of the buttress.
Solo: Pre 1950's   *TR: Pre 1950's*

UK Trad			
4c	**② Starlight**☆☆☆ (f **3c**)		S TR

Marginally harder than Moonlight.
Solo: Pre 1960's

6a	**③ Orangutang**☆☆☆ (f **5c**)		S TR

Much easier when you know how!
Solo: 1970's   *TR: 1967 Greg Morgan*

6b	**④ Brookslight**☆☆ (f **6a+**)		S TR

Technical and very enjoyable, easier for lanky's.
TR: 1965 R Brookes

6b	**⑤ Monkey's Bow**☆☆☆ (f **6a+**)		S TR

A very good stamina outing, especially for shorties.
Solo: 1996 Mike Ball   *TR: Pre 1960's*

6b	**⑥ Primate Shot**☆☆ (f **6c**)		S TR

Damn hard low down.
TR: 1987 Paul Stone

6b	**⑦ Oliver James**☆☆☆ (f **6c**)		S TR

Brutally direct and hard.
TR: 1989 Theseus Gerard

Local chat: A superb leaning wall that is mostly covered with excellent jugs - ho ho! All of the lines are obvious as are the holds, it's just that the angle is rather steep for most. Every part of this wall has been traversed, giving routes of mixed interest.

Top access & Erosion beta: Go to the left of the buttress and access the top via the St. Gotthard Tunnel route. (The Chimney on the right has been climbed - but is disgusting.) There are bolts on top of Orangutang & Moonlight, but you will need a long static rope for setting a belay on the harder routes. Make sure to protect the rounded top of the cliff with sling protectors.

◁ [UK 4b] MOONLIGHT ARETE (font 3b), Billy Beswick

Crag layout map - page 8
Graded tick list - page 10

Left margin tabs (top to bottom): HARRISON'S ROCKS | BOWLES ROCKS | HIGH ROCKS | HIGH ROCKS ANNEXE | HAPPY VALLEY | BULLS HOLLOW | ERIDGE GREEN | UNDER ROCKS | STONE FARM

UK Trad	Fontainebleau colour (font grade)		Slimed
2a ①	Noisome Cleft No.1 (f 2a)		Slime S TR

Rather Yukky

Solo: Pre 1950's   TR: Pre 1950's

3a ②	Noisome Cleft No.2 (f 2b)	Slime S TR

More Yuk.

Solo: Pre 1950's   TR: Pre 1950's

3b ③	The Green Cleft (f 3b)	🗑 Grim Slime S TR

Completely disgusting.

Solo: 2005 Robin Mazinke   TR: 2005 Mike Vetterlein

5b ④	Noisome Wall (f 4c)	Slime S TR

A wandering and greasy experience.

Solo: Pre 1960's

UK Trad	Fontainebleau colour (font grade)		Ticked
6a ⑤	Plagarism (f 6a)		Slime S TR

A bit powerful.

TR: 1992 Robin Mazinke

6a ⑥	Noisome Wall Direct (f 6a)	Slime ✋ S TR

Yukky - technical with small edges.

TR: 1995 Robin Mazinke

6a ⑦	Bostic (f 6a)	Grim Slime S TR

Always hard and doesn't dry out that often.

TR: 1965 P Sorre

6c ⑧	Tempestivity☆☆ (f 7b)	S TR

A fine wall that rarely comes into condition

TR: 1995 John Patterson

Local chat: This sector is less horrendously manky and marginally drier than the Sod section. It is the natural drainage sector of the crag from the hill above. Who knows - it may dry out one day and give excellent climbing - The lines are good. Photo taken in pristine winter condition.

Access & Erosion: Best route to the top is back left along the crag and up the St. Gotthard Tunnel. You will need a long static rope for the belay set up.

Crag layout map - page 8
Graded tick list - page 10

HARRISON'S ROCKS

BOWLES ROCKS

HIGH ROCKS

HIGH ROCKS ANNEXE

HAPPY VALLEY

BULLS HOLLOW

ERIDGE GREEN

UNDER ROCKS

STONE FARM

K Trad	Fontainebleau colour (font grade)			Ticked		UK Trad	Fontainebleau colour (font grade)			Slimed

2a **①** Passage Chimney (f 2a)
Really dark and yukky.
Solo: Pre 1950's   TR: Pre 1950's

5b **②** Squank ⁕ (f 4c)
A dog leg crack.
Solo: 1992 Tim Skinner

5b **③** Tubesnake Boogie (f 4c)
Moderately yukky.
Solo: 1992 Chris Murray

5c **④** Ten Foot Pole (f 5a)
Oozing slime.
Solo: 1992 Tim Skinner

5c **⑤** El Loco (f 5b)
Oozing something nasty.
TR: 1990 Tim Skinner

6a **⑥** The Sod (f 6a)
Very nasty.
Solo: 1980's   TR: 1968 R Brooks

6a **⑦** Sharp Dressed Man (f 6a)
Another outing into gunge.
TR: 1992 Doug Reid

Local chat: This is traditionally the wettest and most diabolical section of the rocks – and not recommended. Included so you know what to avoid.

Access & Erosion: Easiest to go right, around past Niblick and Vice, then up the gully leading to the top of the crag. Belay trees are set well back.

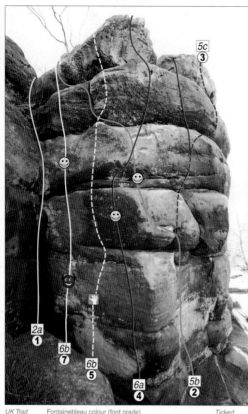

UK Trad   Fontainebleau colour (font grade)   Ticked

2a **(1) Passage Chimney (f 2a)**   S   TR
Really dark and yukky.
Solo: Pre 1940's

5b **(2) Forester's Wall**☆☆☆ **(f 4b)**   S   TR
Very blind climbing - difficult to onsight and steep.
Solo: Pre 1960's   *TR: Pre 1950's*

5c **(3) Bonanza**☆☆☆ **(f 5a)**   S   TR
Superbly exposed, finishing direct is only slightly harder.
Solo: 1960's

6a **(4) Indian Summer**☆☆☆ **(f 5c)**   S   TR
Stay on the left wall until mid height.
    TR: 1987 David Atchison-Jones

6a **(5) Forester's Wall Direct**☆☆☆ **(f 6a)**   S   TR
The low desperate move can be avoided by starting on
Indian summer - a more balanced and easier route.
Solo: 1980's Dan Lewis   *TR:1960's*

6b **(6) Sossblitz**☆☆☆ **(f 6a+)**   Ouch   S   TR
An all time classic, never seems easy.
Solo: 1979 Andy Meyers   *TR: 1965 Trevor Panther*

UK Trad   Fontainebleau colour (font grade)   Ticked

6b **(7) Fowler's Wall**☆☆ **(f 6a+)**   S   TR
The most direct line on the left side of the wall - damp.
    TR: 1978 Mick Fowle

6b **(8) Republic**☆☆☆ **(f 6b)**   S   TR
Confusing and difficult to onsight.
Solo: 1992 Steve Quinton   *TR: 1993 Dan Lew*

6b **(9) What the Butler Saw**☆☆☆ **(f 6b+)**   S   TR
An ingenious and inspired weaving line crossing Sossblit
    TR: 2000 Ian Butle

6b **(10) Bulging Bloody Bonanza**☆ **(f 6c)**   S   TR
Very sandy rock - power through the overhang.
    TR: 1990's Matt Smit

*Local chat: A very tall buttress with classic long routes.
Many have been soloed, but note - not on sight! Lots of
rounded holds and moves that aren't obvious.*

*Access & Erosion: Belay bolts on top - a selection of
long slings should be enough. Go to the right, then
walk up the gully to the right of Vice block. Buttress is
free standing - so watch out for a deep chasm - best
access is by a small step up above Passage Chimney.*

[UK 5c] BONANZA (font 5a), Rachel Hoyland ▷

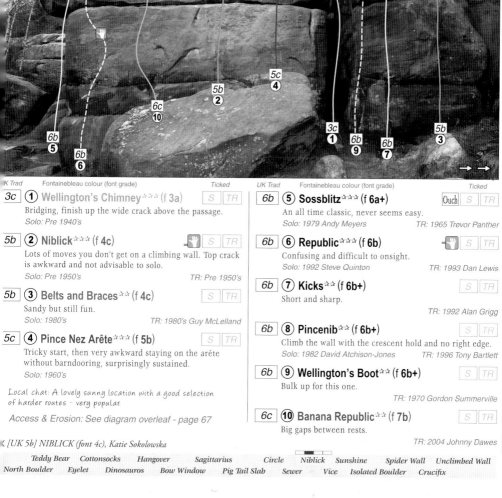

HARRISON'S ROCKS

BOWLES ROCKS

HIGH ROCKS

HIGH ROCKS ANNEXE

HAPPY VALLEY

BULLS HOLLOW

ERIDGE GREEN

UNDER ROCKS

STONE FARM

UK Trad	Fontainebleau colour (font grade)	Ticked

3c **(1) Wellington's Chimney** ☆☆☆ (f **3a**)   S TR

Bridging, finish up the wide crack above the passage.
Solo: Pre 1940's

5b **(2) Niblick** ☆☆☆ (f **4c**)   S TR

Lots of moves you don't get on a climbing wall. Top crack is awkward and not advisable to solo.
Solo: Pre 1950's   *TR: Pre 1950's*

5b **(3) Belts and Braces** ☆☆ (f **4c**)   S TR

Sandy but still fun.
Solo: 1980's   *TR: 1980's Guy McLelland*

5c **(4) Pince Nez Arête** ☆☆☆ (f **5b**)   S TR

Tricky start, then very awkward staying on the arête without barndooring, surprisingly sustained.
Solo: 1960's

Local chat: A lovely sunny location with a good selection of harder routes - very popular.

Access & Erosion: See diagram overleaf - page 67

[UK 5b] NIBLICK (font 4c), Katie Sokolowska

UK Trad	Fontainebleau colour (font grade)	Ticked

6b **(5) Sossblitz** ☆☆☆ (f **6a+**)   Ouch S TR

An all time classic, never seems easy.
Solo: 1979 Andy Meyers   *TR: 1965 Trevor Panther*

6b **(6) Republic** ☆☆☆ (f **6b**)   S TR

Confusing and difficult to onsight.
Solo: 1992 Steve Quinton   *TR: 1993 Dan Lewis*

6b **(7) Kicks** ☆☆ (f **6b+**)   S TR

Short and sharp.
TR: 1992 Alan Grigg

6b **(8) Pincenib** ☆☆ (f **6b+**)   S TR

Climb the wall with the crescent hold and no right edge.
Solo: 1982 David Atchison-Jones   *TR: 1996 Tony Bartlett*

6b **(9) Wellington's Boot** ☆☆ (f **6b+**)   S TR

Bulk up for this one.
TR: 1970 Gordon Summerville

6c **(10) Banana Republic** ☆☆ (f **7b**)   S TR

Big gaps between rests.
TR: 2004 Johnny Dawes

HARRISON'S ROCKS

BOWLES ROCKS

HIGH ROCKS

HIGH ROCKS ANNEXE

HAPPY VALLEY

BULLS HOLLOW

ERIDGE GREEN

UNDER ROCKS

STONE FARM

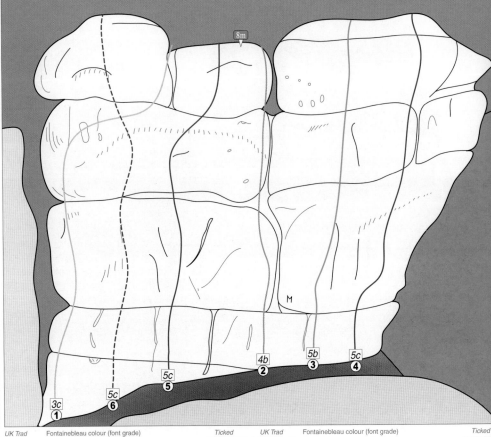

UK Trad		Fontainebleau colour (font grade)	Ticked
3c	**①**	**Wellington's Chimney**✩✩✩ (f 3a)	S · TR

Bridging, finish up the wide crack above the passage.
Solo: Pre 1960's

UK Trad		Fontainebleau colour (font grade)	Ticked
4b	**②**	**Sabre Crack**✩ (f 3b)	S · TR

Often damp crack system.
Solo: Pre 1950's

UK Trad		Fontainebleau colour (font grade)	Ticked
5b	**③**	**Caroline**✩ (f 4b)	S · TR

Pleasant if dry.
Solo: 1980 David Atchison-Jones

UK Trad		Fontainebleau colour (font grade)	Ticked
5c	**④**	**Pete's Reach**✩ (f 5a)	S · TR

Ascend from the ironstone knob.
Solo: 1990's   *TR: 1990 Pete Atkinso*

UK Trad		Fontainebleau colour (font grade)	Ticked
5c	**⑤**	**Lady Jane**✩ (f 5a)	S · TR

Technical in the centre section.
Solo: 1990's   *TR: 1970's Tim Daniel*

UK Trad		Fontainebleau colour (font grade)	Ticked
5c	**⑥**	**Hitchcock's Horror**✩ (f 5b)	S · TR

Tricky in the middle part.
TR: 1997 Rob Hitchcoc

Local chat: This is a dark chimney passage tucked in the South side of Niblick Block. It stays very dank during the winter months, but then improves during the summer because the top part of the wall catches plenty of morning sunshine. It's worth seeking out in a heat wave - but only if you've done the better routes in the area. There are a few other grizzly routes in the dark cleft, best left to cavers.

Access & Erosion: There are many belay bolts on top of Niblick Block, so a selection of long slings should suffice. It is far nicer to belay from the top for these routes since the bottom of the passage is cold and dank.

Crag layout map - page 8
Graded tick list - page 10

Teddy Bear   Cottonsocks   Hangover   Sagittarius   Circle   Niblick   Sunshine   Spider Wall   Unclimbed Wall
North Boulder   Eyelet   Dinosauros   Bow Window   Pig Tail Slab   Sewer   Vice   Isolated Boulder   Crucifix

HARRISON'S ROCKS

BOWLES ROCKS

HIGH ROCKS

HIGH ROCKS ANNEXE

HAPPY VALLEY

BULLS HOLLOW

ERIDGE GREEN

UNDER ROCKS

STONE FARM

UK Trad		Fontainebleau colour (font grade)	Ticked
1b	①	**Boxing Day Cracker** (f 2a)	S TR

Has been climbed.
Solo: 1995 Christine Eades

2b	②	**Flotsam** (f 2b)	S TR

Yukky chimney line to the right.
Solo: 1940's

3b	③	**Jetsam** (f 3a)	S TR

Yukky chimney line on the left.
Solo: 1940's

UK Trad		Fontainebleau colour (font grade)	Ticked
5b	④	**Belts and Braces**✫✫ (f 4c)	S TR

Sandy but still fun.
Solo: 1980's   TR: 1980's Guy McLelland

5c	⑤	**Bootless Buzzard** (f 5a)	S TR

Can be damp often.
Solo: 1993 Tim Skinner   TR: 1991 Doug Reid

5c	⑥	**Soft Cock** (f 5b)	S TR

Mantle somewhere.
Solo: 1993 Tim Skinner   TR: 1991 Doug Reid

6b	⑦	**Kicks**✫✫ (f 6b+)	S TR

Short and sharp.
TR: 1992 Alan Grigg

Niblick Area

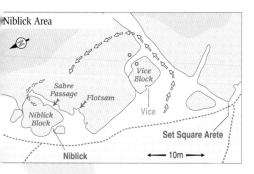

Local chat: A small alcove with big ledges offering climbing of poor quality in general. The easier routes tend to be a natural drain line for run off water – so are not ideal at damp times.

NIBLICK BLOCK: Access & Erosion: Go right along the outcrop, then up and around the Vice Block. Avoid going direct to the top of Niblick Block and falling down Sabre Passage. Bolt belay bolts on top, but you will need 2-3 long slings in addition. For the Flotsam section there is a good bit of heather tuffty stuff at the top, you will need a long static rope to extend the belay from trees set back - and down to the top of the rock.

HARRISON'S ROCKS

BOWLES ROCKS

HIGH ROCKS

HIGH ROCKS ANNEXE

HAPPY VALLEY

BULLS HOLLOW

ERIDGE GREEN

UNDER ROCKS

STONE FARM

| UK Trad | Fontainebleau colour (font grade) | Ticked | | UK Trad | Fontainebleau colour (font grade) | Ticked |

2a ① Tame Corner (f 2a)   S   TR

Climbing the back corner trends to a different belay.
Solo: Pre 1950's   *TR: Pre 1950's*

2b ② Tame Variant (f 2b)   S   TR

Problematical but not difficult.
Solo: Pre 1965's   *TR: Pre 1950's*

4b ③ Toeing the Line (f 3b)   S   TR

Stay on the line without drifting to the jugs on the right.
Solo: 1999 Jan Cholawo

4c ④ Deadwood Crack ☆☆ (f 3c)   S   TR

Not easy at all. Most find the top overhang nails.
Solo: Pre 1960's

5c ⑤ Wildcat Wall ☆☆ (f 5a)   S   TR

If you can reach the holds - it's an easy mantle.
Solo: Pre 1950's   *TR: Pre 1950's*

6b ⑥ Woodside Blossom ☆☆ (f 6a+)   S   TR

Not over supplied with positive holds.
Solo: Early 1970's Mick Fowler

Local chat: This bay is at the corner where Harrison's changes direction, and gets a lot of sunshine. It's very popular with beginners, and makes for a nice picnic spot – if somewhat rather busy with lots of folk trekking by.

Access & Erosion: Go up to the right of Vice block, then up the passage and around in a loop to end up at the top of Deadwood Crack. Make sure to extend the locking karabiner over the edge and minimise the belay rope touching the rock where possible.

Crag layout map - page 8
Graded tick list - page 10

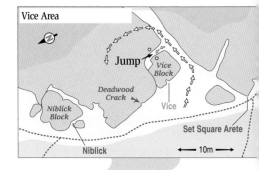

Vice Area

Jump

Vice Block

Deadwood Crack

Vice

Niblick Block

Set Square Arete

Niblick

10m

Cotswold Outdoor
for all your outdoor clothing and equipment needs

95-97 Mount Pleasant Rd,
Royal Tunbridge Wells, Kent, TN1 1QG
Tel: 01892 539 402

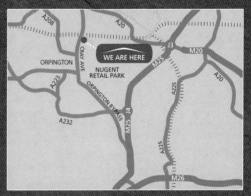

Unit 2, Nugent Shopping Park
Cray Avenue, Orpington, Kent, BR5 3RP
Tel: 01689 885 560

Unit 29, Newnham Court Shopping Village,
Bearsted Road, Maidstone, Kent, ME14 5LH
Tel: 01622 738 381

8m

HARRISON'S ROCKS

BOWLES ROCKS

HIGH ROCKS

HIGH ROCKS ANNEXE

HAPPY VALLEY

BULLS HOLLOW

ERIDGE GREEN

UNDER ROCKS

STONE FARM

K Trad	Fontainebleau colour (font grade)		Ticked
2a	① **Tame Corner**☆ (f 2a)		S / TR

Climbing the back corner goes to a different belay.
Solo: Pre 1950's — *TR: Pre 1950's*

| 4b | ② **The Vice**☆☆☆ (f 3b) | | S / TR |

A climb where the holds truly run out completely!
Solo: Pre 1950's — *TR: Pre 1950's*

| 5b | ③ **The Stag**☆ (f 4c) | | S / TR |

A one move wonder.
Solo: 1982 David Atchison-Jones — *TR: 1970's*

UK Trad	Fontainebleau colour (font grade)		Ticked
5c	④ **Venison Burger** (f 5b)		S / TR

Climbing just the finger crack in the middle of the face.
Solo: 1980's — *TR: 1980's*

| 6a | ⑤ **Toevice**☆☆☆ (f 5c) | | S / TR |

Reasonably difficult, then a heinous mantle.
Solo: 1974 Mick Fowler — *TR: 1974 Mick Fowler*

| 6a | ⑥ **Handvice**☆ ☆☆ (f 6a) | | S / TR |

A very steep climb to try and figure it out as you go.
Solo: 1974 Mick Fowler — *TR: 1966 David Jones*

Local chat: The vice must be the most tried and fallen off route at Harrison's. A classic climb that looks obvious and straightforward, until the holds run out completely. Requires very little effort – simply technique, the more you struggle the less you progress. Its harder compatriots to the right are nasty little buggers – lure you into thinking that you are going to get up them, then spit you off at the last gasp.

Top access & erosion: See map on previous spread - page 68. Getting up and down off the vice block is somewhat interesting. You can climb up the rear by the short route CRACKING UP 2a. Most take a big leap across the gap to descend, leaders of groups should check this LEAP out first. There are several bolt belays in the top of the Vice block that only requires a couple of slings. Check you are happy with the condition of the bolt belays. Note: Ground below Toevice is usually wet, make sure to have a waterproof carpet - clean dry shoes are essential for the toelock.

Crag layout map - page 8
Graded tick list - page 10

◁ [UK 4b] THE VICE (font 3b), Stephanie Fraser

HARRISON'S ROCKS
BOWLES ROCKS
HIGH ROCKS
HIGH ROCKS ANNEXE
HAPPY VALLEY
BULLS HOLLOW
ERIDGE GREEN
UNDER ROCKS
STONE FARM

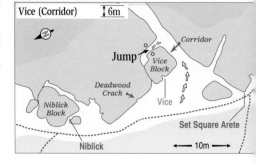

UK Trad   Fontainebleau colour (font grade)   Ticked

2a **(1)** Cracking Up☆ (f 2a)   S   TR
Climb the obvious short wall.
Solo: Pre 1930's   *TR: Pre 1930's*

3b **(2)** Pickled Pogo Stick☆ (f 2b)   S   TR
Climb - or get pickled and attempt on a pogo stick!
Solo: 1982 David Atchison-Jones

4a **(3)** Corridor Route☆ (f 3a)   S   TR
Good beefy short climb.
Solo: Pre 1950's   *TR: Pre 1950's*

5b **(4)** Rhapsody inside a Satsuma☆ (f 4b)   S   TR
Fun name, fun climb.
Solo: 1982 David Atchison-Jones

5b **(5)** Birch Nose☆☆ (f 4c)   S   TR
Rounded and awkward.
Solo: 1982 David Atchison-Jones   *TR: Pre 1950's*

5c **(6)** The Clamp☆ (f 5a)   S   TR
A short wall.
Solo: 1970's Tim Daniells

5c **(7)** Victoria☆ (f 5b)   S   TR
A thumpy little number.
Solo: 1989 Tim Skinner

6a **(8)** Handvice☆☆☆ (f 6a)   [symbol] S   TR
A very steep climb to try and figure it out as you go.
Solo: 1974 Mick Fowler   *TR: 1966 David Jones*

Local chat: The corridor is one of those places that can
easily get overgrown - and consequently remain damp and
esoteric. When it dries out - the routes are pretty good, just
a touch on the short side. The shorter climbs are good fun
as boulder problems.

Top access & erosion beta: Access by route 1.
Descend by leap across gap or descending route 1.
There are belay bolts on top of Vice Block for these
routes at the back, but you will need several slings to
extend the belay karabiner over the top edge.

Vice (Corridor)   ↕6m

Jump   Corridor
    Vice
    Block
Deadwood
Crack   Vice
Niblick
Block
    Set Square Arete
Niblick   ← 10m →

Crag layout map - page 8
Graded tick list - page 10

the reach
climbing wall

A superb indoor climbing centre, with 11 metre high lead walls - 70 lines increasing to 150, and a top of the range bouldering area - up to 500 square metres that will increase in the future.

Crispin Waddy of Living Stone has designed some unique climbing areas for us, including a massive centrepiece - a triple buttress with movable volumes. A huge 4 metre high boulder that rocks on a pivot system.

On site cafe and facilites, make this a full day out at any time of the year.

Unit 6, Mellish Estate, Harrington Way, Woolwich, SE18 5NR   tel: 020 8855 9598

HARRISON'S ROCKS

BOWLES ROCKS

HIGH ROCKS

HIGH ROCKS ANNEXE

HAPPY VALLEY

BULLS HOLLOW

ERIDGE GREEN

UNDER ROCKS

STONE FARM

UK Trad	Fontainebleau colour (font grade)	Ticked

5b ① **Knight's Gambit**☆☆ (f **4c**)   S TR

A very technical step up leads to success.

Solo: Pre 1960's

5b ② **Set Square Arête**☆☆ (f **4c**)   S TR

Awkward moves throughout, most do a knee grovel.

Solo: 1970's   *TR: Pre 1940's*

5c ③ **Knight's Move**☆☆☆ (f **5b**)   ♎ S TR

The wall is often dirty, but the holds remain clean-ish.

Solo: Pre 1960's

Local chat: A west facing wall that seems to attract
green moss and slime unfortunately. The breaks are
quite a long way apart making it very difficult for
shorter climbers. All of the grades are morpho-body
height dependent. Despite the green slime, the routes
are very good and well worth doing - even if some of
the surrounding rock is still a trifle damp.

UK Trad	Fontainebleau colour (font grade)	Ticked

6a ④ **Fat and Middle Aged** (f **6a**)   S TR

A scruffy one - often in poor condition.

Solo: 1989 J. Diplock

6b ⑤ **Skin Job**☆ (f **6b**)   S TR

A problematic wall - often damp.

TR: 1991 Tim Skinner

6b ⑥ **Reach for the Sky**☆☆ (f **6b**)   🖐 S TR

Most tall people even do this with a dyno - grade morpho.

Solo: 1992 Tim Skinner   *TR: 1960's Doug Chase*

*Top access & erosion beta: Go to the left of the
wall, turn sharp right up the narrow passage
to get up to the top. Be careful to set up the
karabiner in a low position for Set Square Arête, ✪
then have an additional karabiner to clip for the
top overhang move.*

Crag layout map - page 8
Graded tick list - page 10

[UK 5c] KNIGHT'S MOVE (font 5b), Fred Chognard ▷

HARRISON'S ROCKS

BOWLES ROCKS

HIGH ROCKS

HIGH ROCKS ANNEXE

HAPPY VALLEY

BULLS HOLLOW

ERIDGE GREEN

UNDER ROCKS

STONE FARM

UK Trad	Fontainebleau colour (font grade)	Ticked

4c (1) **Sunshine Crack**☆☆☆ (f 3c)   S   TR

Very difficult for beginners with no obvious holds.
Solo: Pre 1950's   *TR: Pre 1950's*

5b (2) **Set Square Arête**☆☆ (f 4c)   S   TR

Awkward moves throughout, most do a knee grovel.
Solo: 1970's   *TR: Pre 1940's*

5c (3) **Piecemeal Wall**☆☆☆ (f 5b)   S   TR

The holds have worn increasing the grade substantially.
Solo: Pre 1960's Arthur Dolphin   *TR: Pre 1960's*

6a (4) **The Knam**☆☆☆ (f 6a)   S   TR

More technical than powerful - lovely moves.
Solo: 1980's   *TR: 1968 Trevor Panther*

Local chat: This area opposite a low picnic slab is split in half by Sunshine Crack, a very popular climb that usually defeats even the most energetic beginners. The climbs are completely different in character, and are very good benchmark grades. You don't get any easy ticks on these routes. Fortunately they are easy to finish, but the holds are often sketchy - and the footholds either wet or poor - not ideal soloing territory.

Top access & erosion beta: Go to the left, turn sharp right leading to the corridor, then turn sharp right up the narrow passage for getting to the top. Be careful to set up the belay karabiner in a low position for Set Square Arête, then have an additional karabiner to clip for the top overhang move. ❁

UK Trad	Fontainebleau colour (font grade)	Ticked

6a (5) **The Mank**☆☆ (f 6a)   S   TR

One pretty hard move.
Solo: 1982 Dan Lewis   *TR: 1965 Barry Wyborough*

6b (6) **Sandbag**☆ (f 6b)   S   TR

A long distance between holds - often quoted at 5b.
Solo: 1990 Pete Atkinson   *TR: 1980's Frank Shannon*

6b (7) **Doctor Pepper**☆☆☆ (f 6c)   S   TR

The centre section thwarts most.
                TR: 1982 Steve Quinton

Modern Bouldering Terms:
Beta - Knowing the moves for a problem.
Crimp - Small fingertip hold, generally intensely painful.
Egyptian - Front and back foot like an Egyptian figure.
Gaston - A Crimp, thumb down on with elbow out.
Guppy - A cupped hand on a small prow.
Morpho - Body size dependent.
Match - Joining fingertips of both hands on a rail.
Nails - Hard as Nails - very very desperate.
Pop up - Small dyno for a finger hold.
Press out - Modern term for mantleshelf.
Rail - Small long thin edge for fingers.
Smear - Foot dimple with no edge or noticeable form.
Stow - A hold, a small stalictite/staligmite in a break.
Thumb sprags - Undercut with thumbs facing up, hands open and elbows out.

[UK 5c] PIECEMEAL WALL (font 5b), Kate Mead ▷

UK Trad	Fontainebleau colour (font grade)	Ticked		UK Trad	Fontainebleau colour (font grade)	Ticked

3b **(1) Smooth Chimney**★★★ (f 2c)   S TR
Most of the holds have worn smooth - tricky top.
Solo: Pre 1960's

5a **(2) Two Toed Sloth**★★ (f 4a)   S TR
A classic boulder problem start.
Solo: Pre 1960's

5c **(3) Reverse Traverse**★★ (f 5b)   S TR
Surprisingly absorbing throughout.
Solo: Pre 1960's

5c **(4) Soft Rocker**★★★ (f 5b)   S TR
One move wonder.
Solo:1990 Pete Atkinson

5c **(5) Piecemeal Wall**★★★ (f 5b)   S TR
The holds have worn increasing the grade substantially.
Solo: Pre 1960's Arthur Dolphin   TR: Pre 1960's

6a **(6) The Mank**★★ (f 6a)   S TR
One pretty hard move.
Solo: 1982 Dan Lewis   TR: 1965 Barry Wyborough

6b **(7) Eric**★ (f 6b)   S TR
A nasty top overhang.
Solo: 1992 John Patterson   TR: 1970's

6b **(8) Karen's Condom**★ (f 6b)   S TR
Bulges with long reaches to slopers.
Solo: 1985 Chris Arnold   TR: 1980's Martyn Lewis

6b **(9) Hard Condom**★ (f 6c)   S TR
The direct finish - more nasty to solo.
TR: 1992 Steve Quinton

6b **(10) Doctor Pepper**★★★ (f 6c)   S TR
The centre section thwarts most.
TR: 1982 Steve Quinton

Local chat: The Smooth and Slippery Chimney provides good entertainment for climbers of all ages. The harder routes tend to be rounded horror shows and none too easy. A few of the breaks stay dampish for a while, so some folk take a beer towel with them for cleaning their shoes high up.

Top access & erosion beta: Go to the left and follow around for main gully leading up. Note trees on top of this sector to recognise them when you get up high. A mixture of slings should suffice. If you need a high belay, put a sling around a tree branch, but be sure to back it up with a bombproof other belay.

Crag layout map - page 8
Graded tick list - page 10

◁ *[UK 5a] TWO TOED SLOTH (font 4a), Rob Harbour*

| Teddy Bear | Cottonsocks | Hangover | Sagittarius | Circle | Niblick | Sunshine | Spider Wall | Unclimbed Wall |
| North Boulder | Eyelet | Dinosauros | Bow Window | Pig Tail Slab | Sewer | Vice | Isolated Boulder | Crucifix |

HARRISON'S ROCKS · BOWLES ROCKS · HIGH ROCKS · HIGH ROCKS ANNEXE · HAPPY VALLEY · BULLS HOLLOW · ERIDGE GREEN · UNDER ROCKS · STONE FARM

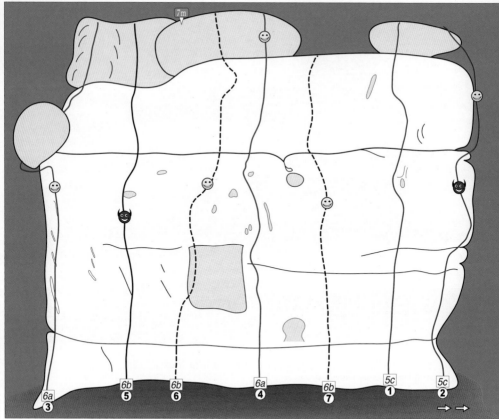

HARRISON'S ROCKS

BOWLES ROCKS

HIGH ROCKS

HIGH ROCKS ANNEXE

HAPPY VALLEY

BULLS HOLLOW

ERIDGE GREEN

UNDER ROCKS

STONE FARM

UK Trad		Fontainebleau colour (font grade)		Ticked

5c ① **Green Fingers** ✩✩✩ (f 5b) 〰 S TR

Pockets and crimps - very shady and cool.
Solo: 1982 Gareth Harding   *TR:1970's Gordon DeLacy*

5c ② **North West Corner** ✩✩✩ (f 5b) S TR

Powerful and delicate at the same time.
Solo: 1960's   *TR: Pre 1960's*

6a ③ **Boysen's Arête** ✩✩✩ (f 5c) 〰 S TR

Only one move that's hard - but hard it is.
Solo: 1960's Martin Boysen

6a ④ **Bloody Fingers** ✩✩✩ (f 6a) 〰 S TR

Not too bad on the crimps.
Solo: Pre 1992 John Patterson   *TR:1976 Martin Randall*

Access & Erosion: Quickest is to go back along the Sunshine sector and use those directions to the top plateau. You have to jump across the passageway to set up the belays for all of these routes. A selection of slings should be ample, but make sure to back up single bolt belays.

UK Trad		Fontainebleau colour (font grade)		Ticked

6b ⑤ **Powder Finger** ✩✩ (f 6a+) 〰 S TR

Just one on-off move.
Solo: 1990 John Patterson   *TR: 1984 Geoff Pearson*

6b ⑥ **Bloody Staircase** ✩✩✩ (f 6b) S TR

Easy to start but requires the odd crimpy move.
TR: 1992 Paul Widdowson

6b ⑦ **Krypton Factor** ✩✩✩ (f 6b) 〰 S TR

Full on crimp city.
TR: 1992 Paul Widdowson

Local chat: Behind the Isolated Boulder is a dark passageway (chimney). One side is flat and clean, with all of the above routes. The other side has rounded breaks and can be climbed anywhere at will – with little interest. The north facing side is slightly overhanging, which makes holding the crimps somewhat tiring. It stays damp and chilly, but in a hot summer can be one of the few places that are good to climb, keep for those really hot summer days. The rock is also very fine grained that offers tiny crimps – enjoy with fresh fingertips. Caution: Topouts are often greasy, so if you solo, beware.

Crag layout map - page 8
Graded tick list - page 10

HARRISON'S ROCKS

BOWLES ROCKS

HIGH ROCKS

HIGH ROCKS ANNEXE

HAPPY VALLEY

BULLS HOLLOW

ERIDGE GREEN

UNDER ROCKS

STONE FARM

UK Trad	Fontainebleau colour (font grade)	Ticked

5c ① **West Wall**☆☆☆ (f **5a**)   S   TR
Many difficult variations but this is the easiest way.
Solo: Pre 1960's   *TR: Pre 1950's*

5c ② **North West Corner**☆☆☆ (f **5b**)   S   TR
Powerful and delicate at the same time.
Solo: 1960's   *TR: Pre 1960's*

6a ③ **South West Corner**☆☆☆ (f **6a**)   S   TR
The low start is just the beginning of the difficulties.
Staying on the left side of the arête keeps the climb more
sustained throughout (font 6a+).
Solo: 1968 Terry Tullis   *TR:1960's*

6b ④ **Storming Cuvier Rempart**☆☆☆ (f **6b**)   S   TR
A good eliminate line. Avoiding arête completely with a
crimpy start, then undercuts, and finish without the big
holds of North West Corner.
     TR: 1982 David Atchison-Jones

Access & Erosion: Bolts belays - several slings needed.

UK Trad	Fontainebleau colour (font grade)	Ticked

6b ⑤ **Wooly Cub**☆☆☆ (f **6b+**)      S   TR
Climb the mid wall on crimps without using the arête.
Solo: 1991 Jasper Sharpe   *TR: 1979 Mick Fowler (6b)*

6b ⑥ **Wooly Jumper**☆☆☆ (f **6c**)   S   TR
Dyno between the two large breaks.
     TR: 1985 Matt Saunders

6b ⑦ **Wooly Bear**☆☆☆ (f **6c**)   S   TR
Span in a static move between the two large breaks.
Solo: 2002 Ally Smith   *TR: 1983 Dan Lewis*

6c ⑧ **Wooly Hat**☆☆☆ (f **7a**)   S   TR
Follow the broken finger flake all the way.
     TR: 1967 Ben Wintringham (6a)

*Local chat: A classic large wall with some superb routes.
You can also make up a lot of easier routes by combining
certain sections together.*

North Boulder   Eyelet   Dinosauros   Bow Window   Pig Tail Slab   Sewer   Vice   **Isolated Boulder**   Crucifix
Teddy Bear   Cottonsocks   Hangover   Sagittarius   Circle   Niblick   Sunshine   Spider Wall   Unclimbed Wall

11m

| UK Trad | Fontainebleau colour (font grade) | | Ticked |

4c ① Isolated Buttress Climb☆☆☆ (f **3c**)   S   TR

Top crack is not nice - or easy.
Solo: 1920's

5b ② Birchden Wall☆☆☆ (f **4c**)   S   TR

A lot harder than this grade if you don't have the beta.
Solo: Pre 1960's   TR: Pre 1950's

5c ③ Edward's Wall☆☆☆ (f **5a**)   S   TR

Try to only use the arête where necessary.
Solo: 1970's   TR: 1960's

5c ④ Birchden Corner☆☆☆ (f **5a**)   S   TR

Steep climbing on good holds.
Solo: 1940's Johnnie Lees

5c ⑤ Diversion☆☆☆ (f **5b**)   S   TR

One damn powerful move - not obvious.
Solo: Pre 1960's Dick Someone or another

Local chat: Birchden Wall is one of the best climbing spots in the south east for the mid grade climber. Lovely long routes that are just on the easy side of vertical. Most local climbers have these routes completely wired and will make them look ridiculously easy – beware!

Crag layout map - page 8
Graded tick list - page 10

| UK Trad | Fontainebleau colour (font grade) | | Ticked |

6a ⑥ Pan☆☆☆ (f **5c**)   S   TR

Originally called Halibut Giblets - a good eliminate.
No holds on either Birchden Wall or Birchden Corner allowed, and goes directly over the top overhang.
TR: 1982 Chris Arnol

6a ⑦ Edwards Effort☆☆☆ (f **5c**)   S   TR

A dainty lower section leads to a confusing flared crack that is sometimes climbed with a jammed middle finger. Finishing left is font 5c, going right is font 6b.
Solo: 1947 Menlove Edwards   TR: 1940*

6a ⑧ Frank's Arête☆☆☆ (f **6a**)   S   TR

Direct up the arête the whole way.
Solo: 1980's Frank Shannon

6b ⑨ Alexander Beetle☆☆☆ (f **6b+**)   S   TR

Originally called 'Alexander Beetle goes shopping on an Airbus to Bombay.' Takes an eliminate line up the wall - only using the side of the crack for the left hand.
TR: 1988 David Atchison-Jone

Access & Erosion: Belay bolts on top - a selection of long slings should be enough. Go to the right, around the next corner, then up the gully having passed Spider Wall. This boulder is free standing - and access is by a leap across a deep rock crevasse (many newcomers throw a complete wobbly).

UK Trad	Fontainebleau colour (font grade)	Ticked
2b	**① Boulder Bridge Route**☆☆☆ (f 2b)	S TR

Bridge anywhere up the back passage.
Solo: Pre 1950's *TR: Pre 1950's*

| 5c | **② Birchden Corner**☆☆☆ (f 5a) | S TR |

Steep climbing on good holds that escapes left.
Solo: 1940's Johnnie Lees

| 5c | **③ Crowborough Corner**☆☆☆ (f 5a) | S TR |

Various trick moves are used to move left onto the arête.
Solo: Pre 1960's *TR: Pre 1950's*

| 6a | **④ Wailing Wall**☆☆☆ (f 5c) | S TR |

Crux holds constantly change shape on this one.
Solo: Pre 1960's *TR: 1960's (5b)*

Local chat: Wailing Wall looks fabulous from a distance, where the angle seems vertical – ho ho! The uneven ground below is very unkind to falling climbers or high ball boulderers! A great spot for morning sunshine and afternoon shade.

| 6a | **⑤ Boysen's Arête**☆☆☆ (f 5c) | S TR |

Only one move that's hard - but hard it is.
Solo: 1960's Martin Boysen

| 6a | **⑥ Frank's Arête**☆☆☆ (f 6a) | S TR |

Direct up the arête the whole way.
Solo: 1980's Frank Shannon

| 6a | **⑦ Gall Stone**☆ (f 6a) | S TR |

Up the crack then the front face of the boulder.
TR: 1989 Paul Widdowson

| 6b | **⑧ Mister Spaceman**☆ (f 6a+) | S TR |

A single boulder problem move.
Solo: 1990 John Patterson *TR: 1994 Geoff Pearson*

| 6b | **⑨ Wailing Wall Eliminate**☆ (f 6b) | S TR |

A crimpy wall leads to a long reach.
Solo: 1988 David Atchison-Jones *TR: 1965*

Access & Erosion: Turn around and go past Spider Wall to reach the top plateau. Wobbly illustrates the leap across the passage. Bolts on top, 4 long slings needed.

HARRISON'S ROCKS
BOWLES ROCKS
HIGH ROCKS
HIGH ROCKS ANNEXE
HAPPY VALLEY
BULLS HOLLOW
ERIDGE GREEN
UNDER ROCKS
STONE FARM

⋀⋀ *[UK 6a] WAILING WALL (font 5c), Buster Martin*   *[UK 6a] BOYSEN'S ARETE (font 5c), Katie Sokolowska* ⋀

HARRISON'S ROCKS

BOWLES ROCKS

HIGH ROCKS

HIGH ROCKS ANNEXE

HAPPY VALLEY

BULLS HOLLOW

ERIDGE GREEN

UNDER ROCKS

STONE FARM

8m

Tricky step up

5c ③

5b ②   6a ⑥   6a ⑦   5b ①

UK Trad   Fontainebleau colour (font grade)   *Ticked*

5b ① **Jagger**☆☆ (f 4b)   S TR
A good technical route when dry.
Solo: 1980's   *TR: 1970's Tim Daniells*

5b ② **Boulder Route**☆☆ (f 4b)   S TR
A dark and greasy experience - good when dry.
Solo: 1970's

5c ③ **Ear-ring**☆ (f 5a)   S TR
Technical wall climbing - short lived.
Solo: 1990's   *TR: 1992 Pete Atkinson*

5c ④ **Plumb Line**☆ (f 5b)   S TR
A dark experience in the passage beneath the jump.
TR: 1993 Pete Atkinson

5c ⑤ **Bad Finger** (f 5b)   Slime Grim S TR
Greasy and slimey walls opposite Bloody Finger.
TR: 1970's

6a ⑥ **Gall Stone**☆ (f 6a)   S TR
Up the crack then the front face of the boulder.
TR: 1989 Paul Widdowson

6a ⑦ **Battle of the Bulge**☆☆☆ (f 6a)   S TR
A very good technical way up this wall.
Solo: 1990's   *TR: 1990 Pete Atkinson*

Local chat: These routes often dry out in summer and give
you climbs that you can never remember how to do. They
aren't anything great, but are certainly worth doing once.

*Access & Erosion: Go around to the right past Spider
Wall, then follow the obvious way up to the top plateau.
A selection of long slings should suffice.*

Grim

Grim

Grim

5c ⑤   5c ④   5b ②

HARRISON'S ROCKS

BOWLES ROCKS

HIGH ROCKS

HIGH ROCKS ANNEXE

HAPPY VALLEY

BULLS HOLLOW

ERIDGE GREEN

UNDER ROCKS

STONE FARM

UK Trad	Fontainebleau colour (font grade)	Ticked

2a **(1) Big Cave Left**★★★ (f 2a)   S TR
A good fun experience for beginners.
Solo: Pre 1940's

2b **(2) Big Cave Right**★★★ (f 2b)   S TR
A slightly more difficult route - exit is a squirm.
Solo: Pre 1940's

5b **(3) Right Under Your Nose**✕ (f 4b)   S TR
The very obvious arête.
TR: 2002 Graham West

5b **(4) Baldrick's Balderdash**✕ (f 4b)   S TR
Bridge your way up using the boulder to the top wall.
Solo: 1990 Pete Atkinson   *TR: 1980's*

UK Trad	Fontainebleau colour (font grade)	Ticked

5b **(5) Rough Boy**★★ (f 4c)   S TR
Climb is better than it looks.
Solo: 1992 Paul Widdowson   *TR: 1992 G. Lulham*

6a **(6) The Wallow**★★ (f 5c)   S TR
Taking the steep wall direct - much easier for tall folk.
Solo: 1992 Tim Skinner   *TR: 1980's Dan Lewis*

Local chat: A couple of very good easy climbs. The harder ones tend to stay damp and gungy.

Access & Erosion: These routes start low down in a cave area. Go up past Spider Wall to your right. Slings only needed for belays.

Crag layout map - page 8
Graded list - page 10

UK Trad	Fontainebleau colour (font grade)	Ticked

4a **(1) Crack and Cave**☆☆☆ (f 3a)   S TR
Originally called Grand Morin. A classic for its grade.
Solo: Pre 1930's

5b **(2) Baldrick's Balderdash**☆ (f 4b)   S TR
A pretty good climb that does need a dry spell.
Solo: 1990 Pete Atkinson   *TR:1980's*

5b **(3) Big Cave Wall**☆☆ (f 4b)   S TR
Climb the wall to start rather than the arête. Then swing
around to continue. Move right at the top to avoid the
really nasty overhang (original line).
Solo: Pre 1960's   *TR: Pre 1950's*

5c **(4) Spider Wall**☆☆ (f 5a)   S TR
Worn footholds make strong fingers essential.
Solo: 1960's   *TR: Pre 1960's*

Local chat: Spider wall on the right photo topo has
become a lot more undercut over the past 10 years, with
the starting footholds wearing away - it now gives very
fierce starts. A nice spot that catches the morning sun.

UK Trad	Fontainebleau colour (font grade)	Ticked

6a **(5) Last Chance**☆☆ (f 5c)   S TR
Leaving the ground is testing, soon easing up.
Solo: Pre 1960's

6a **(6) Forget-me-Knot**☆☆ (f 5c)   S TR
A difficult first move. Top overhang is good fun too.
Solo: 1982 Guy McLelland

6a **(7) Arachnophobia**☆☆☆ (f 6a)   S TR
A direct line up the arête, a very undercut top bulge.
Solo: 1980's Assorted Spiders

6a **(8) Second Chance**☆ (f 6a)   S TR
A dynamic boulder problem, much harder done static.
Solo: Pre 1960's

6b **(9) Black Widdowson**☆☆ (f 6b)   S TR
A crimpy and technical eliminate.
TR: 2002 Paul Widdowson

Top access & erosion beta: Go to the right then
up the passage that leads to the top plateau.
Make sure to set up the belay karabiner below
the top edge for routes on the left.

◁ [UK 6a] LAST CHANCE (font 5c), Livia Popa

HARRISON'S ROCKS

BOWLES ROCKS

HIGH ROCKS

HIGH ROCKS ANNEXE

HAPPY VALLEY

BULLS HOLLOW

ERIDGE GREEN

UNDER ROCKS

STONE FARM

UK Trad	Fontainebleau colour (font grade)	Ticked		UK Trad	Fontainebleau colour (font grade)	Ticked

4a ① **Crack and Cave**☆☆☆ (f **3a**) ☐S ☐TR
Originally called Grand Morin. A classic for its grade.
Solo: Pre 1930's

4b ② **Thingy**☆ (f **3b**) ☐S ☐TR
A short nose.
Solo: 1970's

5a ③ **Grant's Crack**☆☆☆ (f **4a**) ☐S ☐TR
Not that easy or straightforward - easy to fall off.
Solo: 1950's Grant Ingles

5b ④ **Whatsaname**☆ (f **4b**) ☐S ☐TR
A blind crack - often needs to dry out.
Solo: 1981 Geoff Pearson

5b ⑤ **Thingamywobs**☆☆ (f **4b**) ☐S ☐TR
A classic crackline.
Solo: 1970's Trevor Panther

6a ⑥ **Grant's Wall**☆☆☆ (f **6a**) ☐S ☐TR
A testing on-off style of route.
Solo: 1983 Ian Mailer   TR: 1965 Trevor Panther

6a ⑦ **Grant's Groove**☆☆☆ (f **6a**) ☐S ☐TR
Originally called 'Groove Wall Super.'
Solo: 1983 Ian Mailer   TR: 1970 Trevor Panther

6b ⑧ **Tiptoe through the Lichen**☆ (f **6b+**) ☐S ☐TR
When dry - this line is pretty technical.
TR: 1990 Pete Atkinson.

Local chat: Grant's Wall is one of those areas that does dry out more often than not, and offers really good technical climbing that is just on the right side of vertical. (Grants Crack is generally the last route to dry out). All of these routes are difficult to onsight - but really worth keeping - for when you are just good enough to 'just' do them. No stamina required, just very steady footwork.

Access & Erosion: Go up to the right of the wall, steps in the very damp gully - way up for most of the routes in the previous few sectors. Some of the routes require a static rope to set up the belay karabiner- and a tape sling plus protection for the top edge.

Crag layout map - page 8
Graded list - page 10

[UK 5a] GRANT'S CRACK (font 4a), Louise Collings ▷

HARRISON'S ROCKS

BOWLES ROCKS

HIGH ROCKS

HIGH ROCKS ANNEXE

HAPPY VALLEY

BULLS HOLLOW

ERIDGE GREEN

UNDER ROCKS

STONE FARM

7m

| 5a ② | 4b ① | 6b ⑦ | 5b ③ | 5c ⑥ | 5b ④ | 5b ⑤ |

UK Trad Fontainebleau colour (font grade) *Ticked*

4b ① Rum and Ribena (f 3b) Slime | S | TR
More swamp than Caribbean - a rum deal nevertheless.
Solo: 1970's

5a ② Little Cousin (f 4a) Slime | S | TR
A mantle on muck.
Solo: 1992 Tim Skinner

5b ③ Rum and Coke (f 4b) Slime | S | TR
Not recommended.
Solo: 1982 Geoff Pearson

5b ④ Cunning Stunts (f 4b) Slime | S | TR
Dire.
Solo: 1982 Geoff Pearson

UK Trad Fontainebleau colour (font grade) *Ticked*

5b ⑤ Cabbage Patch Blues (f 4b) Slime | S | TR
Dire.
Solo: 1985 Rudi Kane

5c ⑥ Bovver Boot (f 5b) Slime | S | TR
Don't bovver.
TR: 1992 Chris Murra

6b ⑦ Purple Nasty (f 6a+) Slime | S | TR
Nasty for sure.
TR: 1992 Chris Murra

Local chat: This area could clean up if the water run-off was diverted to another part of the cliff. Until this happens, this area is disgusting, rancid and thoroughly putrid.

Top access & erosion beta: The gully to the right or left of the crag allows for an easy ascent. Allow for stagnant water on top, waterproof your ropes first. Short static rope needed for belays.

HARRISON'S ROCKS

BOWLES ROCKS

HIGH ROCKS

HIGH ROCKS ANNEXE

HAPPY VALLEY

BULLS HOLLOW

ERIDGE GREEN

UNDER ROCKS

STONE FARM

UK Trad | Fontainebleau colour (font grade) | Ticked

1b ① Scout Chimney Right (f 2a) | 🗑 S TR
Short & miserable.
Solo: 1940's

2a ② Scout Chimney Left (f 2a) | 🗑 S TR
Longer & more miserable.
Solo: 1940's

3a ③ Back Passage (f 2a) | S TR
A short crack.
Solo: 1966 Tony Bartlett

5a ④ Garden Slab Right (f 4a) | S TR
Fractionally the easier way up.
Solo: 1960's

5a ⑤ Garden Slab Left (f 4a) | S TR
Fractionally the harder way up.
Solo: 1960's

UK Trad | Fontainebleau colour (font grade) | Ticked

5b ⑥ Tiptoe thru the Tulips (f 4b) | S TR
Going direct up the centre.
Solo: 1982 M. Barrett

5c ⑦ Araldite Wall (f 5a) | S TR
Very short unfortunately.
Solo: 1980's | TR: Pre 1960's

5c ⑧ Biceps Buttress ☆☆ (f 5b) | S TR
A good steep climb.
Solo: Pre 1950's | TR: Pre 1950's

5c ⑨ LHT (f 5b) | 🗑 S TR
Slightly less dire.
Solo: 1992 Tim Skinner

Local chat: During the 1970's this area was clean and offered pretty good climbing. Over subsequent years the area has been overgrown and therefore been neglected. With cleaning, the slab offers good delicate climbing. Nothing too fantastic but definitely worth doing.

Top access & erosion beta: Steps lead up the central gully and easily to the top. Short static rope needed to set up good belays.

Crag layout map - page 8
Graded tick list - page 10

North Boulder   Eyelet   Dinosauros   Bow Window   Pig Tail Slab   Sewer   Vice   Isolated Boulder   Crucifix
Teddy Bear   Cottonsocks   Hangover   Sagittarius   Circle   Niblick   Sunshine   Spider Wall   Unclimbed Wall

HARRISON'S ROCKS

BOWLES ROCKS

HIGH ROCKS

HIGH ROCKS ANNEXE

HAPPY VALLEY

BULLS HOLLOW

ERIDGE GREEN

UNDER ROCKS

STONE FARM

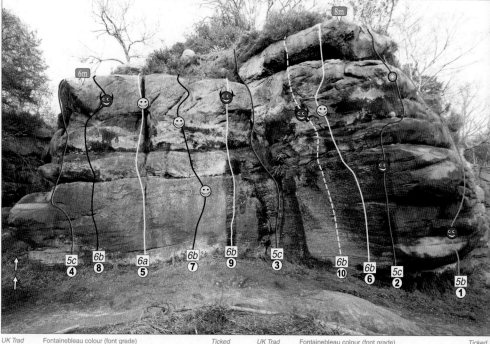

UK Trad	Fontainebleau colour (font grade)	Ticked

5b **①** **Half Crown Corner**☆☆ (f **4b**) ⬚S ⬚TR
A punchy move is needed to get going, then much easier.
Solo: Pre 1940's

5c **②** **Shodan**☆☆☆ (f **5a**) ⬚S ⬚TR
A fingery wall is followed by a puzzling move for many.
Solo: 1960's

5c **③** **The Corner**☆☆ (f **5a**) ⬚S ⬚TR
Most years this is adorned with dampness - fab when dry.
Solo: 1960's

5c **④** **Biceps Buttress**☆☆ (f **5b**) ⬚S ⬚TR
A good steep climb.
Solo: 1960's *TR: Pre 1960's*

6a **⑤** **Muscle Crack**☆ (f **6a**) ⬚S ⬚TR
A wide and nasty crack.
Solo: 1970's *TR: 1960's*

UK Trad	Fontainebleau colour (font grade)	Ticked

6b **⑥** **Phillipa**☆☆☆ (f **6a+**) ⬚S ⬚TR
Many different ways - all awkward.
Solo: 1970's *TR: Pre 1960*

6b **⑦** **Crucifix**☆☆ (f **6a+**) ⬚S ⬚TR
Topping out is generally where it all goes wrong.
Solo: 1992 Tim Skinner *TR: 1968 Trevor Panthe*

6b **⑧** **Finger Popper**☆☆ (f **6b**) ⬚S ⬚TR
Tricky moves at the top, but not that hard (soft touch).
TR: 1985 Ian Maile

6b **⑨** **Hector's House**☆☆☆ (f **6b+**) ⬚S ⬚TR
The short wall, dynamic at the top - usually.
TR: 1982 Guy McLellan

6b **⑩** **Magic Wall**☆☆☆ (f **6c**) ⬚S ⬚TR
Very crimpy lower wall, then direct up the greasy wall.
TR: 1983 Guy McLellan

Local chat: This is a lovely little bay, that catches the afternoon sun and has some cracking short routes. The top outs are pretty fierce - and consequently they are not generally considered as sensible highballs, in fact - I would call them highly dangerous highballs! With the trees trimmed down in front, the full force of the sun gets in and completely dries it out - magic. The angle does not offer anything in the low grades, so keep on walking if you don't feel strong.

Top access & erosion beta: Go to the left and up the large gully to the top plateau. There are some loose blocks at the top, so take care not to belay on these etc. You will need a static rope since good trees are some way back, and please protect the soft top edge. On Shodan and Half Crown Corner, make sure to drop the karabiner a good way down, then clip again for the top overhang. ☺

Crag layout map - page 8
Graded list - page 10

[UK 6b] CRUCIFIX (font 6a+), Liam Halsey ➤

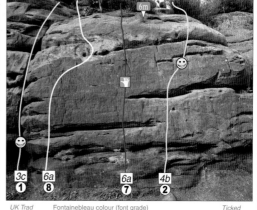

UK Trad	Fontainebleau colour (font grade)	Ticked

3c (1) Birch Tree Crack ☆ (f 3a)   S   TR

The Birch Tree went in the 80's. Now you have to struggle up the crack left. The undercut start is particularly nasty. Good bridging technique solves the problem effortlessly!
Solo: Pre 1940's

4b (2) Birch Tree Wall ☆ (f 3c)   S   TR

An enjoyable short wall - finish delicately.
Solo: Pre 1940's

4c (3) Wanderfall ☆☆ (f 3c)

This direct line seems to have sprouted good holds.
Solo: Pre 1960's

5a (4) Wander at Leisure ☆☆ (f 4a)   S   TR

A few tricky moves to start, getting harder.
Solo: Pre 1960's

Local chat: Unclimbed Wall is the long straight wall at the end of Harrison's. This whole area is very popular, especially as it is one of the first sectors to come into warm morning sunshine - and with a nice selection of routes in the easier grades (don't expect to be on your own here). Nice angled rock that doesn't pump you solid - well maybe. The left end sector used to be called Wander at Leisure, since you could almost anywhere at 5a. Over time, the starts have worn away to be undercut, with some of the holds improving and others denigrating. At present there are 3 pretty good independent lines on the left wall as indicated, but I am sure these will change with wear.

Access & Erosion: The easiest way up is to go to the left of the sector, past Crucifix Wall, then up the passage with steps to your right. There is a scramble up 'Small Crack' at the right edge of the photo-topo, but it isn't that easy to get up whilst carrying ropes etc. Please make sure to extend the belay karabiner down to the top of the climb, and not to rub the rock with the moving rope.

UK Trad	Fontainebleau colour (font grade)	Ticked

5b (5) Half Crown Corner ☆☆ (f 4b)   S   TR

A punchy move is needed to get going, then much easier.
Solo: Pre 1940's

5b (6) Don Juander ☆ (f 4c)   S   TR

Quite a good sustained little number, don't stray off line.
Solo: Pre 1960's

6a (7) Mister Splodge ☆ (f 5c)   S   TR

Good technical climbing but pretty short (stow not in).
Solo: 1960's

6a (8) Dodgepot ☆ (f 6a)   S   TR

Tricky up to the stow, then a sandy grovel.
Solo: 1960's

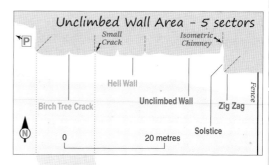

Unclimbed Wall Area - 5 sectors

P   Small Crack   Isometric Chimney

Hell Wall

Birch Tree Crack   Unclimbed Wall   Zig Zag

Fence

Solstice

N   0   20 metres

Crag layout map - page 8
Graded list - page 10

◁ [UK 3c] BIRCH TREE CRACK (font 3a), Sam Rigg

| Teddy Bear | Cottonsocks | Hangover | Sagittarius | Circle | Niblick | Sunshine | Spider Wall | Unclimbed Wall |
| North Boulder | Eyelet | Dinosauros | Bow Window | Pig Tail Slab | Sewer | Vice | Isolated Boulder | Crucifix |

Side tabs: HARRISON'S ROCKS | BOWLES ROCKS | HIGH ROCKS | HIGH ROCKS ANNEXE | HAPPY VALLEY | BULLS HOLLOW | ERIDGE GREEN | UNDER ROCKS | STONE FARM

HARRISON'S ROCKS

BOWLES ROCKS

HIGH ROCKS

HIGH ROCKS ANNEXE

HAPPY VALLEY

BULLS HOLLOW

ERIDGE GREEN

UNDER ROCKS

STONE FARM

UK Trad	Fontainebleau colour (font grade)	Ticked

2a **①** Easy Cleft Left★★ (f 2a) | S | TR

A fun clamber up the giant steps.
Solo: Pre 1940's

3a **②** Charon's Chimney★★★ (f 3a) | S | TR

All beginners struggle on this one.
Solo: Pre 1940's

3a **③** Awkward Cleft Right★★ (f 3a) | S | TR

Technical and troublesome for beginners.
Solo: Pre 1940's

UK Trad	Fontainebleau colour (font grade)	Ticked

4c **④** Hell Wall★★★ ☹ (f 4a) | S | TR

A powerful start leads to an iffy finish for some.
Solo: Pre 1940's

5a **⑤** Senarra★★★ ☹ (f 4a) | S | TR

Much more risky than Hell Wall.
Solo: 1970's

5c **⑥** The Scoop★★ ☹ (f 5b) | S | TR

Very delicate with worn out holds, very sketchy.
Solo: 1960's TR: Pre 1960

6a **⑦** Pullover★★ (f 5c) | S | TR

Powerful - should suit indoor thugs - except the finish.
Solo: 1960's TR: Pre 1960

6a **⑧** Skid Marx (f 6a) | S | TR

Delicate eliminate left of Scoop.
Solo: 1980's

6b **⑨** Demons of Death★★ (f 6a+) | S | TR

Essential mantle practise for Fontainebleau top outs.
Solo: 1980's

Local chat: Hell Wall is significantly lower than most of the outcrop and provides some lovely shorter routes. Many climbs here are also popular highballs, but beware, although the top is not that high, there is a somewhat poignant history of accidents at the base of Hell Wall; consider this very carefully - should you choose a rope free option.

Top access & erosion beta: The easy way up is back to the Crucifix sector then steps in gully to the top plateau. It is also the best descent for beginners since the other ways up and down involve iffy scrambles. Make sure to set up the belay karabiner over the top edge. For some climbs you will need 4 long tape slings.

◁ [3a] AWKWARD CLEFT.

| Teddy Bear | Cottonsocks | Hangover | Sagittarius | Circle | Niblick | Sunshine | Spider Wall | Unclimbed Wall |
| North Boulder | Eyelet | Dinosauros | Bow Window | Pig Tail Slab | Sewer | Vice | Isolated Boulder | Crucifix |

UK Trad	Fontainebleau colour (font grade)	Ticked

5b **①** **Unclimbed Wall**☆☆☆ (f 4b) S TR

Good-ish holds all the way, but a cruncher of a crux right at the end makes it into a fabulous route. The good rest in the middle keeps the grade down.

Solo: 1960's *TR: Pre 1950's*

5b **②** **Far Left**☆☆☆ (f 4c) S TR

Quite sustained for the grade, and definitely a grade harder for shorties. Eliminate to the left is Far Far Left, around 5c but suffers from being wet quite often.

Solo: 1960's *TR: 1963 Max Smart*

5c **③** **Elementary**☆☆☆ (f 5a) S TR

Very tricky onsight, requires stamina & ingenuity.

5c **④** **Baskerville**☆☆☆ (f 5b) S TR

Easy first half, followed by an unobvious technical finish.

TR: 1960'a Ian Asplend

5c **⑤** **My Dear Watson**☆☆☆ (f 5b) S TR

A fine eliminate - with a very awkward start that demands great flexibility. Make every effort to avoid the holds on neighbouring routes.

Solo: Not proven *TR: 1994 Sherlock Holmes*

6a **⑥** **Minnie the Minx**☆☆☆ (f 5c) S TR

Lovely technical climbing leads to a crimp finish

Solo: 1982 David Atchison-Jones *TR: 1980's*

6a **⑦** **Roger the Dodger**☆☆☆ (f 5c) S TR

At the top, the big foothold to the right is not allowed.

Solo: 1982 Dan Lewis *TR: 1980's*

6a **⑧** **Right Unclimbed**☆☆☆ (f 6a) S TR

Make sure to start low to get a better and longer route.

Solo: 1983 Gary Wickham *TR: 1960's*

6a **⑨** **Desperate Dan**☆☆☆ (f 6a) S TR

Pockets combined with weird technique solves desperation.

Solo: 1990 John Patterson *TR: 1982 Dan Lewis*

6b **⑩** **Jingo Wobbly**☆☆☆ (f 6a+) S TR

Very height dependent - grade for tall climbers only. The lower part is a lovely mid grade 5c, and makes a very good direct start to Unclimbed Wall.

Solo: 1990 John Patterson *TR: 1984 Dan Lewis*

6c **⑪** **Dennis the Menace**☆☆☆ (f 7a+) S TR

Small holds to say the least.

TR: 1990's

Local chat: This wall is just about the best single piece of flat rock on Sandstone. It's just off vertical with plenty of pockets, giving a lovely concentration of grade 5c routes that are technical - yet still possible for most good climbers. Virtually all the routes require skill and technique rather than strength & power. It's not the best wall for kids since there are quite a few long reaches unfortunately. Many of the routes have changed names over the years, but more recently the adoption of Beano characters seems good for light hearted fun.

Access & Erosion: Most good climbers find it easy enough to scramble up Isometric Chimney to the top right of the wall. Be sure to set the belay karabiner over the top edge so that the rope doesn't wear the rock. Please make extra effort to step off a clean carpet, and therefore reduce the wear on the footholds. Bolt belays for the easier routes, harder routes tend to require a short static for the belay.

Crag layout map - page 8
Graded tick list - page 10

◁ *[UK 5b] UNCLIMBED WALL (font 4b), Buster Martin*

Teddy Bear   Cottonsocks   Hangover   Sagittarius   Circle   Niblick   Sunshine   Spider Wall   Unclimbed Wall
North Boulder   Eyelet   Dinosauros   Bow Window   Pig Tail Slab   Sewer   Vice   Isolated Boulder   Crucifix

HARRISON'S ROCKS
BOWLES ROCKS
HIGH ROCKS
HIGH ROCKS ANNEXE
HAPPY VALLEY
BULLS HOLLOW
ERIDGE GREEN
UNDER ROCKS
STONE FARM

HARRISON'S ROCKS

BOWLES ROCKS

HIGH ROCKS

HIGH ROCKS ANNEXE

HAPPY VALLEY

BULLS HOLLOW

ERIDGE GREEN

UNDER ROCKS

STONE FARM

UK Trad	Fontainebleau colour (font grade)	Ticked

1b ① Isometric Chimney ✶ (f 2a) ▢ S ▢ TR

An easy scramble up, but much harder to come down.
Solo: Pre 1930's

5a ② Sun Ray ✶ (f 4a) ▢ S ▢ TR

A bit short unfortunately.
Solo: 1960 Ray Stephens

5a ⑤ Zig Zag ✶✶✶ (f 4a) ▢ S ▢ TR

The start is continually wearing away and is pretty tough
to crack these days, may well get harder. By zig zagging,
the grade is kept to a happy & enjoyable 5a.
Solo: 1940's　　　　　　　　　　　*TR: 1930's*

*Local chat: A small wall with some surprisingly good
short routes. Starting any of the routes low on the right
side helps to make the routes longer. The slab is a
classic slide down and seems to be wearing well.*

*Top access & erosion beta: Go up Isometric
Chimney to the left. Bolt belays on top of the
arête, only slings generally needed.*

UK Trad	Fontainebleau colour (font grade)	Ticked

5c ④ Bulging Wall ✶✶ (f 5a) ▢ S ▢ TR

Sometimes called Zig Nose, it's either easy or hard.
Solo: 1960's　　　　　　　　　　　*TR: Pre 1960's*

5c ⑤ Solstice ✶✶ (f 5a) ▢ S ▢ TR

This is a lovely route, but quite short. It can be made a
lot more fun by starting at the lowest point of the arête,
then moving left a bit later.
Solo: 1980's　　　　　　　　*TR: 1977 Martin Randal*

| HARRISON'S ROCKS |
| BOWLES ROCKS |
| HIGH ROCKS |
| HIGH ROCKS ANNEXE |
| HAPPY VALLEY |
| BULLS HOLLOW |
| ERIDGE GREEN |
| UNDER ROCKS |
| STONE FARM |

UK Trad   Fontainebleau colour (font grade)   Ticked

| 5a | **(1) Zig Zag**☆☆☆ (f **4a**) | S | TR |

A lot of going sideways keeps the grade down.
Solo: 1940's   *TR: 1930's*

| 5c | **(2) Bulging Wall**☆☆ (f **5a**) | S | TR |

Sometimes called Zig Nose, it's either easy or hard.
Solo: 1960's   *TR: Pre 1960's*

| 5c | **(3) Witches Broomstick**☆☆ (f **5b**) | S | TR |

A powerful start, easing considerably in the crack.
Solo: 1960's   *TR: 1960's*

| 5c | **(4) Rift**☆☆☆ (f **5b**) | S | TR |

A hard pull to start, then finish either of 3 ways at 5b.
Solo: Pre 1940's   *TR: Pre 1940's*

*Local chat: Nothing here in the lower grades – which
is a pity since the upper wall is very nice and only 5b
territory (lots of eliminate lines also). The undercut
lower part gives unbalanced routes – and usually stays
damp. The rock is also pretty soft in this part due to
the dampness over the years – resulting in very few
holds being left low down.*

*The area to the right of this buttress is fenced off
private land. This is not used for climbing and is very
green and greasy.*

UK Trad   Fontainebleau colour (font grade)   Ticked

| 6a | **(5) Meat Cleaver**☆ (f **6a**) | S | TR |

The crack by the fence - often greasy.
                                          TR: 1982 Dan Lewis

| 6a | **(6) Max**☆☆ (f **6a**) | S | TR |

Very overhanging start, often dynamic.
Solo: 1980's   *TR: 1980's*

| 6b | **(7) Neutral**☆☆ (f **6a+**) | S | TR |

Only marginally harder for a short while.
Solo: 1960's   *TR: 1960's*

| 6b | **(8) Stubble**☆ (f **6b+**) | S | TR |

A powerful start on the steep overhang.
Solo: 1990's   *TR: 1992 Steve Quinton*

| 6b | **(9) The Powerband**☆ (f **6c+**) | S | TR |

A low level traverse of the wall to the arête.
Solo: 2002

*Access & Erosion: Go to the left and up
through Isometric Chimney. You will need a
static rope to set up a correct belay with the
karabiner over the edge. Please always use a
bouldering pad to protect the ground as much
as possible.*

Crag layout map - page 8
Graded tick list - page 10

HARRISON'S ROCKS

BOWLES ROCKS

HIGH ROCKS

HIGH ROCKS ANNEXE

HAPPY VALLEY

BULLS HOLLOW

ERIDGE GREEN

UNDER ROCKS

STONE FARM

Bowles Rocks is a fabulous outcrop with the best quality of Sandstone Rock in the South East of England. It lacks the sheer volume of routes that Harrison's offers, but supplies a concentrated blast of top class routes that are very memorable. The outcrop forms a pleasant series of walls and tiny bays in the lower section, and an intimidating large curving amphitheatre of rock, higher up the grass slope. Bowles catches the sun for most of the day and is a perfect place to climb, relax and picnic. Some 50 plus years ago, the rocks were very overgrown, being set in a small wooded valley that formed part of a Pig Farm. The central walls were sometimes used as a shooting range, hence many of the early route names such as Target, Ricochet at Pig's Nose. The land was then turned into an outdoor centre, along with a dry ski slope at the top of the hill. The original buildings were few and discreet, as was the tiny open air swimming pool for all to enjoy at the foot of the crag. Unfortunately, the development got out of hand and the cliffs are now hemmed in by large buildings. Thankfully in summer, the foliage does its best to mask this torrid urbanization.

The centre for its part, does seem to manage Bowles Rocks exceptionally well, and the area is sparklingly clean and pleasant to visit. There are hefty belay bolts at the top of the crag, and a nice woodland path for access to and from the top. Bowles Outdoor Centre will often set up their own ropes on many of the easier climbs. If you are bringing a large group, contact the centre first.

Location: Bowles Rocks **SAT NAV info**
P1 - Parking Grid reference: **TQ 543 331**
P1 - Postcode **TN3 9LW**
Rocks Grid reference: **TQ 542 330**

Bowles Rocks is just off the main A26, and is situated in a little valley - the noise of the main road is thankfully unheard. There is usually a brown road sign [Bowles Outdoor Centre], to indicate the turning when coming from either Tunbridge Wells or Crowborough. Park in the roomy car park just after the entance, and the rocks are barely a 1 min walk. There is usually a small charge to climb at Bowles which goes into the coffers of the charitable trust that runs and manages the outcrop. For anyone coming by train, there is a nice cross country footpath from Eridge Station, which takes around 20 mins walk.

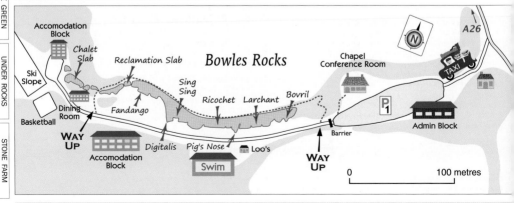

| Bull | Netwall | Fandango | Digitalis | Sing Sing | Ricochet | Pig's Nose | Funnel | Alka | Bovril |
| Chalet Slab | Reclamation | Mick's Wall | Sapper | Carbide | Devaluation | Birch Crack | Larchant | November | |

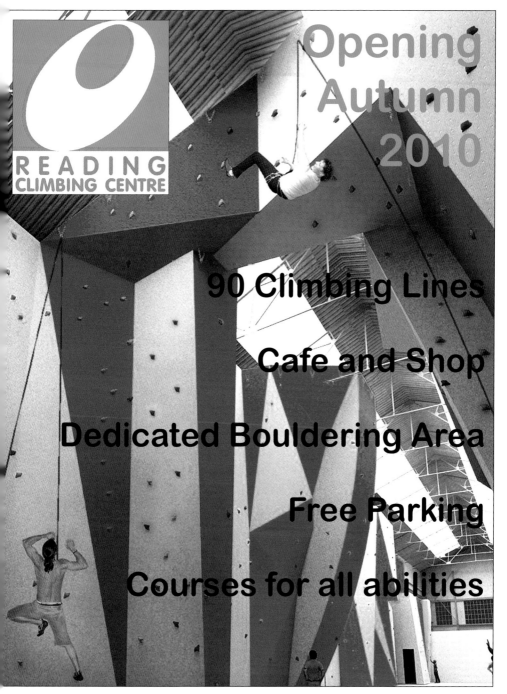

Opening Autumn 2010

90 Climbing Lines

Cafe and Shop

Dedicated Bouldering Area

Free Parking

Courses for all abilities

Unit 33, Britten Road, Robert Cort Industrial Estate
Elgar Road South, Reading, RG2 0AU
www.readingclimbingcentre.com
info@readingclimbingcentre.com

△△ *Banana, Fandango, Mick's Wall and Digitalis sectors.*

[UK 6c] SONIC BLUE (font 7b), Chris 'Orc' Searle - page 121 ▷

⌃ [UK 6b] CARDBOARD BOX (font 6b), Mark Glennie - page 130

⌃ [UK 4c] SAPPER (font 3c), Charlotte Latter - page 126

⌃ [UK 6a] Salamander Slab (font 5c), Suzie Zitter - page 129

HARRISON'S ROCKS

BOWLES ROCKS

HIGH ROCKS

HIGH ROCKS ANNEXE

HAPPY VALLEY

BULLS HOLLOW

ERIDGE GREEN

UNDER ROCKS

STONE FARM

1b
☐ Hot Cross Bun (f 1b) p144
☐ Reclamation G (f 1b) p117
☐ Renison Gully (f 2a) p143
2a
☐ November (f 2a) p144
☐ Badgering (f 2a) p110
☐ Grotty Groove (f 2a) p113
☐ Chelsea Chim (f 2a) p114
☐ Harden Gully (f 2a) p141
☐ Birch Crack (f 2a) p139
2b
☐ Grotto Chimney (f 2a) p122
☐ Rec- Slab Right (f 2b) p117
☐ Running Jump (f 2b) p113
3a
☐ Claire (f 2a) p144
☐ Well's Reach (f 2a) p140
☐ Charlie's Chim (f 2b) p134
☐ Red Peg (f 2a) p144
☐ Sing Sing (f 2b) p129
☐ Skiffle (f 2b) p121
☐ Rec- Slab Left (f 2c) p117
3b
☐ Chalet Slab Left (f 2b) p111
☐ Hibiscus (f 2b) p110
☐ Fragile Wall (f 3b) p143
3c
☐ Funnel (f 3a) p140
☐ Chalet Slab C (f 2c) p111
4a
☐ Rad's Cliff (f 3a) p146
☐ YoYo (f 3a) p126
☐ Corbett Nose (f 3a) p140
☐ Kennard's Climb (f 3a) p139
☐ Barham Boulder (f 3a)
☐ Scirocco Slab (f 3a) p113
☐ Marmite (f 3a) p146
☐ Badger's Head (f 3a) p110
4b
☐ Ballerina (f 3b) p144
☐ Nelson's Col (f 3b) p140
☐ Corbett Slab (f 3b) p140
☐ Scirocco Wall (f 3b) p113
☐ Bovril (f 3b) p146
☐ Sylvie's Slab (f 3b) p141
☐ Dival's Div (f 3b) p140
☐ Babylon (f 3b) p118
☐ Kemp's Delight (f 3b) p122
☐ Roman Nose (f 3b) p112
☐ Netwall (f 3b) p114
☐ Ricochet (f 3b) p132
☐ Wally (f 3b) p146
☐ Elevator (f 4a) p143
4c
☐ Courts Climb (f 3b) p113
☐ Chalet Slab Right (f 3c) p111
☐ Cave Crack (f 3c) p134
☐ Four-by-Two (f 3c) p132

☐ Sapper (f 3c) p126
☐ E.S.Cadet Nose (f 3c) p134
☐ Alka (f 3c) p143
☐ October (f 3c) p141
☐ Six Foot (f 3c) p141
☐ Court's Climb (f 3c) p114
☐ Nealon's (f 4a) p146
5a
☐ Dib (f 4a) p140
☐ Lee Enfield (f 4a) p132
☐ Fragile Arête (f 4a) p141
☐ Helter Skelter (f 4a) p110
☐ Escalator (f 4a) p143
☐ Larchant (f 4a) p141
☐ Pig's Nose (f 4a) p137
☐ G Force (f 4a) p144
☐ P-Perseverance (f 4a) p129
☐ Pull Through (f 4a) p132
☐ Santa's Claws (f 4a) p114
☐ Orr Traverse (f 4a) p125
☐ Barham Boulder (f 4b) p146
5b
☐ Corner Layback (f 4b) p113
☐ Devaluation (f 4b) p134
☐ Drosophila (f 4b) p118
☐ Henn-Heights (f 4b) p141
☐ T.T. (f 4b) p137
☐ Burlap Arete (f 4b) p126
☐ Kalashnikov (f 4b) p132
☐ Abracadabra (f 4b) p131
☐ T.N.T. (f 4b) p118
☐ Two Step (f 4b) p111
☐ Cenotaph C-2 (f 4b) p117
☐ Bull's Nose (f 4b) p110
☐ Chris (f 4b) p139
☐ Gully Wall (f 4c) p139
☐ Mick's Wall (f 4c) p122
☐ Mumbo Jumbo (f 4c) p111
☐ Jackie (f 4c) p129
☐ Seltzer (f 4c) p143
☐ Swastika (f 4c) p131
5c
☐ Kemp's Wall (f 5a) p122
☐ Meager's RH (f 5a) p129
☐ Rib (f 5a) p139
☐ U.N. (f 5a) p140
☐ Jean Genie (f 5a) p112
☐ Aug-Variation (f 5a) p141
☐ Encore (f 5a) p143
☐ Pigs Ear (f 5b) p137
☐ Umbilicus (f 5b) p112
☐ Torreador (f 5b) p110
☐ Coathanger (f 5b) p121
☐ Chalet Slab D (f 5b) p111
☐ Flying Bandit (f 5b) p134
☐ Oliver's Twist (f 5b) p147
☐ Mohrenkop (f 5b) p111
☐ Reclamation Slap (f 5b) p117
☐ Inspiration (f 5b) p126

☐ Spock's Disco (f 5b) p126
☐ August Var-SS (f 5b) p141
6a
☐ Manita (f 5c) p129
☐ Burlap (f 5c) p126
☐ U Tube (f 5c) p140
☐ Nero (f 5c) p129
☐ Target (f 5c) p134
☐ Juanita (f 5c) p126
☐ Pastry (f 5c) p121
☐ Salamander Slab (f 5c) p129
☐ Koffler (f 5c) p139
☐ Perspiration (f 5c) p131
☐ Nealon's Direct (f 5c) p147
☐ Mick's Wall Arête (f 6a) p122
☐ The Big Stretch (f 6a) p134
☐ Mental Balance (f 6a) p117
☐ Aphrodite (f 6a) p114
☐ Banana (f 6a) p118
☐ Nightmare (f 6a) p131
☐ Slyme Cryme (f 6a) p118
☐ Fandango (f 6a) p121
☐ Hate (f 6a) p137
☐ Serenade Arête (f 6a) p125
6b
☐ Digitalis (f 6a+) p125
☐ Fandango R-Hand (f 6a+) p121
☐ Station to Station (f 6a+) p121
☐ Knitwall (f 6a+) p113
☐ Icarus (f 6a+) p121
☐ Blue Moon (f 6a+) p112
☐ Proboscis (f 6a+) p118
☐ Thieving Gypsies (f 6a+) p131
☐ Target Direct (f 6a+) p132
☐ Conjuror (f 6a+) p132
☐ Sugarplum (f 6a+) p121
☐ Lady in Mink (f 6a+) p147
☐ Finale (f 6a+) p143
☐ The Ly'in (f 6a+) p126
☐ Mick's Wall Var (f 6a+) p122
☐ Morpheus (f 6a+) p143
☐ Unbelieveable (f 6a+) p112
☐ Patella (f 6a+) p125
☐ Jack in the Box (f 6b) p146
☐ Kara (f 6b) p132
☐ Bubble Wrap (f 6b) p131
☐ Twilight Zone (f 6b) p129
☐ Geoff's Route (f 6b) p112
☐ Sandman (f 6b) p134
☐ Love (f 6b)
☐ Urban Jock (f 6b+)
☐ Zugabe (f 6b+) p143
☐ Buzzards - Missing (f 6b+) p140
☐ Stoneman (f 6b+) p134
☐ Cardboard Box (f 6b+) p131
☐ McLelland Trav (f 6b+) p125
☐ Coast to Coast (f 6b+) p114
☐ The Thing (f 6b+) p126
☐ Temptation (f 6b+) p125

☐ Watson Watt (f 6b+) p137
☐ Upside Downies (f 6b+) p137
☐ Poff Pastry (f 6c) p121
☐ White Verdict (f 6c) p126
☐ Knuclebones (f 6c) p114
☐ Boiling Point (f 6c) p131
☐ Tobacco Road (f 6c) p121
☐ Banana Hammock (f 6c) p11?
☐ Kinnard (f 6c) p125
☐ Froggatt Fudge (f 6c+) p112
☐ Nutella (f 6c+) p125
6c
☐ Nicotine Alley (f 7a) p121
☐ Zoom (f 7a) p114
☐ London Pride (f 7a) p122
☐ The Wrecker (f 7a) p140
☐ Skallagrigg (f 7a) p134
☐ One Nighter (f 7a+) p126
☐ Rec-Nightmare (f 7a+) p131
☐ Carbide Finger (f 7b) p131
7a
☐ Twisted Vegas (f 7b+) p121
☐ T-Monkey Things (f 7b+) p13?
☐ Phasis (f 7c) p121

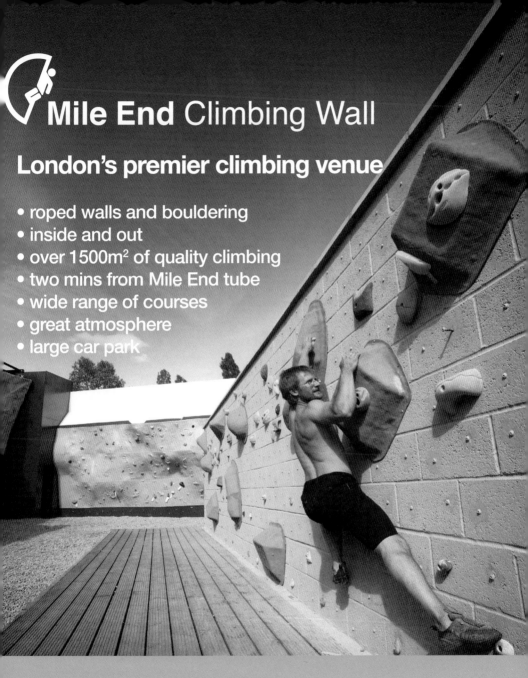

Mile End Climbing Wall

London's premier climbing venue

- roped walls and bouldering
- inside and out
- over 1500m² of quality climbing
- two mins from Mile End tube
- wide range of courses
- great atmosphere
- large car park

www.mileendwall.org.uk
020 8980 0289

UK Trad	Fontainebleau colour (font grade)		Ticked

2a **①** Badgering the Badger (f 2a)   S TR

A simple little slab.
Solo: 1960's

4a **②** Badger's Head ☆ (f 3a)   S TR

A few crimps on a slab.
Solo: 1960's

Local chat: This boulder is situated at the side of a small car park, in front of the top chalet at the end of the tarmac road. It is pretty small and inconsequential, but does offer some little fun problems.

Access & Erosion: There are no belays on top - please use a crash pad to protect the ground.

UK Trad	Fontainebleau colour (font grade)		Ticked

5b **③** Bull's Nose ☆ (f 4b)   S TR

A slightly fiendish mantle.
Solo: 1960's

5c **④** Torreador ☆ (f 5b)   S TR

An eliminate up the arête.
Solo: 1960's

3b **①** Hibiscus ☆ (f 2b)   S TR

An often overgrown area, mantle through the bushes.
Solo: 1960's

5a **②** Helter Skelter ☆ (f 4a)   S TR

A steep small wall with a technical finish.
Solo: 1960's

Local chat: The Hibiscus little sector is just above the west end of the canteen and to the left of Chalet Slab. Nothing great unfortunately, and very awkward with the building so close.

Crag layout map - page 104
Graded list - page 108

HARRISON'S ROCKS

BOWLES ROCKS

HIGH ROCKS

HIGH ROCKS ANNEXE

HAPPY VALLEY

BULLS HOLLOW

ERIDGE GREEN

UNDER ROCKS

STONE FARM

UK Trad   Fontainebleau colour (font grade)   Ticked

3b ① Chalet Slab Left☆ (f 2a)   S TR
  A nice simple slab route.
  Solo: 1960's

3c ② Chalet Slab Centre☆☆☆ (f 2c)   S TR
  A lovely delicate line that escapes left.
  Solo: 1960's

4c ③ Chalet Slab Right☆☆ (f 3c)   S TR
  A slightly fiendish mantle.
  Solo: 1960's

5b ④ Mumbo Jumbo☆ (f 4c)   S TR
  A direct fun finish with a tricky mantleshelf.
  Solo: 1960's

5c ⑤ Chalet Slab Direct☆ (f 5b)   S TR
  A hard finish with an awkward mantleshelf.
  Solo: 1960's

Local chat: A quiet area set behind the dining chalet of the Outdoor Centre, and gets the full whiff of the fish and chips. Lovely texture of rock with a few inset pebbles. Climbing is better than the slightly cramped situation. The topouts look quite tame from below, but beware - they are nasty and spit you off - it is a lot higher than it looks. - a rope is advisable.

Access & Erosion: Easily go up to the left of the sector. 3 slings should be fine for the classic routes, but a short static is handy to keep the belay in position for the harder routes.

5b ① Two Step☆ (f 4b)   S TR
  Two mantles - not much else.
  Solo: 1961 Terry Tullis

5c ② Mohrenkop☆☆ (f 5b)   S TR
  A stiff little number up the front of the block.
  Solo: 1962 Terry Tullis

HARRISON'S ROCKS

BOWLES ROCKS

HIGH ROCKS

HIGH ROCKS ANNEXE

HAPPY VALLEY

BULLS HOLLOW

ERIDGE GREEN

UNDER ROCKS

STONE FARM

UK Trad	Fontainebleau colour (font grade)		Ticked	

4b ① **Roman Nose** ☆ (f **3b**)　　　　 S TR

A fun short climb on big pockets - usually very shady.
Solo: 1961 Terry Tullis

5c ② **Jean Genie** ☆ (f **5a**)　　　　 S TR

Escaping right is the popular finish for boulderers.
Solo: 1970's Mick Fowler

5c ③ **Umbilicus** ☆☆ (f **5b**)　　　　 S TR

Top is a bit iffy.
Solo: 1970's Gordon DeLacy

6b ④ **Blue Moon** ☆☆ (f **6a+**)　　 ♿ S TR

A stiff one arm mantle, easy for some!
Solo: 1970's Gordon DeLacy

6b ⑤ **Unbeliveable** ☆ (f **6a+**)　　　 S TR

Going direct through the roof on undercuts.
TR: 1981 Guy McLelland

6b ⑥ **Geoff's Route** ☆ (f **6b**)　　　 S TR

A long reach to start - slopers.
Solo: 1980's Everyone　　TR: 1980's Geoff Pearson

6b ⑦ **Froggatt Fudge** ☆ (f **6c+**)　　 S TR

Hard start now, up to undercut pocket.
Solo: 1981 David Atchison-Jones

Local chat: A fun little bouldering area, short problems but very hard starts to leave the ground. Soft rock so grades likely to change.

Access & Erosion: The ascent path is just up to the left. 3 slings for the top belays off the holly trees.

Crag layout map - page 104
Graded list - page 108

HARRISON'S ROCKS

BOWLES ROCKS

HIGH ROCKS

HIGH ROCKS ANNEXE

HAPPY VALLEY

BULLS HOLLOW

ERIDGE GREEN

UNDER ROCKS

STONE FARM

UK Trad	Fontainebleau colour (font grade)	Ticked

2a **(1)** Grotty Groove (f 2a)   S TR
Climb the obvious corner.
Solo: Pre 1960's

2b **(2)** Running Jump☆ (f 2b)   S TR
A nice delicate problem - or a running jump.
Solo: Pre 1960's

4a **(3)** Sirocco Slab☆ (f 3a)   S TR
Easiest way up the slab on very non-positive holds.
Solo: Pre 1960's

4b **(4)** Sirocco Wall☆ (f 3b)   S TR
Direct up the wall from the start of the ramp.
Solo: Pre 1960's

UK Trad	Fontainebleau colour (font grade)	Ticked

4b **(5)** Netwall☆ (f 3b)   S TR
Worn holds make this a short tough little problem.
Solo: Pre 1960's

4c **(6)** Court's Climb (f 3b)   S TR
A pretty naff wall.
Solo: 1960's

5b **(7)** Corner Layback☆ (f 4b)   S TR
This corner gets more brutal as the holds wear away.
Solo: 1960's

6b **(8)** Knitwall☆ (f 6a+)   S TR
Boulder problem up the worn holds - grade changes.
Solo: 1981 Guy McLelland

Local chat: A tiny little wall that gives a handful of fun little climbs. Tops can be a bit iffy, so beware. Many of the holds have worn over the years, and there aren't any strict lines to follow for any of the climbs. You can almost climb anywhere at around the same grade.

Top access & erosion beta: Go to the left and continue for some 20 yards then follow the steps up to the top path. There is a top large bolt with wire hawser. 1 sling should be enough.

Bull   Netwall   Fandango   Digitalis   Sing Sing   Ricochet   Pig's Nose   Funnel   Alka   Bovril
Chalet Slab   Reclamation   Mick's Wall   Sapper   Carbide   Devaluation   Birch Crack   Larchant   November

UK Trad	Fontainebleau colour (font grade)		Ticked
2a ①	Chelsea Chimney (f 2a)		S TR

Of very little merit & usually overgrown.
Solo: Pre 1960's

5a ②	Santa's Claws✦✦ (f 4a)	S TR

A few of the granite blocks have pulled out - with care.
Solo: 1960's

5b ③	Corner Layback✦ (f 4b)	S TR

This corner gets more brutal as the holds wear away.
Solo: 1960's

6a ④	Aphrodite✦ (f 6a)	S TR

Not an obvious line, but still good climbing.
Solo: 1982 David Atchison-Jones

UK Trad	Fontainebleau colour (font grade)	Ticked
6b ⑤	**Coast to Coast**✦ (f 6b+)	S TR

A high level traverse, poor footholds.
TR: 1992 Chris Murray

6b ⑥	**Knucklebones**✦✦ (f 6c)	S TR

A wall of monos - certainly suits small fingers.
Solo: 1992 Chris Murray   TR: 1992 Chris Murray

6c ⑦	**Zoom**✦ (f 7a)	S TR

A very steep undercut wall - often done as a dyno.
Solo: 1982 David Atchison-Jones

Local chat: This wall is pretty unmistakeable – with a line of stuck on granite holds. The original intention to make an easy way up a blank wall has transformed into quite a stiff little number, since some of the holds have fallen out and not been replaced. None of the routes in this sector are remotely classics. This said, they do offer some fun moves and a break from the tedium of doing the same old routes at Bowles - again and over again.

Access & Erosion: Follow the outcrop along to the left and ascend up vague steps to a good path that runs along the top of the outcrop. There are several long wire slings attached to big bolts in the rock. You will need a tape sling also to extend the belay karabiner over the edge.

Crag layout map - page 104
Graded list - page 108

[UK 6b] KNUCKLEBONES (font 6c), Ian Bull ▷

UK Trad   Fontainebleau colour (font grade)   *Ticked*

`1b` **(1)** Reclamation Gully (f 1b)   `S` `TR`
An easy way up or down, gets invaded by low tree.
Solo: Pre 1960's

`2b` **(2)** Reclamation Slab★★★ (f 2b)   `S` `TR`
A fun route for beginners - not completely straightforward.
Solo: Pre 1960's

`3a` **(3)** Reclamation Slab Left★★★ (f 2c)   `S` `TR`
Climb the few cut holds with the arête.
Solo: Pre 1960's

Local chat: This slab is a very popular place for beginners, and consequently is used by the outdoor centre a lot of the time. There are several wire slings attached high in the trees above, this forms a yoke to give a suspended belay ring.

Access & Erosion: Some folk solo up and down Reclamation Gully, which involves some large step ups. It is a natural drainage line and can be pretty ugly at the bottom. It is nicer to go left along the outcrop and follow the popular trail to the top of the crag.
The suspended loop is fine for the centre routes, but you will need a short static extension for routes on the left side of the slab; and 3-4 slings for Mental Balance.

Crag layout map - page 104
Graded list - page 108

UK Trad   Fontainebleau colour (font grade)   *Ticked*

`5b` **(4)** Cenotaph Corner Two (f 4b)   `S` `TR`
The grimy corner at the back - yuk.
Solo: 1992 Tim Skinner   *TR: 1992 Brian Kavanagh*

`5c` **(5)** Reclamation Slap⚹ (f 5b)   `S` `TR`
Completely height dependent.
Solo: 1994 Carl Martin   *TR: 1987 Dave Turner*

`6a` **(6)** Mental Balance⚹ (f 6a)   `S` `TR`
Tricky little number.
Solo: 1984 Paul Hayes   *TR: 1984 Paul Hayes*

`6a` **(7)** Slyme Cryme⚹ (f 6a)   `S` `TR`
The top holly tree is a bugger.
Solo: 1980's   *TR: 1980's*

HARRISON'S ROCKS

BOWLES ROCKS

HIGH ROCKS

HIGH ROCKS ANNEXE

HAPPY VALLEY

BULLS HOLLOW

ERIDGE GREEN

UNDER ROCKS

STONE FARM

UK Trad	Fontainebleau colour (font grade)	Ticked

4b (1) **Babylon** (f 3b) 🗑 S TR

Only in an extraordinary summer does this dry out.
Solo: Pre 1960's

5b (2) **Dropsophila**☆☆☆ (f 4b) S TR

A series of cut holds leads upwards. Direct finish font 4c.
Solo: 1960's

5b (3) **TNT**☆ (f 4b) S TR

Technical and nice - if dry. Tends to stay damp & greasy.
Solo: 1970's

5c (4) **Coathanger**☆☆☆ (f 5b) S TR

Start on the face, then later swing up on top of the arête.
Solo: 1960's

Local chat: This small bay is tucked away at the top of the big grassy slope - usually smothered with families picnicing. Many climbers attempt Dropsophila having just ticked the same grade on a climbing wall, only to find that the holds seem mysteriously hidden and evaisory, hence the climb is usually called Drops-off-a-lot. Good clean rock in parts makes the 3 star routes here very popular. Other eliminates are very good and worth seeking out.

Note: There is a UK-4c traverse along the big ramp going up left to right. It is fairly annoying - since it crosses so many other popular routes, plus you need a back rope to stop a possible pendulum into the far wall.

UK Trad	Fontainebleau colour (font grade)	Ticked

6a (5) **Banana**☆☆☆ (f 6a) S TR

A superb shaped depression. Most slip up at the top.
Solo: 1960's (Top crack used to have a chunky tree root.)

6a (6) **Slyme Cryme**☆ (f 6a) 🖐 S TR

The top holly tree is a bugger.
Solo: 1980's   *TR: 1980's*

6b (7) **Proboscis**☆ (f 6a+) S TR

A very good eliminate line.
TR: 1983 J. Mace

6b (8) **Urban Jock**☆ (f 6b+) S TR

A crimpy eliminate, avoid good holds of 'Drops off a lot.'
TR: 1999 Jamie Ogilvie

6b (9) **Banana Hammock**☆ (f 6c) S TR

Low start and follow the line of slopers along the base of the Banana, only slopers all the way to the top exit.
Solo: 2003 Ian Stronghill

Top access & erosion beta: Go left along the outcrop then turn right 15 metres before the buildings to follow the path up and along the top of the crag. Bolts at the top - you only need slings except for Proboscis - this you need a long static to set up quite a complicated belay.

Crag layout map - page 104
Graded list - page 108

Fun in the lower Banana pod ⌃   *[UK 6a] BANANA (font 6a), Suzie Zitter*   *Full on power slap at the top out* ⌃⌃

⟨ HARRISON'S ROCKS
BOWLES ROCKS
HIGH ROCKS
HIGH ROCKS ANNEXE
HAPPY VALLEY
BULLS HOLLOW
ERIDGE GREEN
UNDER ROCKS
STONE FARM

⟨ Trad	Fontainebleau colour (font grade)	Ticked

3a ① **Skiffle**☆☆☆ (f 2b) · S · TR

An easy twisting crack - good fun.
Solo: Pre 1960's

5c ② **Coathanger**☆☆☆ (f 5b)(f ☑ 6c) · S · TR

Start on the face, then later swing up on top of the arête.
Solo: 1960's

6a ③ **Pastry**☆☆ (f 5c) · S · TR

Quite sandy and rounded.
Solo: 1982 David Atchison-Jones   *TR: 1970's*

6a ④ **Fandango**☆☆☆ (f 6a) (☑ f 6a+) · S · TR

Going direct through the roof is excellent fun but harder.
Solo: 1970's Gordon DeLacy (right version 1979 Andy Meyers)

6b ⑤ **Station to Station**☆☆☆ (f 6a+) · S · TR

Tricky start and finish.
Solo: 1983 David Atchison-Jones   *TR: 1982 David A-Jones*

6b ⑥ **Poff Pastry**☆☆☆ (f 6c) · S · TR

A very mean finish to Pastry.
TR: 1983 Guy McLelland

⟨ [UK 5c] COATHANGER (font 5b), David Atchison-Jones

UK Trad	Fontainebleau colour (font grade)	Ticked

6b ⑦ **Tobacco Road**☆☆☆ (f 6c) · S · TR

A superb traverse, nonstop into Fandango Right Hand.
Solo: 1983 David Atchison-Jones   *TR: 1982 Guy McLelland*

6c ⑧ **Nicotine Alley**☆☆☆ (f 7a) · S · TR

Start at T-Road, continue to the arête, then up to jug.
Solo: 1984 Guy McLelland

7a ⑨ **Twisted Vegas**☆ (f 7b+) · S · TR

Steep start to poor holds.
Solo: 1990's Ian Stronghill

7a ⑩ **Phasis**☆ (f ☑ 7c) · S · TR

Big holds only. (Sonic Blue f 7b with mid holds)
Solo: 1990's Ian Stronghill

6b Ⓐ ← **Icarus**☆☆☆ (f 6a+) · S · TR

6b Ⓑ ← **Sugarplum**☆☆☆ (f 6a+) · S · TR

Local chat: This wall is simply paradise for boulderers. It has become a lot more undercut over the years - by 2-3 feet.

Erosion: Go easy on this wall, do not pull outwards on flakes and snap them - think before you crank!

HARRISON'S ROCKS

BOWLES ROCKS

HIGH ROCKS

HIGH ROCKS ANNEXE

HAPPY VALLEY

BULLS HOLLOW

ERIDGE GREEN

UNDER ROCKS

STONE FARM

UK Trad	Fontainebleau colour (font grade)	Ticked

2b ① Grotto Chimney* (f 2a) `S` `TR`
A big wide chimney that often gets very greasy at the top.
Solo: Pre 1960's

3a ② Skiffle*** (f 2b) `S` `TR`
An easy twisting crack - good fun.
Solo: 1960's Terry Tullis

4b ③ Kemp's Delight** (f 3b) `S` `TR`
Add a top running belay for the exit on greasy slab. ✳
Pre 1960's

5b ④ Mick's Wall*** (f 4c) `S` `TR`
Climb the slab avoiding holds on Kemp's Delight.
Overhang can be climbed undercutting or jamming.
Solo: 1960's   *TR:1960's*

*Local chat: The top overhang thwarts easy breeching.
Some very nice climbing all over the bottom part, then
nasty exits for both sides – graunchy to the left, and
disappointing to the right.*

Crag layout map - page 104
Graded list - page 108

UK Trad	Fontainebleau colour (font grade)	Ticked

5c ⑤ Kemp's Wall** (f 5b) `S` `TR`
Climbing the slab direct to the traverse - tricky.
Solo: 1970's   *TR:1960*

6a ⑥ Pastry*** (f 5c) `S` `TR`
Quite sandy and rounded.
Solo: 1982 David Atchison-Jones   *TR: 1971 Nigel Hea*

6a ⑦ Mick's Wall Arête** (f 6a) `S` `TR`
Much easier if you know the numbers.
Solo: 1982 Guy McLelland   *TR: 1970*

6b ⑧ Mick's Wall Variation (f 6a+) `S` `TR`
The top overhang, grade only applies to giraffe's.
Not soloed in current condition   *TR: 2000*

6c ⑨ London Pride (f 7a) `S` `TR`
The top overhang, another for tall climbers.
TR: 1997 Robin Mazink

*Top access & erosion beta: Go left along the crag 80 yds to
the steps and up. For Kemp's Delight, set up belay krab to
point. ● Also put another sling to clip when topping out. ✳*

HARRISON'S ROCKS

BOWLES ROCKS

HIGH ROCKS

HIGH ROCKS ANNEXE

HAPPY VALLEY

BULLS HOLLOW

ERIDGE GREEN

UNDER ROCKS

STONE FARM

Trad	Fontainebleau colour (font grade)		Ticked

2b (1) Grotto Chimney (f 2a) ⬜ S TR
A big wide chimney that often gets very greasy at the top.
Solo: Pre 1960's

6a (3) Serenade Arête ☆☆☆ (f 6a) ⬜ S TR
Now harder with a few missing holds.
Not soloed in current condition TR: 1970's John Durrant

6b (2) Digitalis ☆☆☆ (f 6a+) ⬜ S TR
A few important holds have broken off.
Not soloed in current condition TR: 1960 Martin Boysen

Local chat: This highly impressive wall doesn't offer anything in the lower grades - with the exception of a very good low level traverse. The bigger routes feel big alright, and you are tested both on stamina as well as technique and power. The top moves of Digitalis were originally soloed by the legendary Ron Fawcett - no mean feat, but now represent a far bigger proposition with a substantial amount of climbing on the lower wall, plus the slow disintegration of the crux 'Digitalis' shaped finger holds. Many top sport climbers who crank 8b have tried and failed to tick a direct finish to Digitalis - let's see in the next 10 years.

www.jingowobbly.com
Check out for more Sandstone information

UK Trad	Fontainebleau colour (font grade)		Ticked

6b (4) Patella ☆ (f 6b) 🖐 S TR
An awkward climb, easier for the tall.
Solo: 1984 Paul Hayes TR: 1960's

6b (5) Temptation ☆☆☆ (f 6b+) S TR
Very striking line up this blank wall - mono time.
Solo: 1987 Matt Saunders TR: 1983 Dave Turner

6b (6) Nutella ☆☆☆ (f 6c+) 🖐 S TR
All sorts of difficulties - often damp in the break.
TR: 1987 Dave Turner

Traverses

6b (A) → Kinnard ☆☆☆ (f 6c) S TR
Usually start up Patella & finish up Digitalis.

5a (B) → Orr Traverse ☆☆☆ (f 4a) S TR
Use all good holds, around to Serenade Arête.

6b (C) → McLelland Traverse ☆☆☆ (f 6b+) S TR
Use only the tiny holds at all times & bad footholds.

Access & Erosion: Quickest way to the top is left and up the road/slope to the top access steps. Some bolts on top, but you will also need a short static rope for Nutella and Temptation.

[UK 6b] DIGITALIS (font 6a+), Suzie Zitter

PETZL

Crag layout map - page 104
Graded list - page 108

HARRISON'S ROCKS

BOWLES ROCKS

HIGH ROCKS

HIGH ROCKS ANNEXE

HAPPY VALLEY

BULLS HOLLOW

ERIDGE GREEN

UNDER ROCKS

STONE FARM

11m

UK Trad	Fontainebleau colour (font grade)	Ticked

4a **(1) Yo Yo**☆☆☆ (f 3a)   S TR

The left hand crack line - a fab little route.
Solo: Pre 1960's

4c **(2) Sapper**☆ (f 3c)   S TR

A fun route up through a very bizarre and awkward hole.
Solo: Pre 1960's

5b **(3) Burlap Arête**☆☆☆ (f 4b)   S TR

A fab way up the prominent arête, direct start UK-5c.
Solo: 1981 David Atchison-Jones   *TR: Pre 1960's*

5c **(4) Inspiration**☆☆☆ (f 5b)   S TR

A fun lower half leads to a spectacular finish - wow.
Solo: 1960 Terry Tullis   *TR: Pre 1960's*

5c **(5) Spock does the Bump at the Space Disco**☆☆ (f 5b)   S TR

Only using the left arête, excellent and technical.
Solo: 1981 David Atchison-Jones   *TR: 1980 David A-J*

6a **(6) Burlap**☆☆ (f 5c)   S TR

Climb the technical wall without touching the arête.
Solo: 1981 David Atchison-Jones   *TR: 1960 Terry Tullis*

Local chat: If you want to catch plenty of attention, attempt one of these routes going over the big roofs. The Thing is probably the most fallen off route in the South East, and requires all of those techniques that you simply don't come across on an indoor wall. The arete climbs are all very good and should not be missed.

Crag layout map - page 104
Graded list - page 108

UK Trad	Fontainebleau colour (font grade)	Ticked

6a **(7) Juanita**☆☆ (f 5c)   S TF

A giant jamming crack in the sky - may get harder.
TR: 1960

6a **(8) Serenade Arête**☆☆☆ (f 6a)   S TF

Now harder with a few missing holds.
Not soloed in current condition   *TR: 1970's John Durra*

6b **(9) The Ly'in**☆ (f 6a+)   S TF

The slab on the right side without the arête.
Solo: 1998 John Patterson   *TR: 1984 Chris Arno*

6b **(10) The Thing**☆☆ (f 6b+)   Ouch S TF

There are 4 different ways of climbing this - very morph
Solo up for grabs!   *LED: 1980 Andy Meye*

6b **(11) White Verdict**☆☆ (f 6c)   S TF

The slab on the left side without the arête.
Solo: 1994 John Patterson   *TR: 1983 David Atchison-Jone*

6c **(12) One Nighter**☆☆ (f 7a+)   ♎ S TF

A mantleshelf in the sky.
TR: 1986 Matt Saunde

Top access & erosion beta: Go left up the road, turning right up steps just before the big dining hut on the right. The Thing - make sure to setup belay krab 2 foot from the top cracks (you need the crack as a hold). Please use tape slings and protect the edge - falling off these routes is common. A selection of bolts on top, but you will require a short static rope also.

[UK 6b] THE THING (font 6b+), Steve Glennie

◁ [UK 4a] Yo Yo, Bo Ishojer

15m
12m

HARRISON'S ROCKS
BOWLES ROCKS
HIGH ROCKS
HIGH ROCKS ANNEXE
HAPPY VALLEY
BULLS HOLLOW
ERIDGE GREEN
UNDER ROCKS
STONE FARM

◁ [UK 3a] SING SING, Anaïs Surridge

UK Trad   Fontainebleau colour (font grade)   *Ticked*

3a   **(1) Sing Sing**★★ (f **2b**)   S   TR

The much easier of the two cracks.
Solo: Pre 1960's

4a   **(2) Yo Yo**★★★ (f **3a**)   S   TR

The left hand crack line - a fab little route.
Solo: Pre 1960's

5a   **(3) Pete's Perseverance**★★★ (f **4a**)   S   TR

A nice easy wandering route up the slab.
Solo: 1960's John Smoker

5b   **(4) Jackie**★★★ (f **4c**)   S   TR

A fun lower half leads to a spectacular finish - wow.
Solo: 1970's   *TR: 1970's*

5c   **(5) Meager's Right Hand** (f **5a**)   S   TR

Climb the right arête on its own.
Solo: 1983 David Atchison-Jones   *TR: 1972 Nigel Head*

5c   **(6) Spock does the Bump at the Space Disco**★★ (f **5b**)   S   TR

Only using the left arête, excellent and technical.
Solo: 1981 David Atchison-Jones   *TR: 1980 David A-J*

6a   **(7) Manita**★★ (f **5c**)   S   TR

Climbing the wall strictly without the arête, has a crux.
Solo: 1970's Gordon DeLacy   *TR: 1970's*

UK Trad   Fontainebleau colour (font grade)   *Ticked*

6a   **(8) Nero** (f **5c**)   S   TR

A somewhat long reach to finish.
Solo: 1983 Paul Stone   *TR: 1970's*

6a   **(9) Salamander Slab**★★ (f **5c**)   S   TR

Top moves exercise the back muscles.
Solo: 1960's   *TR: 1960's*

6a   **(10) Perspiration**★★ (f **5c**)   S   TR

A very overhanging crack - on a hot day induces......
Solo: 1960's   *TR: 1960's John Smoker*

6b   **(11) The Ly'in**★ (f **6a+**)   S   TR

The slab on the right side without the arête.
Solo: 1998 John Patterson   *TR: 1984 Chris Arnold*

6b   **(12) Twilight Zone**★ (f **6b**)   S   TR

Direct up the slab 2 metres left of Perspiration.
Solo: 2000's   *TR: 2002 Trevor Nagler*

6b   **(13) White Verdict**★★ (f **6c**)   S   TR

The slab on the left side without the arête.
Solo: 1994 John Patterson   *TR: 1983 David Atchison-Jones*

Local chat: Some of the best slab problems
on Sandstone. Lots of variations possible
alongside the straightforward lines.

Bull   Netwall   Fandango   Digitalis   **Sing Sing**   Ricochet   Pig's Nose   Funnel   Alka   Bovril

Chalet Slab   Reclamation   Mick's Wall   Sapper   Carbide   Devaluation   Birch Crack   Larchant   November

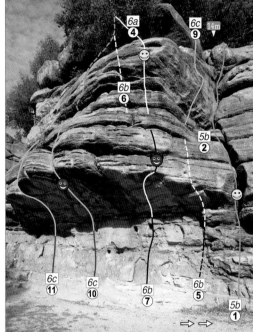

HARRISON'S ROCKS

BOWLES ROCKS

HIGH ROCKS

HIGH ROCKS ANNEXE

HAPPY VALLEY

BULLS HOLLOW

ERIDGE GREEN

UNDER ROCKS

STONE FARM

UK Trad	Fontainebleau colour (font grade)	Ticked

5b ① Abracadabra✩✩ (f **4b**)   S TR
An off width curving crack is fiendishly awkward.
Solo: 1960's   *TR: 1960's*

5b ② Swastika✩✩✩ (f **4c**)   S TR
A lovely excursion onto the top wall.
Solo: 1960's   *TR: 1960's*

6a ③ Perspiration✩✩ (f **5c**)   S TR
A very overhanging crack - on a hot day induces.......
Solo: 1960's   *TR: 1960's John Smoker*

6a ④ Nightmare✩✩ (f **6a**)   S TR
A direct way up the top wall.
Solo: 1994 John Patterson   *TR: 1972 John Durrant*

6b ⑤ Thieving Gypsies✩ (f **6a+**)   S TR
The lower overhang just left of the crack.
Solo: 2001 Various boulderers   *TR: 2001 James Wade*

6b ⑥ Bubble Wrap (f **6b**)   S TR
A poor eliminate.
                                      TR: 1996 Robin Mazinke

*Local chat: This series of giant overhangs offers peculiar
routes. You have fiendishly hard problems low down, and
a very pleasant wall above. Because of the massive grade
imbalance, it is best to make up your own combinations
to suit your own level of climbing.*

UK Trad	Fontainebleau colour (font grade)	Ticked

6b ⑦ Cardboard Box✩✩ (f **6b+**)   S TR
A spectacular cut loose, then a dyno slap, great fun.
Solo: 1995 Guy McLelland   *TR: 1983 Dave Turner*

6b ⑧ Boiling Point✩✩ (f **6c**)   S TR
Nice position - nice grade.
                           TR: 1982 David Atchison-Jones

6c ⑨ Recurring Nightmare✩ (f **7a+**)   S TR
A crimpy boulder problem in the sky - grade uncertain!
                                      TR: 1986 Paul Hayes

6c ⑩ Carbide Finger✩✩ (f **7b**)   S TR
A long crack in the roof which succumbs easily to jams.
Solo: 1987 Matt Saunders   *TR: 1981 Julien Morgan*

6c ⑪ Them Monkey Things✩✩ (f **7b+**)   S TR
A short boulder problem in the sky.
Solo: 2000 Ian Stronghill   *TR: 1980 Johnny Woodward*

*Access & Erosion: This sector is in the middle of the
crag, choose steps at either end for access. 3 slings are
ample for the belay. The lower overhang can easily be
bouldered, but you need a good team of spotters. Take
care on a top rope - when falling from the very back wall
under the roof - you pendulum out and hit the ground, so
take precautions for the first few moves. Please continue
up the easy slabs - rather than lowering off which carves
grooves in the rock.*

Crag layout map - page 104
Graded list - page 108

◀ *[UK 6b] CARDBOARD BOX (font 6b+), Mark Glennie*

Crag layout map - page 104
Graded list - page 108

UK Trad   Fontainebleau colour (font grade)   Ticked

4b ① Ricochet☆☆ (f 3b)   S   TR

The jugs at the start are slowly disappearing - hence this is now the crux of Ricochet.
Solo: 1960's   *TR: 1960's*

4c ② Four by Two☆☆☆ (f 3c)   S   TR

Marginally harder than Ricochet, with more demanding technical moves.
Solo: 1960's   *TR: 1960's*

5a ③ Lee Enfield☆☆ (f 4a)   S   TR

A few sandy holds on the ramp but quite easy until the last move, soft rock so may change grade.
Solo: 1960's   *TR: 1960's*

5a ④ Pull Through☆☆☆ (f 4a)   S   TR

Plenty of good climbing in the top part.
Solo: 1960's   *TR: 1960's*

5b ⑤ Kalashnikov☆☆☆ (f 4b)   S   TR

The most direct line up the slab from the Cairn, technical.
Solo: 1960's   *TR: 1960's*

Local chat: This central wall at Bowles is highly popular with some excellent long routes. It was once the backdrop for a shooting range, hence the peppering with shot holes and respective route names. The lower band of overhanging rock is very soft, but is thankfully bypassed with the use of a cairn. The crisp edges of the shot dimples have worn over the years, and many routes have changed grade.

6a ⑥ Target☆☆☆ (f 5c)   S   TR

Starts beneath the hanging arête, climbed on the right then left with hands in the break. This first part is sustained and spits off most candidates, top is easier.
Solo: 1970's Gordon DeLacy   *TR: 1960'*

6a ⑦ The Big Stretch☆☆ (f 6a)   S   TR

An amusing start to Target. A technical tip toe up the opposite wall, then a bridge too far for most.
         TR: 1980 David Atchison-Jone

6b ⑧ Target Direct☆ (f 6a+)   S   TR

Only one hard move, but on sandy rock that is wearing.
Solo: 1970's Gordon DeLacy

6b ⑨ Conjuror☆☆ (f 6a+)   S   TR

Holds that magically are disappearing over the years.
Solo: 1980's   *TR: 1980's Tim Daniell*

6b ⑩ Kara☆ (f 6b)   S   TR

Direct through the roof - sandy and grade will change.
Solo: 2001 Lawrence King

Top access: Best via steps at the beginning of the outcrop. Wire slings at the top for some routes, 4 long slings essential for some routes. Belay is more complicated for Target area - needs a short static rope.

[UK 5a] LEE ENFIELD (font 4a), Mike Smith ▷

HARRISON'S ROCKS | BOWLES ROCKS | HIGH ROCKS | HIGH ROCKS ANNEXE | HAPPY VALLEY | BULLS HOLLOW | ERIDGE GREEN | UNDER ROCKS | STONE FARM

BOWLES ROCKS - Devaluation

HARRISON'S ROCKS
BOWLES ROCKS
HIGH ROCKS
HIGH ROCKS ANNEXE
HAPPY VALLEY
BULLS HOLLOW
ERIDGE GREEN
UNDER ROCKS
STONE FARM

UK Trad	Fontainebleau colour (font grade)	Ticked

3a ① Charlie's Chimney★★ (f 2b)   S TR
One of those classic chimneys to thrutch up, face either way.
Solo: 1950's   TR: 1950's

4c ② Cave Crack★★★ (f 3c)   S TR
Starts at the very back of the cave, then squirm upwards and outwards - fist jams come in use.
Solo: 1960's   TR: 1960's

4c ③ ES Cadet Nose★★★ (f 3c)   S TR
Starting direct up the nose is quite beefy, but soon has good rests and enjoys a lovely position on the nose. (Crack on L is 5a, right wall start is 5c).
Solo: 1960's   TR: 1960's

5b ④ Devaluation★★★ (f 4b)   S TR
Holds are good, but come in an awkward manner.
Solo: 1960's   TR: 1960's

Local chat: Devaluation is the mid grade classic of the crag, unfortunately the holds seem to be wearing away quite considerably. The hard routes in this sector were all climbed by tall climbers!

Top access: Best via steps at the beginning of the outcrop. Wire slings at the top for some routes, 1 long sling for central routes, short static essential for Target area routes.

5c ⑤ The Flying Bandit★ (f 5b)   S TR
The high nose finish to ES Cadet Nose.
TR: 1970

6a ⑥ Target★★★ (f 5c)   S TR
Starts beneath the hanging arête, climbed on the right then left with hands in the break. This first part is sustained and spits off most candidates, top is easier.
Solo: 1970's Gordon DeLacy   TR: 1960

6a ⑦ The Big Stretch★★ (f 6a)   S TR
Pleasant mid grade 5 climbing for the start and finish, bu with a bridge too far for most in the crux section.
TR: 1980 David Atchison-Jone

6b ⑧ Sandman★★ (f 6b)   S TR
Font 6c for the short.
Solo: 1983 Dan Lewis   TR: 1977 Martin Boyse

6b ⑨ Stoneman★ (f 6b+)   S TR
The direct finish for Sandman.
TR: 1986 Ed Ston

6c ⑩ Skallagrigg★ (f 7a)   S TR
A rather blank wall.
TR: 1994 John Patterso

Crag layout map - page 104
Graded list - page 108

Chalet Slab	Reclamation	Mick's Wall	Sapper	Carbide	Devaluation	Birch Crack	Larchant	November
Bull	Netwall	Fandango	Digitalis	Sing Sing	Ricochet	Pig's Nose	Funnel	Alka	Bovril

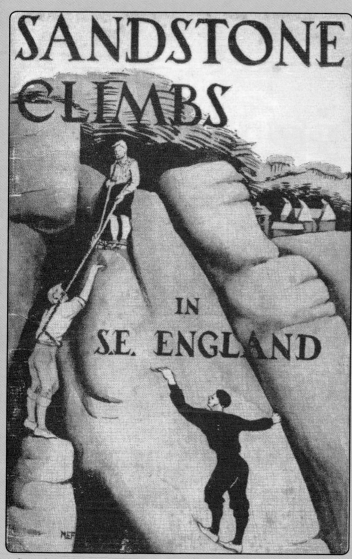

Crag layout map - page 104
Graded list - page 108

UK Trad   Fontainebleau colour (font grade)   Ticked   UK Trad   Fontainebleau colour (font grade)   Ticked

3a   **(1)** Charlie's Chimney** (f 2b)   S   TR

One of those classic chimneys to thrutch up, face either way.

Solo: 1950's   *TR: 1950's*

5a   **(2)** Pig's Nose*** (f 4a)   S   TR

The lower arête is a delight, and the top overhang feels wild and out there - an amazing position on giant jugs.

Solo: 1950's   *TR: 1950's*

5b   **(3)** TT*** (f 4b)   S   TR

Some very fine wall climbing between the nose and crack to the L, going fairly direct over the overhang to top out.

Solo: 1960's Terry Tullis   *TR: 1960 Terry Tullis*

5c   **(4)** Pig's Ear*** (f 5b)   S   TR

Follow the obvious crack but don't drift too far right. Climb the overhang quite direct to end up at the crack.

Solo: 1960's   *TR: 1960's*

6a   **(5)** Hate*** (f 6a)   S   TR

A classic testpiece with several crux's.

Solo: 1975 Mick Fowler   *TR: 1960 John Smoker*

6b   **(6)** Love* (f 6b)   S   TR

Nice lower arête climbed on the right, then damn tricky.

Solo: 1982 David Atchison-Jones   *TR: 1970's Blob Wyvill*

6b   **(7)** Watson Watt* (f 6b+)   S   TR

A good eliminate avoiding big holds in the area.

     TR: 2004 Dave Potts

6b   **(8)** Upside Downies*** (f 6b+)   S   TR

Climb the lower wall without holds in the crack - ouch. Going over the overhang requires amusing toe hooks and strange contortions.

     TR: 1989 David Atchison-Jones

Local chat: One of the best pieces of rock in the South East.

Top access: Steps up at the start of the outcrop. Bolt belays at top - 2 long slings for most routes - short static for Love & clean the top groove first.

◁ [UK 6a] HATE (font 6a), Carrie Atchison-Jones

HARRISON'S ROCKS
BOWLES ROCKS
HIGH ROCKS
HIGH ROCKS AN'EXE
HAPPY VALLEY
BULLS HOLLOW
ERIDGE GREEN
UNDER ROCKS
STONE FARM

Bull   Netwall   Fandango   Digitalis   Sing Sing   Ricochet   **Pig's Nose**   Funnel   Alka   Bovril

Chalet Slab   Reclamation   Mick's Wall   Sapper   Carbide   Devaluation   Birch Crack   Larchant   November

HARRISON'S ROCKS

BOWLES ROCKS

HIGH ROCKS

HIGH ROCKS ANNEXE

HAPPY VALLEY

BULLS HOLLOW

ERIDGE GREEN

UNDER ROCKS

STONE FARM

UK Trad   Fontainebleau colour (font grade)   Ticked

2a **(1) Birch Crack** ★★★ (f **2a**)   S | TR

Much more of a chimney than a crack. Not straightforward and lacking obvious jugs, a fun outing.
Solo: 1950's   *TR: 1950's*

4a **(2) Kennard's Climb** ☆ (f **3a**)

A nice route, technical but not strenuous.
Solo: 1960's   *TR: 1960's*

5a **(3) Pig's Nose** ☆☆☆ (f **4a**)

The lower arête is a delight, and the top overhang feels wild and out there - an amazing position on giant jugs.
Solo: 1950's   *TR: 1950's*

5b **(4) Chris** ☆ (f **4b**)

This lower wall give very nice climbing on small rails, followed by a steeper wall with a difficult top out.
Solo: 1970's   *TR: 1970's*

Local chat: Birch Crack is one of the classic full length routes at Bowles for beginners and is highly popular. Pig's Nose is a very striking and prominent landmark - and is also very popular. Koffler is one of those routes that some find easy, and those with big fat fingers find desperate - lovely wall climbing - if only it went on longer and there were more routes like it.

UK Trad   Fontainebleau colour (font grade)   Ticked

5b **(5) Gully Wall** ☆☆ (f **4c**)   S | TR

Avoid climbing on the opposite wall entirely. This feels like a big wall climb, nice and long.
Solo: 1970's   *TR: 1960's*

5c **(6) Rib** ☆ (f **5a**)   S | TR

This overhanging start is sandy and requires moderate power, thereafter much easier. The crack to the right (Dib) is UK-5a, and makes a far more balanced route.
Solo: 1970's   *TR: 1970's*

6a **(7) Koffler** ☆☆☆ (f **5c**)   S | TR

Avoid the ramp on the right for the feet. The crux uses a mono (a grade easier if 2 fingers go in the hole); going straight up adds another hard move and is more testing.
Solo: 1980's   *TR: 1970's*

*Top access: Best via steps at the beginning of the outcrop. [1] Birch Crack, [2] Kennard's Climb, [3] Pig's Nose & [7] Koffler have top belay points. For routes [4] & [6], extending the belay with a rope down to the mid terrace is a good idea if the candidates are likely to fail on the route - but includes a running belay * to clip. [5] Gully Wall belay - use the big tree set back: use a short static rope plus a wide sling over the edge.*

BOREAL

◁ *[UK 6a] KOFFLER (font 5c), Mark Glennie*

Crag layout map - page 104
Graded list - page 108

Chalet Slab   Reclamation   Mick's Wall   Sapper   Carbide   Devaluation   **Birch Crack**   Larchant   November
Bull   Netwall   Fandango   Digitalis   Sing Sing   Ricochet   Pig's Nose   Funnel   Alka   Bovril

HARRISON'S ROCKS

BOWLES ROCKS

HIGH ROCKS

HIGH ROCKS ANNEXE

HAPPY VALLEY

BULLS HOLLOW

ERIDGE GREEN

UNDER ROCKS

STONE FARM

UK Trad   Fontainebleau colour (font grade)   *Ticked*

3a ① Wells Reach* (f 2a)   S TR

Crack or slab climbing up to the high bolt.
Solo: 1960's   TR: 1960's

3c ② Funnel*** (f 3a)   S TR

Access the shallow scoop easily from the right.
Solo: 1960's   TR: 1960's

4a ③ Corbett's Nose** (f 3a)   S TR

The first beefy bulge is the only hard part.
Solo: 1960's   TR: 1960's

4b ④ Nelson's Column** (f 3b)   S TR

A nice wall climb - start bulge is UK 5a - get a bunk up.
Solo: 1960's   TR: 1960's

4b ⑤ Corbett's Slab** (f 3b)   S TR

Slightly harder than the Nose.
Solo: 1960's   TR: 1960's

4b ⑥ Dival's Diversion*** (f 3b)   S TR

The best route up the slab, short climbers start to the R.
Solo: 1960's   TR: 1960's

5a ⑦ Dib** (f 4a)   S TR

A very difficult start to a very easy crack line, better
finish is up the wall rather than the easy 3a crackline.
Solo: 1960's   TR: 1960's

UK Trad   Fontainebleau colour (font grade)   *Ticked*

5c ⑧ UN*** (f 5a)   S TR

Lower wall is fun, but top out is a real nasty and feels
damn steep. Holds keep on coming but none too big.
Solo: 1960's   TR: 1960

6a ⑨ U Tube*** (f 5c)   S TR

The obvious variant to UN. Climb the slab without the
edge of funnel, the climb the top arête on the L - beasty.
    TR: 1980

6b ⑩ One of our Buzzards is Missing (f 6b+) TR

A powerful roof.
    TR: 1994 Robin Mazink

6c ⑪ The Wrecker* (f 7a)   S TR

A big roof with an awkward crack. Many will jam and
loose skin, stronger climbers will just power through.
    TR: 1960's John Smoke

*Local chat: A very popular area for beginners with a good
selection of easy climbs. The starts are both awkward and
powerful. Further up they have few positive holds - so soloing
can be pretty scary & hazardous.*

*Top access: Best via steps at the beginning of the
outcrop. Bolt belays at the top - except for The
Wrecker Overhang - short static needed.*

| Bull | Netwall | Fandango | Digitalis | Sing Sing | Ricochet | Pig's Nose | **Funnel** | Alka | Bovril |
| Chalet Slab | Reclamation | Mick's Wall | Sapper | Carbide | Devaluation | Birch Crack | Larchant | November |

HARRISON'S ROCKS

BOWLES ROCKS

HIGH ROCKS

HIGH ROCKS ANNEXE

HAPPY VALLEY

BULLS HOLLOW

ERIDGE GREEN

UNDER ROCKS

STONE FARM

UK Trad	Fontainebleau colour (font grade)		Ticked

2a **(1) Harden Gully**✶✶✶ (f 2a) S TR
Not that difficult but plenty of easy climbing, one of the best easy climbs at Bowles.
Solo: 1950's *TR: 1950's*

4b **(2) Sylvie's Slab**✶✶ (f 3b) S TR
Straightforward and fun.
Solo: 1960's *TR: 1960's*

4c **(3) October**✶ (f 3c) S TR
A good stiff start on a very steep wall for the grade, soon easing thereafter.
Solo: 1950's

4c **(4) Six Foot**✶✶ (f 3c) S TR
Nice wall climbing that remains enjoyably sustained.
Solo: 1970's *TR: 1970's*

Local chat: This sector is certainly one of the most popular areas of Bowles - and deservedly so. The wall is just over 7 metres high and gives sustained climbing throughout. There are countless traverses and undercut different starts to the routes above. plenty to keep the boulderer entertained for a few hours.

UK Trad	Fontainebleau colour (font grade)		Ticked

5a **(5) Fragile Arête**✶✶ (f 4a) S TR
Climbing the lower wall is very nice on incut holds, nothing too hard - just a bit of stamina required.
Solo: 1970's

5a **(6) Larchant**✶✶ (f 4a) S TR
A lovely wall with holds of increasing awkwardness.
Solo: 1960's *TR: 1962 Terry Tullis*

5b **(7) Hennessy Heights**✶✶ (f 4b) S TR
Very good wall climbing with plenty of holds.
Solo: 1960's *TR: 1960's*

5c **(8) August Variation**✶✶✶ (f 5a)(f ⌀5b) S TR
Using a sit start makes this a good endurance outing. Eliminate at the top, not touching holds from H-Heights.
Solo: 1980's *TR: 1982 Malcolm McPherson*

Top access: Best via steps at the beginning of the outcrop. When walking along the top you need to drop down a large gully to access the bolt belays on the top terrace. The upper walls can be climbed but don't offer anything great. Just a couple of slings required for belays.

Crag layout map - page 104
Graded list - page 108

HARRISON'S ROCKS

BOWLES ROCKS

HIGH ROCKS

HIGH ROCKS ANNEXE

HAPPY VALLEY

BULLS HOLLOW

ERIDGE GREEN

UNDER ROCKS

STONE FARM

UK Trad	Fontainebleau colour (font grade)		Ticked

1b ① Renison Gully★★ (f 2a) · S · TR

The straightforward corner cracks- top rope cord usually.
Solo: 1960's · *TR: 1960's*

3b ② Fragile Wall★★ (f 2b) · S · TR

A classic lovely route of this sector.
Solo: 1960's · *TR: 1960's*

4b ③ Elevator★★ (f 4a) · S · TR

Excellent slab moves keeping away from the crack.
Solo: 1960's · *TR: 1960's*

4c ④ Alka★★★ (f 3c) · S · TR

About as fierce a 4c that you are likely to find.
Solo: 1960's · *TR: 1950's Nea Morin*

5a ⑤ Fragile Arête★★★ (f 4a) · S · TR

The direct line sucks the stamina out of you.
Solo: 1960's · *TR: 1960's*

5a ⑥ Escalator★★★ (f 4a) · S · TR

An excellent route if slightly eliminate.
Solo: 1970's · *TR: 1960's*

UK Trad	Fontainebleau colour (font grade)		Ticked

5b ⑦ Seltzer★★★ (f 4c) · S · TR

A pleasant beginning leads to a highly intimidating top wall, which feels very exposed and scary.
Solo: 1960's · *TR: 1950's Nea Morin*

5c ⑧ Encore★★ (f 5a) · S · TR

The lower wall can prove very troublesome, and the top wall is simply hard.
Solo: 1981 David Atchison-Jones · *TR: 1950's*

6b ⑨ Finale★★ (f 6a+) · S · TR

Nothing hard up to the overhang, then it all starts unravelling rather quickly, finish left or direct.
Solo: 2002 Ally Smith · *TR: 1960's*

6b ⑩ Morpheus (f 6a+) · S · TR

A very good eliminate with a difficult high rockover.
TR: 2002 Dave Potts

6b ⑪ Zugabe (f 6b+) · S · TR

Not suited for the short.
Solo: 1994 John Patterson · *TR: 1991 Tim Skinner*

Top access: Go right, bolt belays only for easier routes.

◁ [UK 6b] FINALE (font 6a+), Adrian Paisey

Bull	Netwall	Fandango	Digitalis	Sing Sing	Ricochet	Pig's Nose	Funnel	Alka	Bovril
Chalet Slab	Reclamation	Mick's Wall	Sapper	Carbide	Devaluation	Birch Crack	Larchant	November	

HARRISON'S ROCKS

BOWLES ROCKS

HIGH ROCKS

HIGH ROCKS ANNEXE

HAPPY VALLEY

BULLS HOLLOW

ERIDGE GREEN

UNDER ROCKS

STONE FARM

15m

2a
②

5a
⑥

1a
①

4b
⑤

3a
④

3a
③

UK Trad	Fontainebleau colour (font grade)	Ticked

1b ① Hot Cross Bun★★ (f 1b)   S TR

The easy gully in the centre, a steep scramble.

Solo: 1950's   TR: 1950's

2a ② November★★ (f 2a)   S TR

A classic gully route.

Solo: 1950's   TR: 1950's

3a ③ Claire★ (f 2a)   S TR

Very straightforward climbing on rounded holds.

Solo: 1950's   TR: 1950's

3a ④ Red Peg★★ (f 2a)   S TR

Easy if you are tall, desperate if your tiny.

Solo: 1950's   TR: 1950's

4b ⑤ Ballerina★ (f 3b)   S TR

The central slab, tests your friction skills.

Solo: 1950's   TR: 1950's

5a ⑥ G Force (f 4a)   S TR

An excellent pillar and fun top wall. Top wall can also by climbed purely by crimps alone (font 6a+).

Solo: 1970's   TR: 1960's (f 6a+ 2009 George Jones)

Local chat: An ideal spot for complete beginners, many climbs are a lot harder for kiddie size. climbers.

Top access: Steps at the beginning of the outcrop. There are hanging belay rings at the top of routes 1-5.

RED PEG 3a, Chloê Surridge

[UK 4b] WALLY (font 3b), Jeannie Van Der Weyden; route overleaf ▷

HARRISON'S ROCKS

BOWLES ROCKS

HIGH ROCKS

HIGH ROCKS ANNEXE

HAPPY VALLEY

BULLS HOLLOW

ERIDGE GREEN

UNDER ROCKS

STONE FARM

UK Trad	Fontainebleau colour (font grade)	Ticked

3a   ① **Claire**☆ (f 2a)   S   TR

Very straightforward climbing on rounded holds.

Solo: 1950's   *TR: 1950's*

4a   ② **Rad's Cliff**☆☆ (f 3a)   S   TR

A short boulder problem on sandy rock.

Solo: 1960's   *TR: 960's*

4a   ③ **Marmite**☆☆ (f 3a)   S   TR

Climbing the wall just to the right of the arête is fun. Go left higher up, but then swing out onto the nose to finish.

Solo: 1960's   *TR: 1960's*

4b   ④ **Bovril**☆☆ (f 3b)   S   TR

Climbing the front face is more direct and technical, but maybe not so enjoyable.

Solo: 1960's   *TR: 1960's*

UK Trad	Fontainebleau colour (font grade)	Ticked

4b   ⑤ **Wally**☆☆ (f 3b)   S   TR

Climb the central part of the flat wall on good holds, the drift into the hanging chimney - exit left to the top of the tower with a bolt belay on top. (Photo on previous page)

Solo: 1960's   *TR: 1960*

4c   ⑥ **Nealon's**☆☆ (f 4a)   S   TR

This steep overhanging groove requires technique, but additionally power too. Top is an easy delight.

Solo: 1960's   *TR: 1960*

5a   ⑦ **Barham Boulder**☆☆ (f 4b)   S   TR

Climbing this direct up the front face is both tricky and sandy. Holds may deteriorate, many variations possible.

Solo: 1960's   *TR: 1960*

Top access: Best via steps at the beginning of the outcrop. There is a belay ring suspended between the trees at point a *Whilst this is useful, aspirant climbers have been seen to fall off routes [1] and [7], and pendulum into the chimney to the right - with crunching and sobbing results. Be cautious and use a side rope from below to prevent this.*

Crag layout map - page 104
Graded list - page 108

Bull	*Netwall*	*Fandango*	*Digitalis*	*Sing Sing*	*Ricochet*	*Pig's Nose*	*Funnel*	*Alka*	*Bovril*
Chalet Slab	*Reclamation*	*Mick's Wall*	*Sapper*	*Carbide*	*Devaluation*	*Birch Crack*	*Larchant*	*November*	

HARRISON'S ROCKS

BOWLES ROCKS

HIGH ROCKS

HIGH ROCKS ANNEXE

HAPPY VALLEY

BULLS HOLLOW

ERIDGE GREEN

UNDER ROCKS

STONE FARM

K Trad   Fontainebleau colour (font grade)   Ticked

5c   (8) **Oliver's Twist**☆☆☆ (f 5b)   S   TR

A lot meaner climb than it looks. Moving across the wall up to the groove is not so easy.

Solo: 1993 Tim Skinner   *TR: 1989 Matt Smith*

6a   (9) **Nealon's Direct**☆ (f 5c)   S   TR

This direct finish to Nealon's gives some fun jug hauling over this intimidating overhang.

TR: 1990's

Local chat: This is the first area that you come to as you walk up the driveway from the carpark. Even though it's seen by everyone, it's often overlooked by climbers rushing to find their mates further up the crag. It's a pretty good spot with a nice mixture of routes across the grades - and that can be top roped from the same belay - ideal for a mixed group of climbers. Gets a lot of shade in summer, so is ideal on a hot day - as opposed to the central part of Bowles which can boil.

Top access: Best via steps at the beginning of the outcrop. Belay bolts on top - 2 slings should be fine. A static rope and extension sling are needed to get an ideal belay on top of routes [9] and [10].

UK Trad   Fontainebleau colour (font grade)   Ticked

6b   (10) **Lady in Mink**☆☆ (f 6a+)   S   TR

The hard section is pretty obvious. Much harder for the shorter climber - verging on 6b. Various other ways up the headwall to the right at UK-6b.

Solo: 1994 John Patterson   *TR:1970's Johnny Woodward*

6b   (11) **Jack in the Box**☆ (f 6b)   S   TR

A boulder problem in the sky. Climb straight over the nose without holds around to the L, powerful mantleshelf technique required.

TR: 2009 David Atchison-Jones

Bull   Netwall   Fandango   Digitalis   Sing Sing   Ricochet   Pig's Nose   Funnel   Alka   Bovril
Chalet Slab   Reclamation   Mick's Wall   Sapper   Carbide   Devaluation   Birch Crack   Larchant   November

High Rocks is the premier outcrop for top level climbers in the South East. It has a superb combination of fiendishly hard bouldering for powerful lightweights, and big blank pocketed walls to reward those climbers who are well trained. In addition, there are squirmy slithery chimneys for the lower grade climber who doesn't mind getting ruffed up a tad. It's a bizarre situation, since the land is owned by the High Rocks Inn and is run as a vibrant wedding venue by Giuseppe. The plus side is that both climbers and wedding guests seem to cohabit the magnificent rocks in perfect harmony, don't be surprised to meet a white meringue & photographer at some point in the afternoon. Admittedly, the combination of an "entry fee," combined with the severity of the climbing - reduces traffic massively - and the rock shows it. Local climbers work in conjunction with Giuseppe to keep the undergrowth at bay, which is both practical and pleasing to the eye. It is an area best reserved for the very finest of days in a dry period, when the rock is at its strongest and you are cranking like a inspired demon.

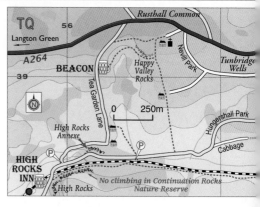

High Rocks Annexe is just a small distance back along the small road to Tunbridge Wells. It's on private land, which is also open access. Do not use the private car park at High Rocks, there are 2 small spots for a couple of cars on the lane.

Location: High Rocks **SAT NAV info**
P - Parking Grid reference: **TQ 558 382**
P - Postcode **TN3 9JJ**
High Rocks Annexe Grid reference: **TQ 562 385**

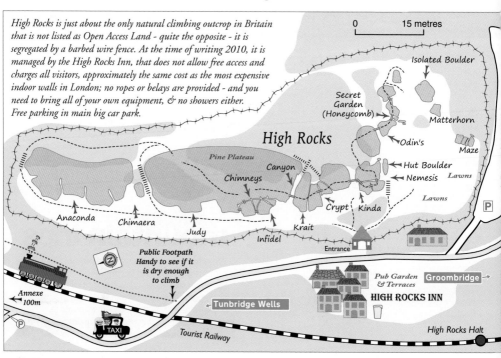

High Rocks is just about the only natural climbing outcrop in Britain that is not listed as Open Access Land - quite the opposite - it is segregated by a barbed wire fence. At the time of writing 2010, it is managed by the High Rocks Inn, that does not allow free access and charges all visitors, approximately the same cost as the most expensive indoor walls in London; no ropes or belays are provided - and you need to bring all of your own equipment, & no showers either. Free parking in main big car park.

High Rocks

Isolated Boulder
Secret Garden (Honeycomb)
Matterhorn
Odin's
Maze
Hut Boulder
Nemesis
Lawns
Lawns
Pine Plateau
Canyon
Chimneys
Crypt
Kinda
Anaconda
Chimaera
Krait
Judy
Infidel
Entrance
Public Footpath Handy to see if it is dry enough to climb
TAXI
Annexe 100m
Tunbridge Wells
Pub Garden & Terraces
Groombridge
HIGH ROCKS INN
Tourist Railway
High Rocks Halt

HIGH ROCKS - Visual Tour

Entrance to High Rocks Central Canyon

A fun high walkway

Chez George on ATOMIC MUSHROOM (font 7b)

Mark Croxall needing a rest on a 2b

Danie Rushmer on OLD KENT ROAD (font 7a)

Mark Glennie on KRAKEN (font 6b+)

Side tabs: HARRISON'S ROCKS | BOWLES ROCKS | HIGH ROCKS | HIGH ROCKS ANNEXE | HAPPY VALLEY | BULLS HOLLOW | ERIDGE GREEN | UNDER ROCKS | STONE FARM

1a
- ☐ Hands Free (f 1a) p217
- ☐ Green Ernie (f 2a) p198

2a
- ☐ Short Ch. (f 2a) p181
- ☐ Warning Rock Ch. (f 2a) p164
- ☐ Orion Chimney (f 2a) p154
- ☐ Shelter Ch. (f 2b) p176

2b
- ☐ Slab Chimney (f 2b) p164
- ☐ Deadwood Ch. (f 2c) p164
- ☐ Colorado Crack (f 3a) p174
- ☐ Chockstone Ch. (f 3a) p160

3a
- ☐ Hut Passage Ch. (f 3a) p185
- ☐ Silly Corner (f 3a) p198
- ☐ Eft Chimney (f 3a) p160
- ☐ Recess Wall (f 3a) p160
- ☐ Easy Crack (f 3a) p197
- ☐ Clipboard Ch.(f 3a) p160
- ☐ Brushwood Ch. (f 3a) p186
- ☐ Rufrock Ch. (f 3a) p191

3b
- ☐ One-Ch.-Missing (f 3b) p164
- ☐ Spider Chimney (f 3b) p164
- ☐ Rhody Route (f 3a) p198

4a
- ☐ Outside Edge Rte (f 3a) p217
- ☐ Turner (f 3a) p218
- ☐ Florentino (f 3a) p218
- ☐ Camile (f 3a) p218
- ☐ Ordinary Route (f 3a) p211
- ☐ Emile (f 3a) p218
- ☐ Crypt Crack (f 3a) p181
- ☐ Giant's Stride (f 3b) p164
- ☐ Cobra Chimney (f 3b) p158
- ☐ Smooth Chim (f 3b) p164
- ☐ Wye Chimney (f 3b) p164

4b
- ☐ Boa by the Back (f 3b) p157
- ☐ Crown of Thorns (f 3b) p164
- ☐ Balcony Direct (f 3b) p170
- ☐ Dirty Dick (f 3b) p181
- ☐ Bush Arête (f 3b) p198
- ☐ Rattlesnake (f 3b) p174
- ☐ Yellimo (f 3b) p203

4c
- ☐ Orion Crack (f 3c) p154
- ☐ Bell Rock Chim (f 3c) p164
- ☐ Puzzle Corner (f 3c) p206
- ☐ Crack Route (f 3c) p194
- ☐ Quirkus (f 3c) p179
- ☐ Alfred (f 3c) p218
- ☐ Boxing Day Ch. (f 3c) p164

5a
- ☐ Corot (f 4a) p218
- ☐ Rodin (f 4a) p218
- ☐ Hut Pass Arête (f 4a) p185
- ☐ Bold Finish (f 4a) p197

- ☐ Bell Rock Pass. (f 4a) p164
- ☐ Bell Rock Bridge (f 4a) p164
- ☐ Issingdown (f 4a) p175
- ☐ Zola (f 4a) p218
- ☐ Spoon (f 4a) p198
- ☐ Harold Hill Arete (f 4a) p174
- ☐ Holly Slab (f 4a) p203
- ☐ Windy Corner (f 4a) p203
- ☐ Helyatosis (f 4a) p198
- ☐ The Chute (f 4a) p164
- ☐ Roof Route (f 4a) p196
- ☐ North Wall (f 4a) p208
- ☐ Testimony (f 4a) p203
- ☐ Rhino's Eyebrow (f 4a) p192
- ☐ Greasy Crack (f 4a) p205
- ☐ Bow Crack (f 4a) p201
- ☐ Strangler (f 4a) p164
- ☐ Simian Progress (f 4a) p214
- ☐ Birthday Arête (f 4a) p196
- ☐ Anaconda Ch. (f 4b) p157

5b
- ☐ Degenerate (f 4b) p203
- ☐ Tricky Dicky (f 4b) p203
- ☐ Awkward Corner (f 4b) p201
- ☐ Open Groove (f 4b) p198
- ☐ Cough Drop (f 4b) p192
- ☐ Advertis-Wall (f 4b) p179
- ☐ Viper Crack (f 4b) p191
- ☐ Wishful Thinking (f 4b) p206
- ☐ Mamba Crack (f 4b) p174
- ☐ Bright Eyes (f 4b) p174
- ☐ Gaugin (f 4c) p218
- ☐ Reynolds (f 4c) p218
- ☐ Barbizon (f 4c) p218
- ☐ Nose Grime (f 4c) p203
- ☐ Effie (f 4c) p174
- ☐ Python Crack (f 4c) p175
- ☐ Henry the Ninth (f 4c) p170
- ☐ Scrap Arête (f 4c) p203
- ☐ The Gibbet (f 4c) p172
- ☐ Hidden Arête (f 4c) p164
- ☐ Geoff's Bald (f 4c) p160
- ☐ Sorrow (f 4c) p159
- ☐ Pure Arête (f 4b) p154
- ☐ Boa-Constrictor (f 4c) p157
- ☐ Barbed Wire F. (f 4c) p203
- ☐ Krankenkopf (f 4c) p167
- ☐ Moore Arete (f 4c) p218
- ☐ Steps Crack (f 4c) p159
- ☐ Simian Face (f 4c) p214
- ☐ Beanstalk (f 4c) p175
- ☐ Swing Face (f 4c) p196
- ☐ Brian Arête (f 4c) p154
- ☐ Z'mutt (f 4c) p217

5c
- ☐ Milly (f 5a) p218
- ☐ Hornet (f 5a) p198
- ☐ Miss Embassy (f 5a) p217
- ☐ Delirium (f 5a) p203

- ☐ Obi-Wan-Kenobi (5a) p182
- ☐ Pussyfoot (f 5a) p194
- ☐ Profiterole (f 5a) p203
- ☐ Orrer Crack (f 5a) p201
- ☐ Advertis-Wall D. (f 5a) p179
- ☐ Onions (f 5a) p160
- ☐ The Carcass (f 5a) p175
- ☐ Brenva (f 5b) p217
- ☐ Simian Mistake (f 5b) p208
- ☐ Odin's Wall (f 5b) p201
- ☐ Sunzilla (f 5b) p160
- ☐ Knife (f 5b) p213
- ☐ Fork (f 5b) p213
- ☐ Monkey Nut (f 5b) p208
- ☐ Peace on Earth (f 5b) p154
- ☐ Lady of the Light (f 5b) p154
- ☐ Coronation Crack (f 5b) p176
- ☐ Orion Arête (f 5b) p154
- ☐ Climbers-Badly (f 5b) p201
- ☐ Navy Way (f 5b) p201
- ☐ Sequins of Cosmic (f 5b) p196
- ☐ Bludnok Wall (f 5b) p194
- ☐ Long Stretch (f 5b) p194
- ☐ Seaman's Wall (f 5b) p198
- ☐ Simian Face Direct (f 5c) 214
- ☐ Shelter Arête (f 5b) p176
- ☐ Amnesia Variation (f 5b) p186
- ☐ Shotgun Wedding (f 5b) p176
- ☐ Diamonds in Orion (f 5b) p196
- ☐ Lucita (f 5b) p172
- ☐ Dinner Plate (f 5b) p213
- ☐ Celebration (f 5b) p188
- ☐ Dysentery (f 5b) p168
- ☐ Pinchgrip (f 5b) p194
- ☐ Canyon Crack (f 5b) p174
- ☐ Graveyard Groove (f 5b) p211

6a
- ☐ Delacroix (f 5c) p218
- ☐ Simian Crack Direct (f 5c) 214
- ☐ The Ghost (f 5c) p201
- ☐ Breakfast (f 5b) p214
- ☐ Mayfair (f 5c) p217
- ☐ Hull Motors (f 5c) p198
- ☐ Engagement Wall (f 5c) p179
- ☐ Effie Left Fork (f 5c) p174
- ☐ Cumberland (f 5c) p203
- ☐ Heat-on-Cooper (f 5c) p218
- ☐ Rockney (f 5c) p196
- ☐ Orca (f 5c) p170
- ☐ Slap Happy (f 5c) p203
- ☐ Steps Crack Direct (f 5c) p159
- ☐ Another back pass. (f 5c) p164
- ☐ Sputnik (f 5c) p208
- ☐ Cut Steps Crack (f 5c) p163
- ☐ Effie RH Finish (f 5c) p174
- ☐ Monkey Business (f 5c) p208
- ☐ Boysen's Crack (f 5c) p170
- ☐ Elephant (f 6a) p218
- ☐ Vingt-et-Un (f 6a) p203

- ☐ Picasso (f 6a) p218
- ☐ Sweaty Pussy (f 6a) p196
- ☐ Jaws (f 6a) p170
- ☐ Thrust (f 6a) p203
- ☐ Coronation Crack-R (f 6a) p1?
- ☐ Tequila Marquita (f 6a) p172
- ☐ Bow Spirit (f 6a) p201
- ☐ Bludgeon (f 6a) p188
- ☐ The Sphinx (f 6a) p208
- ☐ Tool Wall (f 6a) p213
- ☐ Woofus Weejects (f 6a) p206
- ☐ Mulligan's Wall (f 6a) p188
- ☐ Step On (f 6a) p198
- ☐ Fresh Air Finish (f 6a) p163
- ☐ Lunge'n'shelf (f 6a) p206
- ☐ Ides of March (f 6a) p206
- ☐ Marathon Man (f 6a) p207
- ☐ The Diver (f 6a) p207
- ☐ Meat and 2 Veg (f 6a) p186
- ☐ Dry Martini (f 6a) p188
- ☐ Slant Eyes (f 6a) p172
- ☐ Monkey Nutter (f 6a) p214
- ☐ Firebird (f 6a) p188
- ☐ Oven-R-Freddy (f 6a) p208
- ☐ Temple of Doom (f 6a) p213
- ☐ Mike's Left Knee (f 6a) p197
- ☐ Dagger Crack (f 6a) p205
- ☐ Rum, Bum and Bis (f 6a) p20
- ☐ Tilley Lamp Crack (f 6a) p191
- ☐ Something Crack (f 6a) p201
- ☐ Ockendon Slab (f 6a) p174
- ☐ Scimitar (f 6a) p155
- ☐ The Oligarchy (f 6a) p176
- ☐ Toothpick (f 6a) p213
- ☐ Id (f 6a) p194
- ☐ P.M.A. (f 6a) p174
- ☐ Conchita (f 6a) p172
- ☐ Guy's Problem (f 6a) p217
- ☐ Stalag (f 6a) p217
- ☐ Jabberwocky (f 6a) p217
- ☐ Ragged Trade (f 6a)
- ☐ The Dragon (f 6a) p167

6b
- ☐ Lobster (f 6a+) p170
- ☐ Moss Side Story (f 6a+) p203
- ☐ JPS (f 6a+) p217
- ☐ Metaphysical P. (f 6a+) p194
- ☐ Genevieve (f 6a+) p179
- ☐ Simian Crimp (f 6a+) p208
- ☐ Infidel (f 6a+) p170
- ☐ Craig-Y-Blanco (f 6a+) p205
- ☐ Roobarb (f 6a+) p186
- ☐ Too Tall for Tim (f 6a+) p163
- ☐ Pegasus (f 6a+) p160
- ☐ Too Crimpy for C (f 6a+) p163
- ☐ Devastator (f 6a+) p211
- ☐ Adder (f 6a+) p158
- ☐ Champagne C. (f 6a+) p188
- ☐ Robin's Route (f 6a+) p167

☐ Village Life (f 6b) p203
☐ The Kop (f 6b) p167
☐ Knock on Blood (f 6b) p194
☐ Rattlesnake II (f 6b) p157
☐ Touch too Much (f 6b) p191
☐ Beer Gut Shuffle (f 6b) p207
☐ Corsican Proposal (f 6b) p192
☐ Honeycomb (f 6b) p205
☐ So What (f 6b) p167
☐ Too Hard for Dave (f 6b) p163
☐ Natterjack (f 6b) p182
☐ Moving Staircase (f 6b) p159
☐ Green Goblin (f 6b) p217
☐ Senile Walk (f 6b) p164
☐ Death Cap (f 6b) p182
☐ Lamplight (f 6b) p191
☐ Educating Airlie (f 6b) p185
☐ Unfinished Bus (f 6b) p197
☐ Mervin Direct (f 6b) p182
☐ Dali (f 6b+) p218
☐ Prangster (f 6b+) p168
☐ Tom's Mantle (f 6b+) p217
☐ Barracuda (f 6b+) p205
☐ Kraken (f 6b+) p167
☐ Nemesis (f 6b+) p191
☐ Roofus (f 6b+) p192
☐ Firefly (f 6b+) p188
☐ Strangler D-Finish (f 6b+) p164
☐ Peapod (f 6b+) p175
☐ Crossing the Rub (f 6b+) p163
☐ Shattered (f 6b+) p191
☐ Monkey Sphincter (f 6b+) p208
☐ Designer Label (f 6b+) p160
☐ Malcolm's Cod (f 6b+) p160
☐ The Purvee (f 6b+) p154
☐ Sloping Beauty (f 6b+) p218
☐ Rag Trade (f 6b+) p160
☐ Telegram Sam (f 6b+) p160
☐ Tubby Fats Waller (f 6b+) p155
☐ Boonoonoo (f 6b+) p186
☐ Bolt to Bolt (f 6b+) p157
☐ Extender (f 6c) p203
☐ Crucible (f 6c) p217
☐ Leglock (f 6c) p163
☐ Early Breakfast (f 6c) p214
☐ Mysteries - Org (f 6c) p211
☐ Plantaganet (f 6c) p211

☐ Carbon Fibre (f 6c) p203
☐ Barbed Wire Kiss (f 6c) p203
☐ Cheetah (f 6c) p176
☐ The Full Monty (f 6c) p213
☐ First Crack (f 6c) p155
☐ The Blues (f 6c) p211
☐ Morpho (f 6c) p160
☐ Whiff Whaff (f 6c) p201
☐ Chez's Arete (f 6c) p218
☐ Dyno-Sore (f 6c) p179
☐ Look Sharp (f 6c) p181
☐ VS M-Staircase (f 6c) p159
☐ Elysium (f 6c) p198
☐ Krait Arête (f 6c) p176
☐ Spanked (f 6c) p167
☐ The Gangster (f 6c+) p168
☐ Fungal Smear (f 6c+) p157
☐ Salad Days (f 6c+) p163
☐ Can Opener (f 6c+) p203
☐ Honeypot (f 6c+) p205
☐ Orc's Dyno (f 6c+) p218
☐ Growing Pains (6c+) p175
☐ Slowhand (f 6c+) p170
☐ Kranked (f 6c+) p167
☐ Missing Link (f 6c+) p157
☐ Kinda Wanders (f 6c+) p185
☐ Bad Blood D (f 6c+) p176
☐ Sharpe Dyno (f 6c+) p185

6c
☐ Judy (f 7a) p160
☐ Orcanyon (f 7a) p174
☐ Smoke (f 7a) p188
☐ Jug of Flowers (f 7a) p197
☐ Return of the Mojo (f 7a) p211
☐ Honeycomb Direct (f 7a) p205
☐ Going Going (f 7a) p203
☐ Magnetic (f 7a) p170
☐ The Real Slim Shady (f 7a) p163
☐ Renascence (f 7a) p158
☐ Superman (f 7a) p160
☐ Old Kent Road (7a) p217
☐ I'll be Back (f 7a) p185
☐ Oak Tree Corner (f 7a) p218
☐ Kinda Lingers (f 7a) p185
☐ Mocasyn (f 7a) p172
☐ Yoda (f 7a) p182
☐ Brenva Sit Start (f 7a) p217

☐ A Bridge Too Far (f 7a+) p203
☐ Chez's Dyno (f 7a+) p188
☐ Superfly (f 7a+) p167
☐ Greenside Boulder (f 7a+) p218
☐ Happy Days (f 7a+) p214
☐ Kinda Lingers Direct (f 7a+) p185
☐ Ponytail Pearson (f 7a+) p197
☐ Bad Blood (f 7a+) p176
☐ Punch (f 7a+) p160
☐ Slick City (f 7a+) p203
☐ Acid Test (7a+) p217
☐ Pammy (f 7a+) p158
☐ Darth Vader (f 7a+) p186
☐ Fat Start (f 7a+) p170
☐ Wonder Boy (f 7a+) p157
☐ The Rip (f 7b) p167
☐ Atomic Mushroom (f 7b) p163
☐ The Gob (f 7b) p205
☐ Mojo (f 7b) p211
☐ Sinbad (f 7b) p198
☐ Unforgettable (f 7b) p186
☐ Bone Machine (f 7b) p157
☐ Porg's Progress (f 7b) p181

7a
☐ Mish Bell (f 7b+) p164
☐ Yoda Sit Start (f 7b+) p182
☐ Clown's Pocket (f 7b+) p155
☐ Cool Bananas (f 7b+) p174
☐ Vandal (f 7b+) p160
☐ Cont-Adventures of Porg (f 7b+)
☐ Resurrection (f 7b+) p158
☐ Pet Cemetery (f 7b+) p163
☐ Hale Bopp (f 7b+) p176
☐ Dog Town (f 7b+) p163
☐ Crosstown Traffic (f 7c) p203
☐ Kinda Lingers Sit Start (f 7c) p185
☐ Mish Bell (f 7c) p164
☐ Second Generation (f 7c) p158
☐ Final Destination (f 7c+) p206
☐ Bum Dragon (f 7c+) p203
☐ The Wish (f 7c+) p217
☐ Chimaera (f 7c+) p159
☐ The Slow Pull (f 7c+) p217
☐ The Snowdrop (f 7c+) p168
☐ Poppet's Persistance (f 7c+) p168
☐ Dont Pierdol (8a+) p217

HARRISON'S ROCKS
BOWLES ROCKS
HIGH ROCKS
HIGH ROCKS ANNEXE
HAPPY VALLEY
BULLS HOLLOW
ERIDGE GREEN
UNDER ROCKS
STONE FARM

PEGLERS

◁ *[UK 6a] MEAT AND TWO VEG (font 6a), Jérôme Curoy bridged on the classic testpiece - page 186.*

HARRISON'S ROCKS
BOWLES ROCKS
HIGH ROCKS
HIGH ROCKS ANNEXE
HAPPY VALLEY
BULLS HOLLOW
ERIDGE GREEN
UNDER ROCKS
STONE FARM

UK Trad	Fontainebleau colour (font grade)		Ticked

2a **(1) Orion Chimney** (f 2a)   S TR
Not the best route in the world.
Solo: Pre 1960's

4c **(2) Orion Crack** ☆ (f 3c)   S TR
Often very greasy and pretty disgusting.
Solo: Pre 1960's

5b **(3) Pure Arête** ☆ (f 4b)   S TR
The obvious left arête.
Solo: 1960's

5b **(4) Brian Arête** ☆ (f 4c)   S TR
Relies on good friction, how lucky do you feel?
Solo: 1998 Chris Arnold

Local chat: This is the farthest block of rock, just inside
the boundary fence. It's tucked away in a corner and
doesn't dry out quickly at all. The breaks tend to be
too far apart unfortunately for most climbers of normal
height. In a hot dry summer, this area does dry out and
the moss can be cleaned off successfully.

*Top access & erosion beta: Go to the L and
easily up the gully to the top. You will need
a short static rope for all belays, and an
additional long static to make a yoke for the
top of Orion Buttress.*

Crag layout map - page 148
Graded list - page 150

UK Trad	Fontainebleau colour (font grade)		Ticked

5c **(5) Peace on Earth** ☆☆ (f 5b)   S TR
Hand traverse the break with feet sliding.
TR: 1970's Tim Daniell

5c **(6) Lady of the Light Bulb** ☆☆ (f 5b)   S TR
Quite technical.
Solo: 2005 Tim Skinner   *TR: 1992 Doug Rei*

5c **(7) Orion Arête** ☆ (f 5b)   S TR
Greenish often - mediocre.
Solo: 1970's

6a **(8) Scimitar** ☆ (f 6a)   Slime S TR
Very green and greasy, impossible to grade.
Solo: 1960's

6b **(9) The Purvee** (f 6b+)   S TR
Rather reachy.
TR: 1990 Gary Wickham

HARRISON'S ROCKS

BOWLES ROCKS

HIGH ROCKS

HIGH ROCKS ANNEXE

HAPPY VALLEY

BULLS HOLLOW

ERIDGE GREEN

UNDER ROCKS

STONE FARM

10m

6a ①

6b ②

12m

6b ③

7a ④

K Trad   Fontainebleau colour (font grade)   Ticked

6a ① **Scimitar**☆ (f **6a**)
Very green and greasy, impossible to grade.
Soly: 1960's

6b ② **Tubby Hayes is a Fats Waller**☆☆ (f **6b+**)
Technical with pockets.

TR: 1990 Dave Turner

6b ③ **First Crack**☆ (f **6c**)
Gnarly and painful - often slimey.

TR: 1978 Mick Fowler

7a ④ **Clown's Pocket**☆ (f **7b+**)
Big dyno up the wall, finishing at the break.
Solo: 2005 Chez George

Local chat: In the late 1970's, First Crack was regarded as the hardest route in the South East, and very much the route you had to do if you fancied yourself as a top climber. Luckily these days, there are much harder and far more enjoyable routes to be found. This sector gets little sun and dries very slowly. On the rare occasion that it dries out, there isn't likely to be a massive rush – I don't think you'll have to queue.

Top access & erosion beta: Go to the L and easily up the gully to the top. Big trees are set well back and you will need 2 static ropes to set up a yoke, and keep the belay karabiner over the top of the route perfectly.

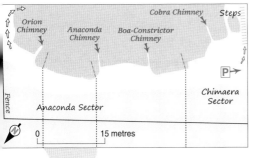

Orion Chimney

Anaconda Chimney

Boa-Constrictor Chimney

Cobra Chimney   Steps

Fence

P

Anaconda Sector

Chimaera Sector

0   15 metres

Crag layout map - page 148
Graded list - page 150

Anaconda   Judy   Dragon   Canyon   Advertisement   Kinda Lingers   Nemesis   Odin's Wall   Isolated Boulder   Maze
Chimaera   Chimneys   Infidel   Krait Arête   Crypt   Darth Vader   Hut Boulder   Honeycomb   Matterhorn

HARRISON'S ROCKS

BOWLES ROCKS

HIGH ROCKS

HIGH ROCKS ANNEXE

HAPPY VALLEY

BULLS HOLLOW

ERIDGE GREEN

UNDER ROCKS

STONE FARM

Trad | Fontainebleau colour (font grade) | Ticked

4b ① **Boa by the Back**★★ (f 3b)   S   TR
A squeezy slither, easiest at the back of the chimney.
Solo: Pre 1950's

5a ② **Anaconda Chimney**★★★ (f 4b)   S   TR
A tight and slithery squirm.
Solo: Pre 1950's

5b ③ **Boa-Constrictor Chimney**★★★ (f 4c)   S   TR
The flared start makes things awkward.
Solo: Pre 1950's

6b ④ **Rattlesnake 2**★★★ (f 6b)   S   TR
Leaving the chimney at the first break, climb the arête.
TR: 1986 Ian Mailer

Local chat: Anyone who is planning to go to the big canyon areas in the USA, check out your chimney techniques on these classic squeeze chimneys. If you can squirm well on these greasy buggers, you can cope with anything. The other routes are substantially harder and generally only come into condition towards the end of a dry spell. The nose of Bone Machine remains unclimbed!

Top access & erosion beta: Go to the R and easily up the gully via the steps. You will need a short static rope plus slings for setting up a belay.

UK Trad | Fontainebleau colour (font grade) | Ticked

6b ⑤ **Bolt to Bolt** (f 6b+)   S   TR
Boulder up the old bolt holds to the mid break.
Solo: 1990's

6b ⑥ **Fungal Smear**★★ (f 6c+)   S   TR
Climbs the obvious technical ramp line.
TR: 1990 Gary Wickham

6b ⑦ **Missing Link**★★★ (f 6c+)   S   TR
Lots of climbing, often difficult to clean lower break.
TR: 1990 Gary Wickham

6c ⑧ **Wonder Boy**★★ (f 7a+)   S   TR
A direct start to Fungal Smear via holes.
Solo: 2008 Ian Stronghill

6c ⑨ **Bone Machine**★★★ (f 7b)   S   TR
The exceptionally steep wall but finishing up the crack.
TR: 1993 Gary Wickham

Crag layout map - page 148
Graded list - page 150

[UK 6b] MISSING LINK (font 6c+), Ben Read

HARRISON'S ROCKS

BOWLES ROCKS

HIGH ROCKS

HIGH ROCKS ANNEXE

HAPPY VALLEY

BULLS HOLLOW

ERIDGE GREEN

UNDER ROCKS

STONE FARM

UK Trad	Fontainebleau colour (font grade)	Ticked

4a **(1) Cobra Chimney**☆☆ (f **3b**)   S TR

A wide bridging chimney, lovely when it's dry.
Solo: Pre 1950's

6b **(2) Adder**☆ (f **6a+**)   S TR

An excellent climb but is usually humongously greasy.
TR: 1976 Gordo DeLacy

6c **(3) Renascence**☆☆☆ (f **7a**)   S TR

The huge and imposing prow - a classic line.
TR: 1990 Dave Turner

UK Trad	Fontainebleau colour (font grade)	Ticked

6c **(4) Pammy**☆ (f **7a+**)   S TR

A sit start boulder problem finishing at the break.
Solo: 2002 Chez George

7a **(5) Resurrection**☆ (f **7b+**)   S TR

A boulder problem to the break, short but hard.
Solo: 2005 Ian Stronghill

7a **(6) Second Generation**☆☆☆ (f **7c**)   S TR

Continuous difficulty - plus a figure of four needed.
TR: 1990 Jasper Sharp

Local chat: A couple of highly impressive buttresses that give exceptional climbing in the top grades. Second Generation was given the sport climbing grade of 8a at the time of the first ascent – done in rapid style by an incredibly young Jasper Sharpe – who had only just turned 16.

Top access & erosion beta: Access the top via the steps to the right, then turn L to climb the short little gully. Tree belays quite a way back, you will need a static rope plus a sling and protection for the top edge (Quite a few routes only need 4 slings though).

UK Trad	Fontainebleau colour (font grade)	Ticked

5b **(1) Sorrow** (f **4c**)   S | TR

The front of the buttress - needs hot dry conditions.

Solo: 1980's   *TR: 1979 Tim Daniells*

5b **(2) Steps Crack** ☆☆(f **4c**)   S | TR

A classic crack line.

Solo: Pre 1950's   *TR: 1920's*

6a **(3) Steps Crack Direct** ☆ (f **5c**)   S | TR

An obvious more difficult finish.

TR: 1980's Unknown

Local chat: Not many routes in this sector, just a bit too blank for comfort. The ramp of Moving Staircase tends to stay pretty damp, however it does clean up well after a good dry spell - generally needing the warmth of summer months for the mossy footholds to dry out. The hard route Chimaera is a contorted classic, offering holds that are brittle and friable - please go carefully - best avoided by heavyweights.

UK Trad	Fontainebleau colour (font grade)	Ticked

6b **(4) Moving Staircase** ☆☆☆ (f **6b**)   S | TR

The start is draining, but sketchy reach is the simple key.

TR: 1986 Martin Boysen

6b **(5) Very Steep Moving Staircase** ☆☆☆ (f **6c**)   S | TR

A direct start compounds problems.

TR: 1980's Guy McLelland

7a **(6) Chimaera** ☆☆ (f **7c+**)   S | TR

A very tricky groove that spits out most - very morpho. Short and flexible climbers will find this a grade easier - perhaps.

TR: 1990 Dave Turner

Top access & erosion beta: Access the top via the steps to the left. Tree belays are quite a way back, you will need a short static rope plus a sling and protection for the top edge. Falling off the start to Moving Staircase gives you quite a swing into open space.

Crag layout map - page 148
Graded list - page 150

HARRISON'S ROCKS

BOWLES ROCKS

HIGH ROCKS

HIGH ROCKS ANNEXE

HAPPY VALLEY

BULLS HOLLOW

ERIDGE GREEN

UNDER ROCKS

STONE FARM

HARRISON'S ROCKS

BOWLES ROCKS

HIGH ROCKS

HIGH ROCKS ANNEXE

HAPPY VALLEY

BULLS HOLLOW

ERIDGE GREEN

UNDER ROCKS

STONE FARM

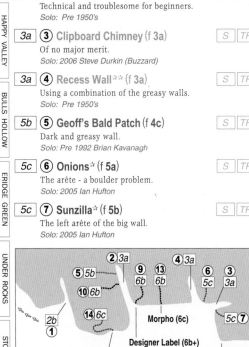

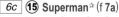

UK Trad	Fontainebleau colour (font grade)	Ticked		UK Trad	Fontainebleau colour (font grade)	Ticked

2b ① **Chockstone Chimney**☆☆☆ (f 3a)   S   TR
Straightforward chimney - but quite dirty & squirmy.
Solo: Pre 1950's

3a ② **Eft Chimney**☆ (f 3a)   S   TR
Technical and troublesome for beginners.
Solo: Pre 1950's

3a ③ **Clipboard Chimney** (f 3a)   S   TR
Of no major merit.
Solo: 2006 Steve Durkin (Buzzard)

3a ④ **Recess Wall**☆☆ (f 3a)   S   TR
Using a combination of the greasy walls.
Solo: Pre 1950's

5b ⑤ **Geoff's Bald Patch** (f 4c)   S   TR
Dark and greasy wall.
Solo: Pre 1992 Brian Kavanagh

5c ⑥ **Onions**☆ (f 5a)   S   TR
The arête - a boulder problem.
Solo: 2005 Ian Hufton

5c ⑦ **Sunzilla**☆ (f 5b)   S   TR
The left arête of the big wall.
Solo: 2005 Ian Hufton

6b ⑧ **Pegasus**☆☆☆ (f 6a+)   S   TR
A superb line finishing up the arête.
TR: 1990 Paul Widdowson

6b ⑨ **Designer Label** (f 6b+)   S   TR
Start on the left side of the arête to finish up the front.
Solo: 1987 Ian Mailer

6b ⑩ **Malcolm's Codpiece** (f 6b+)   S   TR
The bolder problem on the left wall inside the chimney.
Solo: 1992 Paul Widdowson

6b ⑪ **Ragtrade**☆ (f 6b+)   S   TR
Holds seem to have worn off this making the start hard.
TR: 1980 Mick Fowler

6b ⑫ **Telegram Sam**☆☆ (f 6b+)   S   TR
The obvious blunt arête - sketchy high slab finish.
TR: 1990 Paul Widdowson

6b ⑬ **Morpho**☆ (f 6c)   S   TR
A height and body dependent boulder problem.
Solo: 2005 Chez George

6c ⑭ **Judy**☆☆☆ (f 7a)   S   TR
An overhanging and stupendous line.
TR: 1982 Guy McLelland

6c ⑮ **Superman**☆ (f 7a)   S   TR
Damp and on soft rock - may not last that long.
Solo: 2005 Ian Stronghill

6c ⑯ **Punch**☆☆ (f 7a+)   S   TR
Most just do this as a 7a boulder problem to the break.
TR: 1995 Luc Perciva

7a ⑰ **Vandal**☆ (f 7b+)   S   TR
The rather steep arête, very morpho.
Solo: 2003 Jim Wardle

Local chat: A very imposing and steep sector.

Crag layout map - page 148
Graded list - page 150

Access: Up to the left - static rope needed.

[UK 6c] JUDY (font 7a), Steve Pearson

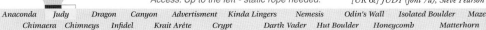

Anaconda   Judy   Dragon   Canyon   Advertisement   Kinda Lingers   Nemesis   Odin's Wall   Isolated Boulder   Maze
Chimaera   Chimneys   Infidel   Krait Arête   Crypt   Darth Vader   Hut Boulder   Honeycomb   Matterhorn

HARRISON'S ROCKS

BOWLES ROCKS

HIGH ROCKS

HIGH ROCKS ANNEXE

HAPPY VALLEY

BULLS HOLLOW

ERIDGE GREEN

UNDER ROCKS

STONE FARM

Trad	Fontainebleau colour (font grade)	Ticked

5c (1) **Sunzilla** ☆ (f 5b) S TR
The left arête of the big wall.
Solo: 2005 Ian Hufton

6a (2) **Cut Steps Crack** ☆☆☆ (f 5c) S TR
Whacky climbing from one side to another - use 2 belays.
TR: 1970's Gordon DeLacy

6a (3) **Fresh Air Finish** ☆☆☆ (f 6a) S TR
An even better out there finish - two belays essential.
TR: 2005 Robin Mazinke

6b (4) **Too Tall for Tim (Daniells)** ☆☆☆ (f 6a+) ✋ TR
Only possible for the very tall.
TR: 1984 Chris Arnold

< [UK 6b] SALAD DAYS (font 6c+), James O'Neil

UK Trad	Fontainebleau colour (font grade)	Ticked

6b (5) **Too Crimpy for Chris (Arnold)** ☆☆☆ (f 6a+) S TR
The high traverse, finishing up the arête of Salad Days.
TR: 2008 Tim Daniells

6b (6) **Too Hard for Dave (Turner)** ☆☆☆ (f 6b) S TR
The powerful and problematic overhanging arête.
TR: 1990 Paul Widdowson

6b (7) **Crossing the Rubicon** ☆☆ (f 6b+) S TR
Not always dry - but good all the same.
TR: 1990's

6b (8) **Leglock** ☆ (f 6c) S TR
Can often be greasy and horrible.
TR: 1980 Andy Meyers

6b (9) **Salad Days** ☆☆☆ (f 6c+) S TR
This classic arête start - looses holds regularly!
TR: 1982 Guy McLelland

6c (10) **The Real Slim Shady** ☆ (f 7a) S TR
Solo: 2005 Ian Stronghill

6c (11) **Atomic Mushroom** ☆ (f 7b) S TR
Solo: 2005 Giles Taylor

7a (12) **Pet Cemetery** ☆☆ (f 7b+) S TR
Going up via the gaston, usually finishing at the break.
Solo: 1995 Luc Percival

7a (13) **Dogtown** ☆☆ (f 7b+) S TR
Full on power.
Solo: 2005 Ian Stronghill

Local chat: A full on bouldering area of tough nuts to crack.
Access: Left or right - 2 static ropes for some routes.

Anaconda   Judy   Dragon   Canyon   Advertisement   Kinda Lingers   Nemesis   Odin's Wall   Isolated Boulder   Maze
Chimaera   Chimneys   Infidel   Krait Arête   Crypt   Darth Vader   Hut Boulder   Honeycomb   Matterhorn

Left margin tabs: HARRISON'S ROCKS · BOWLES ROCKS · HIGH ROCKS · HIGH ROCKS ANNEXE · HAPPY VALLEY · BULLS HOLLOW · ERIDGE GREEN · UNDER ROCKS · STONE FARM

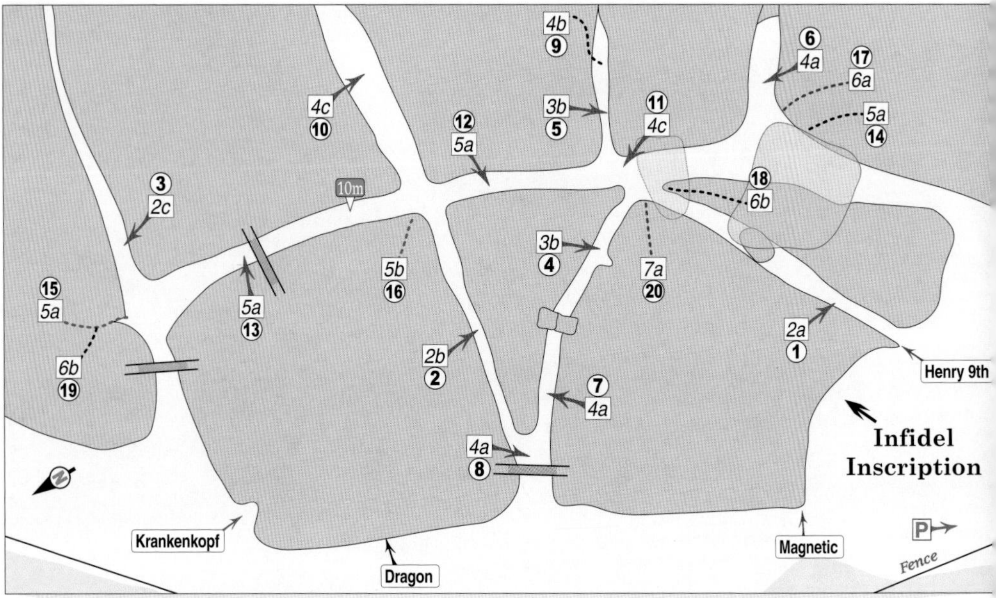

Map labels: 10m, Krankenkopf, Dragon, Magnetic, Henry 9th, **Infidel Inscription**, Fence, P

UK Trad		Fontainebleau colour (font grade)	Ticked
2a	①	**Warning Rock Chimney**✭✭ (f 2a)	S TR
		A fun way up and usually dry.	
2b	②	**Slab Chimney**✭✭✭ (f 2b)	S TR
		No shortage of contortions required.	
2c	③	**Deadwood Chimney**✭✭ (f 2c)	S TR
		Can be climbed almost anywhere.	
3b	④	**One of our Chimney's is Missing**✭ (f 3a)	S TR
		Name is more amusing than the climbing.	
3b	⑤	**Spider Chimney**✭✭✭ (f 3a)	S TR
		Full of creepy crawlies, arachnophobics keep out.	
4a	⑥	**Giant's Stride**✭✭✭ (f 3b)	S TR
		Easiest way up hereabouts.	
4a	⑦	**Smooth Chimney**✭✭✭ (f 3b)	S TR
		As the name suggests.	
4a	⑧	**Wye Chimney**✭✭✭ (f 3b)	S TR
		Wyde bridging is the key to this one.	
4b	⑨	**Crown of Thorns** (f 3b)	Slime BVZZ S TR
		This route exits via a hole in the ground - caving.	
4c	⑩	**Bell Rock Chimney**✭ (f 3c)	S TR
		Classic dark and dank chimney.	
4c	⑪	**Boxing Day Chimney**✭✭✭ (f 3c)	S TR
		To be ascended on Boxing Day of course.	
5a	⑫	**Bell Rock Passage**✭✭✭ (f 4a)	S TR
		Entertaining and demanding bridging anywhere here.	
5a	⑬	**Bell Rock Bridge Route**✭✭✭ (f 4a)	S TR
		Mixture of techniques to arrive at the bridge.	

UK Trad		Fontainebleau colour (font grade)	Ticked
5a	⑭	**The Chute** (f 4a)	S TR
		A slanting crack then chimney to finish.	
5a	⑮	**Strangler**✭✭ (f 4a)	S TR
		Can be good, but usually dank and dirty.	
5b	⑯	**Hidden Arete**✭ (f 4c)	S TR
		Only good in a mega heat wave.	
6a	⑰	**Another Back Passage** (f 6a)	S TR
		Uninspiring.	
6b	⑱	**Senile Walk**✭ (f 6b)	S TR
		A Technical and interesting arête - hot summer only.	
			TR: 1992 Martin Boyse
6b	⑲	**Strangler Direct Finish**✭ (f 6b+)	S TR
		Finish via the thin crack.	
			TR: 1992 Paul Widdowso
7a	⑳	**Mish Bell**✭ (f 7c)	S TR
		Finish via the thin crack.	
			TR: 2007 Chez Georg

Local chat: The chimneys and complex labyrinth sector of High Rocks is unique in Britain. The routes I have illustrated are broad suggestions, since you can climb just about anywhere in these passages at a reasonable grade, and individual route-lines are only applicable at the very top grades. These chimney style routes are excellent fun – so long as you are willing to put up with sore knees after the bridging, and green clothes from the old moss on the walls. In winter they ooze dankness. In summer they remain chilly and somewhat dark. In a max out heat wave, this is a damn good place to come, but be prepared for kids playing hide and seek - and asking endless questions!

Access & Erosion: The bridges may look secure, but it is advised to back up belays from substantial trees.

[UK 5a] BELL ROCK BRIDGE ROUTE, Mike Pollack ❯

HARRISON'S ROCKS

BOWLES ROCKS

HIGH ROCKS

HIGH ROCKS A'NNEXE

HAPPY VALLEY

BULLS HOLLOW

ERIDGE GREEN

UNDER ROCKS

STONE FARM

K Trad	Fontainebleau colour (font grade)		Ticked

4a (1) **Wye Chimney**☆☆☆ (f 3b)   S TR
The big wide chimney - anywhere you can.
Solo: Pre 1950's

5b (2) **Krankekopf Crack**☆ (f 4c)   S TR
The steep and gnarly crack just off to the R.
Solo: 1970's *TR: 1954 Billy Maxwell*

6a (3) **The Dragon**☆☆☆ (f 6a)   S TR
A classic route with a difficult start, middle and finish.
Solo: 1980's *TR: 1959 John Smoker*

6b (4) **Robin's Route**☆☆☆ (f 6a+)   S TR
The top crack is often damp - not a nice solo.
Solo: 1980 Mick Fowler *TR: 1960's Robin Harper*

6b (5) **So What**☆☆☆ (f 6b)   S TR
More steep bulges.
TR: 1990 Paul Hayes

6b (6) **Kraken**☆☆☆ (f 6b+)   S TR
Find the easiest way up the bulges, finish up the arête.
TR: 1990 Paul Widdowson

6b (7) ✍ **Spanked** (f 6c)   S TR
Start just right of Krankenkopf, go up to the arête bulge.
✍: 2005 Ian Stronghill

Local chat: A hard sector by the fence.

◁ *[UK 6a] THE DRAGON (font 6a), Rachel Hoyland*

UK Trad	Fontainebleau colour (font grade)		Ticked

6c (8) **Kranked**☆ (f 6c+) (✍ **Superfly** f 7a+)   S TR
The direct start to Kraken.
Solo: 1995 Luc Percival *✍: 2005 Ian Hufton*

6c (9) **The Rip**☆☆☆ (f 7b)   S TR
The traverse into and up Kranked.
Solo: 2005 Ian Stronghill

Belays: Multi static

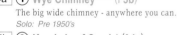

HARRISON'S ROCKS
BOWLES ROCKS
HIGH ROCKS
HIGH ROCKS ANNEXE
HAPPY VALLEY
BULLS HOLLOW
ERIDGE GREEN
UNDER ROCKS
STONE FARM

UK Trad	Fontainebleau colour (font grade)	Ticked		UK Trad	Fontainebleau colour (font grade)	Ticked

5c ① **Dysentery** (f **5b**)   S TR

This can be unpleasant.

TR: 1970's Nigel Head

6b ② **The Prangster**☆☆☆ (f **6b+**) 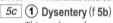 S TR

The lower bulge is a popular font 6b/6b+ bloc problem.

TR: 1992 Steve Quinton

6c ③ **The Gangster**☆☆ (f **6c+**)   S TR

The lower bulge to the break.

Solo: 1990's Climber's various

7a ④ **Snowdrop**☆☆ (f **7c+**)   S TR

Up to the break is straightforward font 6c+. The top nose is a classic mantle and body swerve, a Dawes special.

TR: 1997 Johnny Dawes

7a ⑤ **Poppet's Persistence**☆☆ (f **7c+**)   S TR

A high groove on the wall appears almost holdless.

TR: 2006 James Pearson

Local chat: The down side for this buttress is that it really gets wet during the winter months and the route Dysentery lives up to its name somewhat. The overhanging and undercut nature of the buttress makes it popular as a bouldering spot. The upper wall contains some real test piece routes that rarely get ascended – might be easy ticks though, not enough ascents to confirm difficulty. After a dry spring the wall dries out and can easily be cleaned to give excellent routes. An old route The Prang started around the corner to the right, linking Magnetic & Prangster, but now seems superseded.

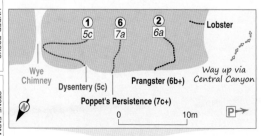

Access & Erosion: Go to the right and up the central canyon. Top has good belay trees but set well back - a long static rope does the job. Please use a crash pad at all times when bouldering here, and leave it alone when the rock is damp please.

Crag layout map - page 148
Graded list - page 150

[UK 6b] THE PRANGSTER (font 6b+), Paul MacCallum »

HARRISON'S ROCKS
BOWLES ROCKS
HIGH ROCKS
HIGH ROCKS ANNEXE
HAPPY VALLEY
BULLS HOLLOW
ERIDGE GREEN
UNDER ROCKS
STONE FARM

UK Trad	Fontainebleau colour (font grade)		Ticked	UK Trad	Fontainebleau colour (font grade)		Ticked
4b ①	**Balcony Direct**☆☆ (f **3b**)		S TR	**6b** ⑥	**Lobster**☆☆☆ (f **6a+**)		S TR
	Bridge up the open part of the passage - finishing left. *Solo: Pre 1950's*				Needs a bit of a dry spell for full enjoyment. *TR: 1959 John Smoke*		
5b ②	**Henry the Ninth**☆☆☆ (f **4c**)		S TR	**6b** ⑦	**Infidel**☆☆☆ (f **6a+**)		S TR
	Arête can be climbed on the left - or au cheval. *Solo: 1977 Mick Fowler* *TR: 1960's*				Increasingly technical as the holds wear away. *Solo: 1985 Mick Fowler* *TR: 1977 Mick Fowle*		
6a ③	**Orca**☆☆ (f **5c**)		S TR	**6b** ⑧	**Slowhand**☆☆ (f **6c+**)		S TR
	Start up Balcony but then finish only on the head wall. *Solo: 2005 Tim Skinner* *TR: 1990 Paul Widdowson*				Increasingly brutish as the holds wear away. *TR: 1990 Paul Widdowso*		
6a ④	**Boysen's Crack**☆☆ (f **5c**)		S TR	**6c** ⑨	⚡ **Magnetic** (f **7a**)		S TR
	Way harder if slimey and grimey. *Solo: 1994 Chris Arnold* *TR: 1970's Martin Boysen*				Well chalked up line of rising slopers. *Solo: 2003 Boulderers - Various*		
6a ⑤	**Jaws**☆☆☆ (f **6a**)		S TR	**6c** ⑩	**Fat Start** (f **7a+**)		S TR
	The lower bulge is a popular font 6b bloc problem. *Solo: 1980's* *TR: 1970's Tim Daniells*				The direct start to Jaws. *Solo: 1997 Johnny Dawes*		

Local chat: Even though the right hand photo-topo is crowded, the inset bay does dip in some way and the routes are pretty obvious. It's a very good sector with a couple of mega classics. This alcove stays cool on hot days - making it an ideal venue during a hot summer. A super hard crimpy route has been done using the carved lettering on the wall, however, I've resisted listing it as a route to tick. Grinding away at the carving will only destroy the delicate nature of the inscription (which ain't too bad after all), so perhaps best to give the letters a miss.

Access & Erosion: Get to the top by going right and up through the central canyon. You will definitely need an extra static rope for many of the belays. Also protect the rock where possible. For the route of Infidel, make sure the belay karabiner is at position illustrated. ✹

Crag layout map - page 148
Graded list - page 150

[UK 6c] MAGNETIC (font 7a), Giles Taylor ▷

UK Trad	Fontainebleau colour (font grade)		Ticked

5b ① **The Gibbet**✩✩ (f 4c) S TR
Obvious crack line, generally going left around the tree.
Solo: 1957 Philip Gibson

5c ② **Lucita**✩✩✩ (f 5b) S TR
The crack offers plenty of ugly jams.
Solo: 1960's *TR: 1958 John Smoker*

6a ③ **Tequila Marquita**✩✩✩ (f 6a) S TR
It all starts going wrong when the crack finishes.
Solo: 2005 Tim Skinner *TR: 1958 John Smoker*

6a ④ **Slant Eyes**✩✩✩ (f 6a) S TR
Is more difficult than it looks.
Solo: 1980's *TR: 1978 Mick Fowler*

UK Trad	Fontainebleau colour (font grade)		Ticked

6a ⑤ **Conchita**✩✩ (f 6a) S TR
More tricky than difficult.
TR: 1958 John Smoke

6c ⑥ **Mocasyn** (f 7a) S TR
Follow Slant Eyes to the 4th pocket, then gain a mono ar
crank desperately to the obvious pocket in the centre of
the wall (do not use large break of Slant Eyes out right).
TR: 1995 Luc Perciv

7a ⑦ **Cool Bananas** (f 7b+) S TR
A technical flat wall beneath the bridge.
TR: 1987 Dave Turne

Local chat: Here are some classic hand jamming routes that many who enjoy the Peak District will excel on. The tops however do not give in easily, plus you have an added slime factor at various times of the year. The whole bay area in front of the central canyon is a lovely area to enjoy the sunshine and relax on a summers day.

Access & Erosion: Get to the top by going right and up through the central canyon. You will definitely need an extra static rope for these belays. Also protect the rock where possible. Make sure the belay karabiner is around the positions illustrated.

Crag layout map - page 148
Graded list - page 150

[UK 6a] EFFIE LEFT FORK (font 5c), Dick Glazzard
Route overleaf from topo on page17

Left margin tabs: HARRISON'S ROCKS · BOWLES ROCKS · HIGH ROCKS · HIGH ROCKS ANNEXE · HAPPY VALLEY · BULLS HOLLOW · ERIDGE GREEN · UNDER ROCKS · STONE FARM

UK Trad		Fontainebleau colour (font grade)	Ticked	
2b	①	**Colorado Crack** ☆ (f 3a)	S	TR

Obvious crack going up to the ledge on the right.
Solo: Pre 1950's

4b	②	**Rattlesnake** ☆ (f 3b)	S	TR

Not much of a bite to this one.
Solo: Pre 1950's

5a	③	**Harold Hill Arête** (f 4a)	S	TR

The small arête.
Solo: 2005 Robin Mazinke   TR: 2005 Mike Vetterlein

5b	④	**Mamba Crack** ☆☆ (f 4b)	S	TR

Another grizzly nasty.
Solo: Pre 1950's

5b	⑤	**Bright Eyes** ☆ (f 4b)	S	TR

A short route, going up to the left.
Solo: 1970's Tim Daniells

5b	⑥	**Effie** ☆☆☆ (f 4c)	S	TR

A classic crack, then escaping easily left.
Solo: 1960's George Clark

5c	⑦	**Canyon Crack** (f 5b)	S	TR

Exiting up a crack after a high traverse from Effie.
TR: 1976 Mick Fowler

6a	⑧	**Effie Left Fork** ☆☆ (f 5c)	S	TR

Going left is a lot harder - requiring advanced technique.
TR: 1975 Mick Fowler

6a	⑨	**Effie Right Hand Finish** (f 5c)	S	TR

Exiting up a crack after a high traverse from Effie.
TR: 1976 Mick Fowler

6a	⑩	**Ockendon Slab** ☆ (f 6a)	S	TR

A slab with a tricky finish.
Solo: 1997 Robin Mazinke   TR: 1989 S. Allen

6a	⑪	**PMA** ☆ (f 6a)	S	TR

An awkward top out.
TR: 1987 Paul Hayes

6c	⑫	**Orcanyon** ☆ (f 7a)	S	TR

A boulder problem slab.
Solo: 2005 Chez George

7a	⑬	**Cool Bananas** ☆☆ (f 7b+)	S	TR

A very technical wall that stays in the shade.
TR: 1987 Dave Turner

Local chat: The central canyon is sometimes referred to as Grand Canyon - a tad misleading. It is generally dark and damp, but fortunately just dark - in a heat wave. Apart from an hour in the morning, the sun never gets in here. A good selection of routes for an appropriate day.

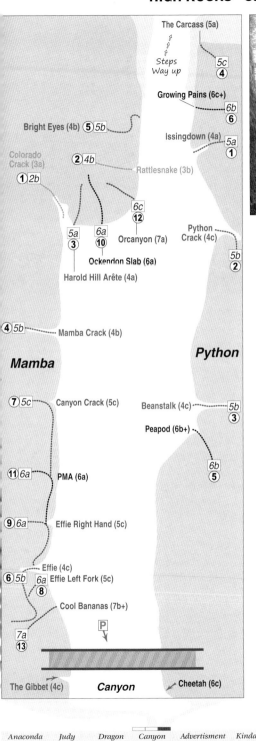

The Carcass (5a)

Steps
Way up

5c ④

Growing Pains (6c+)
6b ⑥

Bright Eyes (4b) ⑤ 5b

Issingdown (4a)
5a ①

Colorado
Crack (3a)

② 4b

Rattlesnake (3b)

① 2b

6c ⑫

Python
Crack (4c)

5a ③

6a ⑩

Orcanyon (7a)

5b ②

Ockendon Slab (6a)

Harold Hill Arête (4a)

④ 5b — Mamba Crack (4b)

Mamba

Python

⑦ 5c — Canyon Crack (5c)

Beanstalk (4c) 5b ③

Peapod (6b+)

6b ⑤

⑪ 6a — PMA (6a)

⑨ 6a — Effie Right Hand (5c)

Effie (4c)

⑥ 5b 6a Effie Left Fork (5c)

⑧

Cool Bananas (7b+)

7a ⑬

P

The Gibbet (4c)

Canyon

Cheetah (6c)

UK Trad   Fontainebleau colour (font grade)   Ticked

5a ① **Issingdown** (f **4a**)   S TR
Done first when it was raining.
Solo: 1960's

5b ② **Python Crack** (f **4c**)   S TR
A squeezy little number of substance.
Solo: 1960's   *TR: Pre 1950's*

5b ③ **Beanstalk** ☆ (f **4c**)   S TR
A grizzly and green wide crack.
Solo: 1960's   *TR: 1957 Philip Gordon*

5c ④ **The Carcass** (f **5a**)   S TR
A short boulder problem.
Solo: 2005 Ian Stronghill

6b ⑤ **Peapod** ☆ (f **6b+**)   S TR
Often damp and green unfortunately.
TR: 1986 Martin Boysen

6b ⑥ **Growing Pains** ☆ (f **6c+**)   S TR
A boulder problem up the greasy wall
Solo: 2005 Chez George

HARRISON'S ROCKS

BOWLES ROCKS

HIGH ROCKS

HIGH ROCKS ANNEXE

HAPPY VALLEY

BULLS HOLLOW

ERIDGE GREEN

UNDER ROCKS

STONE FARM

UK Trad	Fontainebleau colour (font grade)	Ticked

2b ① Shelter Chimney☆☆☆ (f 2b) `S` `TR`
This gets harder the deeper you go into the darkness.
Solo: Pre 1950's

5c ② Coronation Crack☆☆☆ (f 5b) `S` `TR`
If the wall for your feet is dry - then it's easy.
Solo: 1979 Mick Fowler   *TR: 1954 Billy Maxwell*

5c ③ Shelter Arête☆☆ (f 5b) `S` `TR`
Climbs the left wall then the top wall going left.
Solo: 1996 John Patterson   *TR: 1970's*

5c ④ Shotgun Wedding☆☆☆ (f 5b) `S` `TR`
An superb eliminate climb. Climb the arête, but avoid
using any of the square cut holds completely - interesting
higher up. No Advertisement - hence the name.
Solo: 1980's   *TR: 1960's*

6a ⑤ Coronation Crack Escape☆☆☆ (f 5c) `S` `TR`
Missing out the top crack is actually harder.
Solo: 1978 Stevie Haston   *TR: 1960's*

6a ⑥ The Oligarchy (f 6a) `S` `TR`
Sometimes feels good, sometimes trivial.
TR: 1991 Mike Vetterlein

Local chat: A superb sweep of rock at the entrance to
the Central Canyon. The obvious line of Coronation Crack
will definitely appeal to those thugs who love jamming.
The harder climbs are a big step up in difficulty, so
expect difficult progress.

6b ⑦ Cheetah☆☆ (f 6c) `S` `TR`
The damp rock here has disintegrated.
TR: 1974 Mick Fowle

6b ⑧ Krait Arête☆☆☆ (f 6c) `S` `TR`
'Easily move onto the arête' is not a common phrase.
TR: 1980's Martin Boyser

6b ⑨ Bad Blood Direct☆☆☆ (f 6c+) `S` `TR`
A more fitting start to the harder route above.
Solo: 1997 Johnny Dawes

6c ⑩ Bad Blood☆☆☆ (f 7a+) `S` `TR`
An eliminate - mostly without using the top arête.
TR: 1991 Jasper Sharpe

7a ⑪ Hale Bopp☆ (f 7b+) `S` `TR`
Fun climbing, as yet without a finish, two different starts
TR: 1997 Johnny Dawes

*Top access & erosion beta: Get to the top by
going through the Canyon then turning right on
obvious trails. Top belays are trees, so you will
need 6 slings for Krait or a static rope - please
additionally protect the edge - especially on
Krait Arête which usually spits you off low down
and at regular intervals - i.e. on every attempt.
Coronation Crack requires 2 static ropes to make
a yoke from 2 big trees.*

BOREAL

[UK 6b] KRAIT ARÊTE (font 6c), Stephen Glennie ▷

Crag layout map - page 148
Graded list - page 150

HARRISON'S ROCKS

BOWLES ROCKS

HIGH ROCKS

HIGH ROCKS ANNEXE

HAPPY VALLEY

BULLS HOLLOW

ERIDGE GREEN

UNDER ROCKS

STONE FARM

JK Trad   Fontainebleau colour (font grade)   Ticked   UK Trad   Fontainebleau colour (font grade)   Ticked

4c **(1)** **Quirkus** (f 3c)   `S` `TR`
Takes the easiest line up the right hand side.
Solo: 1960's

5b **(2)** **Advertisement Wall** ☆☆☆ (f 4b)   `S` `TR`
Takes the easiest way up using any combination of holes.
Solo: Pre 1960's   *TR: 1956 Paul Smoker*

5c **(3)** **Advertisement Wall Direct** ☆ (f 5a)   `S` `TR`
Holds wearing away on direct start - grade may change.
Solo: 1960's

5c **(4)** **Shotgun Wedding** ☆☆☆ (f 5b)   `S` `TR`
A superb eliminate climb. Climb the arête, but avoid using
any of the square cut holds for hands or feet; interesting
higher up. No Advertisement - hence the name.
Solo: 1960's   *TR: 1960's*

6a **(5)** **Engagement Wall** ☆☆☆ (f 5c)   `S` `TR`
Not hard moves when you know how.
Solo: 1990 John Godding   *TR: 1958 Paul Smoker*

6b **(6)** **Genevieve** ☆☆ (f 6a+)   `S` `TR`
Quite awkward.
     TR: 1990 Paul Widdowson

6b **(7)** **Dynosore** ☆☆ (f 6c)   `S` `TR`
Very height dependant.
     TR: 1987 Dave Turner

*Access & Erosion: Go to the left and up through the
Central Canyon for the summit plateau. Please take
care to protect the top square cut edge. You will need 2
static ropes to set up the belay for these routes.*

Local chat: This wall is so called because in the Victorian era,
the square holes used to support a rather obnoxious advertising
hoarding. Fortunately the sandstone around the holes has weathered
and they can be used as reasonable holds. Catches the sunshine for
most of the year and is always a popular spot to hang out.

BOREAL

◁ [UK 6b] DYNOSORE (font 6c), Mark Glennie

Crag layout map - page 148
Graded list - page 150

Anaconda   *Judy*   *Dragon*   *Canyon*   *Advertisment*   *Kinda Lingers*   *Nemesis*   *Odin's Wall*   *Isolated Boulder*   *Maze*
Chimaera   *Chimneys*   *Infidel*   *Krait Arête*   *Crypt*   *Darth Vader*   *Hut Boulder*   *Honeycomb*   *Matterhorn*

HARRISON'S ROCKS

BOWLES ROCKS

HIGH ROCKS

HIGH ROCKS ANNEXE

HAPPY VALLEY

BULLS HOLLOW

ERIDGE GREEN

UNDER ROCKS

STONE FARM

UK Trad   Fontainebleau colour (font grade)   *Ticked*

2a **(1) Short Chimney** (f 2a)   S   TR
Up or down, quite a fun little outing.
Solo: Pre 1960's

4a **(2) Crypt Crack** (f 3a)   S   TR
Often damp and not that brilliant.
Solo: Pre 1960's

4b **(3) Dirty Dick** (f 3b)   S   TR
Often very dirty and not that brilliant.
Solo: Pre 1960's

UK Trad   Fontainebleau colour (font grade)   *Ticked*

6b **(4) Look Sharp**⋆⋆ (f 6c)   S   TR
A classic arête problem of leaving the ground. Those who
are on the short side will find this defyingly difficult - but
more often impossible.
Solo: 1985 Barry Knight   *TR: 1984 Guy McLelland*

6c **(5) Porg's Progress**⋆ (f 7b)   S   TR
A fiendish boulder problem.
Solo: 1997 Johnny Dawes   *TR: 1992 Paul Widdowson*

7a **(6) Continuing Adventures of Porg**⋆ (f 7b+)   S   TR
More difficult bouldering.
Solo: 1997 Johnny Dawes   *TR: 1995 Luc Percival*

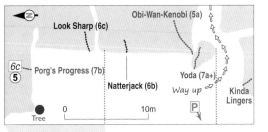

*Local chat: Not an area to go out of your way for if
you climb in the lower grades. A couple of classic
boulder problems though in the upper grades.*

*Access & Erosion: Please use boulder pads to protect
the ground, and don't thrash away at these if you don't
stand a chance, the rock isn't that strong - thanks. If
you are thin, Short Chimney curves around and you
can walk through it to the top, otherwise go to the
right. Two static ropes are needed for the top belays.*

Crag layout map - page 148
Graded list - page 150

◁ *[UK 6b] LOOK SHARP (font 6c), Mark Croxall*

Chimaera   *Chimneys*   *Infidel*   *Krait Arête*   *Crypt*   *Darth Vader*   *Hut Boulder*   *Honeycomb*   *Matterhorn*
Anaconda   *Judy*   *Dragon*   *Canyon*   *Advertisment*   *Kinda Lingers*   *Nemesis*   *Odin's Wall*   *Isolated Boulder*   *Maze*

UK Trad	Fontainebleau colour (font grade)	Ticked

2a ① Short Chimney (f 2a)   S TR
Up or down, quite a fun little outing.
Solo: Pre 1960's

5c ② Obi-Wan-Kenobi☆ (f 5a)   S TR
Ascend corner crack and follow the arête direct.
Solo: 1980's

6b ③ Natterjack☆ (f 6b)   S TR
Left end of square cut holds.
TR: 1990's

6b ④ Death Cap☆ (f 6b)   S TR
Tricky.
TR: 1990's

UK Trad	Fontainebleau colour (font grade)	Ticked

6b ⑤ Mervin Direct☆☆ (f 6b)   S TR
Right end of the square cut holds.
TR: 1985 Gary Wickham

6b ⑥ Look Sharp☆☆ (f 6c)   S TR
A classic arête problem of leaving the ground.
Solo: 1985 Barry Knight   TR: 1984 Guy McLelland

6c ⑦ Yoda☆☆ (f 7a) (⌀ f 7b+)   S TR
The delectable front nose of the leaning block.
Solo: 2005 Chez George   ⌀ : 2006 Ian Stronghill

Local chat: This wall is set high above the lower path and the ground is slowly dropping away. The height is just a bit too high for comfortable bouldering, plus the holds are mostly artificial square cut - and remain damp. Needs a good dry spell to come into condition.

Top access & erosion beta: Go up the passage to the right of Yoda block. A selection of big trees is set slightly back, a short static is ample for setting up the belay.

Crag layout map - page 148
Graded list - page 150

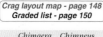

Sidebar tabs: HARRISON'S ROCKS | BOWLES ROCKS | HIGH ROCKS | HIGH ROCKS ANNEXE | HAPPY VALLEY | BULLS HOLLOW | ERIDGE GREEN | UNDER ROCKS | STONE FARM

HARRISON'S ROCKS

BOWLES ROCKS

HIGH ROCKS

HIGH ROCKS ANNEXE

HAPPY VALLEY

BULLS HOLLOW

ERIDGE GREEN

UNDER ROCKS

STONE FARM

JK Trad	Fontainebleau colour (font grade)	Ticked

3a (1) **Hut Passage Chimney**☆☆☆ (f **3a**)   S TR
Sometimes called "Hut Transverse Passage Ordinary Route!"
Solo: Pre 1960's

5a (2) **Hut Passage Arête**☆ (f **4a**)   S TR
Short and fun if it has dried out.
Solo: Pre 1960's

6b (3) **Educating Airlie**☆ (f **6b**)   S TR
It's a pity that this route normally stays greasy.
TR: 1991 Mike Vetterlein

6b (4) **Kinda Wanders**☆ (f **6c+**)   S TR
Traverse in to the arête on the obvious line, then finish
Kinda Lingers top arête. Still involves a technical and
difficult 6c+ move high up.
TR: 1980's Gary Wickham

Local chat: The Kinda Lingers arete gives a hard
move high up – but is more popular with boulderers for
the lower section of hard starts and good problems.
The big wall to the right seems just a bit too blank
unfortunately.

Crag layout map - page 148
Graded list - page 150

UK Trad	Fontainebleau colour (font grade)	Ticked

6b (5) **Sharpe Dyno**☆ (f **6c+**)   S TR
The obvious dyno - then to the pockets.
Solo: 1990 Jasper Sharpe

6c (6) **I'll Be Back**☆☆ (f **7a**)   S TR
A technical wall.
TR: 1991 Jasper Sharpe

6c (7) **Kinda Lingers**☆☆☆ (f **7a**)   S TR
The original start uses a figure of 4 to span up to pockets.
TR: 1980's Gary Wickham

6c (8) **Kinda Lingers Direct**☆☆☆ (f **7a+**)   S TR
The more logical start at font 7a (7b without a jump).
TR: 1990 Jasper Sharpe

7a (9) ✍ **Kinda Lingers Sit Start**☆ (f **7c**)   S TR
A sit start direct from below - or more recently from left.
Solo: 2003 Unknown

Access & Erosion: Go up the gully to the left for the
top. Big trees set back, you will need a static rope also.
The tops of the routes here usually need cleaning, and
remain damp, so wait for a good dry spell.

◁ [UK 6b] SHARPE DYNO (font 6c+), Mark Croxall

HARRISON'S ROCKS

BOWLES ROCKS

HIGH ROCKS

HIGH ROCKS ANNEXE

HAPPY VALLEY

BULLS HOLLOW

ERIDGE GREEN

UNDER ROCKS

STONE FARM

UK Trad   Fontainebleau colour (font grade)   *Ticked*

| **3a** ① **Brushwood Chimney**☆☆ (f 3b) | S | TR |

A fine chimney with lots of different techniques.
Solo: Pre 1950's

| **5c** ② **Amnesia Variation**☆☆ (f 5b) | S | TR |

Leaving the chimney high up to finish up the head wall.
TR: 1992 M. Gallagher

| **6a** ③ **Meat & Two Veg**☆☆☆ (f 6a) | S | TR |

Originally called "All that meat but only two veg." A
typical mad day out with Matt Saunders. Bridge the gap
between the tree & rock, then ascend both. (Photo p 152)
TR: 1980's Matt Saunders

| **6b** ④ **Roobarb**☆☆ (f 6a+) | S | TR |

Climbs the centre of the wall behind the tree to the high
break - sandy holds wearing away. Then drift around to
the chimney and climb the slab direct.
Solo: 1980's   *TR: 1978 Mick Fowler*

*Local chat: This highly imposing section at the centre of the
crag and is often the first place you arrive at. It is one of the
highest parts of High Rocks and will feel pretty high to most.
A complete mixture of routes with few being easy.*

UK Trad   Fontainebleau colour (font grade)   *Ticked*

| **6b** ⑤ **Boonoonoonoonoos**☆☆☆ (f 6b+) | S | TR |

A stamina classic of the crag, slightly overhanging which
should not feel hard - crux is very reach dependent.
TR: Late1980's Dave Turner

| **6c** ⑥ ✍ **Darth Vader**☆☆ (f 7a+) | S | TR |

The striking arête to the high break (font 6c with stand
start making it a much poorer problem).
Solo: 2005 Chez George

| **6c** ⑦ **Unforgettable**☆☆ (f 7b) | S | TR |

A sustained big number, mostly technical, some thug.
TR: 1989 Paul Hayes

*Access & Erosion: Either left of right. Arranging a top
rope belay is not straightforward and you will need 2
static rope belays. Please protect the edge of the crag
here since most fall off, and the rope acts as a saw into
the rock. The top outs to the routes are not hard, so
make sure the karabiner is nicely below the edge.*

[UK 6c] UNFORGETTABLE (font 7b), Dave Potts ▷

Chimaera   Chimneys   Infidel   Krait Arête   Crypt   Darth Vader   Hut Boulder   Honeycomb   Matterhorn
Anaconda   Judy   Dragon   Canyon   Advertisement   Kinda Lingers   Nemesis   Odin's Wall   Isolated Boulder   Maze

HARRISON'S ROCKS
BOWLES ROCKS
HIGH ROCKS
HIGH ROCKS ANNEXE
HAPPY VALLEY
BULLS HOLLOW
ERIDGE GREEN
UNDER ROCKS
STONE FARM

UK Trad	Fontainebleau colour (font grade)		Ticked

3a ① Rufrock Chimney ☆☆ (f 3a)   S   TR

A damn good chimney outing, further inside is more diff.
Solo: Pre 1950's

5c ② Celebration ☆☆☆ (f 5b)   S   TR

A superb line in an impressive position.
Solo: 1970's   TR: 1959 Paul Smoker

6a ③ Bludgeon ☆☆☆ (f 6a)   S   TR

A real stamina test on a magnificent natural line without
any individual hard moves - ho ho! (Originally called
Bloodgeon but now known locally as Bludgeon.)
TR: 1959 Martin Boysen

6a ④ Mulligan's Wall ☆☆☆ (f 6a)   S   TR

After the crack line, veer slightly right to finish direct.
5c Route originally went left to the tree - bit of a cop out
and misses the final crux.
TR: 1959 Don Ingrey (5c)

6a ⑤ Dry Martini ☆ (f 6a)   S   TR

A squeezed in route next to the tree.
TR: 1980 David Atchison-Jones

*Local chat: This buttress is in the sun for the hottest part of
the day - making it great in the spring, but horrible in high
summer. The rock quality low down is poor, but really improves
as you ascend. The routes on the left side feel very long and
steep (from the foot of the steps), watch out for taking a
crunching swinger into the steps from the start of Bludgeon
- spotter advised.*

UK Trad	Fontainebleau colour (font grade)		Ticked

6a ⑥ Firebird ☆☆☆ (f 6a)   S   TR

A more sustained route than Mulligan's Wall, but with
individually easier moves.
TR: 1970's Tim Daniel.

6b ⑦ Champagne Celebration ☆☆ (f 6a+)   S   TR

Going direct up the wall on crimps.
Solo: 1983 David Atchison-Jones   TR: 1981 Guy McLellan

6b ⑧ Firefly ☆ (f 6b+)   S   TR

A nasty move at the first crack on poor rock.
TR: 1977 Mick Fowle

6c ⑨ Smoke ☆ (f 7a)   S   TR

Poor soft rock unfortunately.
TR: 1992 Alan Grigg

6c ⑩ Chez's Dyno ☝ ☆☆ (f 7a+)   S   TR

A whopping giant dyno between the markers. ⦿
Solo: 2002 Chez George

*Access & Erosion: Go to the right past Hut Boulder,
then left up to the top plateau (See plan on page 192).
Setting up belays here is complicated and best left
to those good at ropework. You will need 2 static
rope belays set to trees quite a way back. Top belay
karabiner needs to be well over the somewhat rounded
top edge - co-ordinate with climbers below for setting in
the best position.*

Crag layout map - page 148
Graded list - page 150

The Arch
Climbing Wall

Central London's only dedicated indoor climbing centre.

100+ boulder problems and **4 circuits** reset monthly by guest setters including Gaz Parry, Andy Earl and Johnny Dawes.

Open until 10pm 7 days a week including bank holidays. Only 1 minute walk from London Bridge station.

Tel: 020 7407 0999
THE ARCH CLIMBING WALL
6 BERMONDSEY STREET SE1 2ER
www.archclimbingwall.com

HARRISON'S ROCKS
BOWLES ROCKS
HIGH ROCKS
HIGH ROCKS ANNEXE
HAPPY VALLEY
BULLS HOLLOW
ERIDGE GREEN
UNDER ROCKS
STONE FARM

UK Trad   Fontainebleau colour (font grade)   *Ticked*

3a (1) **Rufrock Chimney** ☆☆☆ (f 3a)   S   TR

This is the open front part of the passage - historically called Hut Transverse Passage. Many possibilities to climb up anywhere at varying grades 3a-4a.
Solo: Pre 1950's

5b (2) **Viper Crack** ☆☆ (f 4b)   S   TR

Often dry these days and good fun.
Solo: 1960's   *TR: 1950's*

6a (3) **Tilley Lamp Crack** ☠☠ ☆☆☆ (f 6a)   S   TR

Sorting out the exit from the crack - is not obvious.
Solo: 1996 John Patterson   *TR: 1960's George Clark*

6b (4) **A Touch Too Much** ☠ ☆☆☆ (f 6b)   S   TR

Pockets combined with awkwardness.
Solo: 1986 Gary Wickham   *TR: 1985 Matt Saunders*

UK Trad   Fontainebleau colour (font grade)   *Ticked*

6b (5) **Lamplight** ☆☆☆ (f 6b)   S   TR

An eliminate line with excellent climbing.
TR: 1996 Barry Knight

6b (6) **Nemesis** ☠☠ ☆☆☆ (f 6b+)   S   TR

The crux has 'slightly' poor footholds.
Solo: 2002 Giles Taylor   *TR: 1986 Gary Wickham*

6b (7) **Shattered** ☠ ☆☆ (f 6b+)   S   TR

A classic arête with rounded holds to start, followed by classic sandstone techniques. One of many routes to be aptly named after Rolling Stones hits.
Solo: 1982 David Atchison-Jones   *TR: 1982 David A-Jones*

Access & Erosion: Go up to the right past Hut Boulder, then turn L and follow main gully up and around - taking a short cut is awkward with ropes and stuff. (See plan on page 192). You will need a static rope in addition to long slings for the belays, some routes like Tilley Lamp require 2 static ropes to form a yoke.

Local chat: In the 1950's, this bay was filled with a Tea House, which eventually fell down but does explain the tarmac in front of the wall – highly useful to sunbathe on spring days. The area became heavily overgrown during the 1970's. It was so damp that the classic low traverse of the wall called 'Lord' and graded 6b – considered as a gruesome test piece on Sandstone in the early 1980's. Now dry, it goes at a comfortable font 5c. Even though nearly all of the routes have been soloed, don't underestimate them - they are very dangerous highballs and were done by some of the top local climbers when going well.

[UK 6b] NEMESIS (Font 6b+), Matt Burke

Anaconda   Judy   Dragon   Canyon   Advertisement   Kinda Lingers   Nemesis   Odin's Wall   Isolated Boulder   Maze

Chimaera   Chimneys   Infidel   Krait Aréte   Crypt   Darth Vader   Hut Boulder   Honeycomb   Matterhorn

HARRISON'S ROCKS

BOWLES ROCKS

HIGH ROCKS

HIGH ROCKS ANNEXE

HAPPY VALLEY

BULLS HOLLOW

ERIDGE GREEN

UNDER ROCKS

STONE FARM

UK Trad	Fontainebleau colour (font grade)		Ticked

5a ① **Rhino's Eyebrow**☆☆ (f **4a**)   S   TR

Stays a bit mossy on the back of this large boulder.

Solo: 1960's   *TR: 1953 Vic Hayden*

5b ② **Cough Drop**☆☆ (f **4b**)   S   TR

North facing - best left for a hot summers day.

Solo: 1960's   *TR: 1953 Doug Stone*

UK Trad	Fontainebleau colour (font grade)		Ticked

6b ③ **Corsican Proposal**☆ (f **6b**)   S   TR

The blunt nose.

     TR: 1996 Chris Arno

6b ④ **Roofus**☆☆☆ (f **6b+**)   S   TR

Not too bad up to the final lip, skill and fitness required.

     TR: 1993 Guy McLellar

Top access & erosion beta: This pinnacle is isolated with no easy way up. It is locally considered good form, for the best climber in the group to solo up a route, and then set up top ropes (4 sets of bolts on top), with karabiners well over the edge in order that the moving rope does not rub or wear the rock. I recommend that you take all the safety precautions that you are happy with, and make sure not to unduly damage the rock in any way. Most of the time you don't need to top out, but remember to lower off the routes with care please, placing your feet gently. Check with other climbers before stripping the boulder of top ropes. Do not abseil off and pull the ropes through the top bolts - either downclimb, or go hand over hand on a double rope draped over the low shoulder.

Local chat: This is a lovely free standing boulder, so named after the tea hut that was adjacent during the Victorian Era. There are relatively easy ways up the dark passage side, but they often remain damp and greasy, not ideal for climbing without a rope. The noses at either end - are difficult. On the Front Face, there is a central crack line - this is easyish until the top where it becomes awkward, and the rock sounds rather hollow! At the left end there is the route Long Stretch page 194. This route has the crux low down fortunately - so with a few spotters and crash pads, this is normally the classic solo to the top of the block.

[UK 6b] ROOFUS (font 6b+), Joe Heasman >

HARRISON'S ROCKS
BOWLES ROCKS
HIGH ROCKS
HIGH ROCKS ANNEXE
HAPPY VALLEY
BULLS HOLLOW
ERIDGE GREEN
UNDER ROCKS
STONE FARM

UK Trad	Fontainebleau colour (font grade)	Ticked

4c ① Crack Route★★★ (f 3c) `S` `TR`

The two high crux's make this an iffy solo for many.
Solo: Pre 1960's *TR: 1930's*

5c ② Pussyfoot★★★ (f 5a) `S` `TR`

Worn out holds present a few problems.
Solo: 1960's *TR: 1953 Kevin Day*

5c ③ Bludnok Wall★ (f 5b) `S` `TR`

A one move wonder.
Solo: 1969 Martin Boysen *TR: 1958 John Smoker*

5c ④ Long Stretch★★★ (f 5b) `S` `TR`

Awkward.
Solo: 1960's *TR: 1958 John Smoker*

5c ⑤ Pinchgrip★★★ (f 5b) `S` `TR`

Rounded and awkward - easy when wired.
Solo: 1970's *TR: 1970's*

Access & Erosion: See previous page 192 for access directions. Always make sure that top belay karabiner sits below the edge. ✳

6a ⑥ Sweaty Pussy★★ (f 6a) `S` `TR`

A direct line up Pussyfoot.
Solo: 1982 Various Lads *TR: 1981 David Atchison-Jones*

6a ⑦ Id★★ (f 6a) `S` `TR`

Follow up the arête the same as for Roofus, then at the top swing right to finish at a reasonable grade. Escaping right at the top might be judged Ego (Freud).
Solo: 1980's *TR: 1962 Graeme Hughes*

6b ⑧ Metaphysical Poets★★ (f 6a+) `S` `TR`

A very good eliminate when bored with Pinchgrip.
TR: 1988 Carrie Atchison-Jones

6b ⑨ Knock on Blood★ (f 6b) ✋ `S` `TR`

A direct line up the slab - very reach dependent.
TR: 1997 Robin Mazink

Local chat: The front face of Hut Boulder is certainly the busiest part of High Rocks where you are likely to bump into friends etc. A handy place to meet since it nicely gets the sun around lunchtime. Routes here dry out quickly and are all worth doing.

Caution: High Rocks is an "outdoor climbing environment." All bolt rings or chains can only be considered as totally reliable on the day of insertion. Thereafter, the holding power will remain hidden from view and will be unknown. Use at your own risk and if you are in any doubt at all, do not rely on them.

[UK 4c] CRACK ROUTE (font 3c), Philippa Speirs ▷

HARRISON'S ROCKS

BOWLES ROCKS

HIGH ROCKS

HIGH ROCKS ANNEXE

HAPPY VALLEY

BULLS HOLLOW

ERIDGE GREEN

UNDER ROCKS

STONE FARM

UK Trad   Fontainebleau colour (font grade)   Ticked

5a **(1) Roof Route**☆☆☆ (f **4a**)   [S] [TR]
The natural slanting break using everything available.
Solo: Pre 1960's   *TR: Pre 1950's*

5a **(2) Birthday Arête**☆☆☆ (f **4a**)   [S] [TR]
Soon swing left and get into balance.
Solo: 1960's   *TR: 1953 Doug Stone*

5b **(3) Swing Face**☆ (f **4c**)   [S] [TR]
Overhang is reasonable when you have the beta.
Solo: Pre 1960's   *TR: Pre 1950's*

5c **(4) Sequins of Cosmic Turbulence**☆☆ (f **5b**) [S] [TR]
An intergallactic route (big hold left of wobbly is out).
Solo: 1993 Tim Skinner   *TR: 1982 David Atchison-Jones*

5c **(5) Diamonds in Orion**☆☆ (f **5b**)   [S] [TR]
Good for hot days.
Solo: 1980's   *TR: 1980's*

6a **(6) Rockney**☆☆☆ (f **5c**)   [S] [TR]
Many different ways - all awkward.
Solo: 1980's   *TR: 1982 Barry Franklin*

6a **(7) Sweaty Pussy**☆☆ (f **6a**)   [S] [TR]

Access & Erosion: See previous page 192.

HARRISON'S ROCKS

BOWLES ROCKS

HIGH ROCKS

HIGH ROCKS ANNEXE

HAPPY VALLEY

BULLS HOLLOW

ERIDGE GREEN

UNDER ROCKS

STONE FARM

JK Trad	Fontainebleau colour (font grade)	Ticked

3a (1) **Easy Crack** ☆☆ (f **3a**)   S TR
The very obvious damp crackline.
Solo: Pre 1950's

5a (2) **Bold Finish** ☆☆ (f **4a**)   S TR
Not the most pleasant of top outs.
Solo: 1960's   *TR: 1960's*

5b (3) **Viper Crack** ☆☆ (f **4b**)   S TR
Often dry these days and good fun.
Solo: 1960's   *TR: 1950's*

6a (4) **Mike's Left Knee** ☆ (f **6a**)   S TR
A high crux - powerful.
Solo: 2007 Tim Skinner   *TR: 1990 Paul Widdowson*

UK Trad	Fontainebleau colour (font grade)	Ticked

6b (5) **Unfinished Business** ☆ (f **6b**)   S TR
Boulder wall to the right of Bold Finish.
Solo: 2005 Ian Stronghill

6b (6) **Shattered** ☆☆ (f **6b+**)   S TR
A classic boulder semi-high ball.
Solo: 1982 David Atchison-Jones   *TR: 1982 David A-Jones*

6c (7) **Jug of Flowers** ☆☆ (f **7a**)   S TR
Two alternative starts possible.
TR: 1980's Guy McLelland

6c (8) **Ponytail Pearson** ☆☆ (f **7a+**)   S TR
A bit too blank for most.
TR: 1991 Jasper Sharpe

Local chat: The wall behind Hut Boulder stays heavily in the shade all year. It does dry out in summer and the light green dust can easily be wiped off. A real mixture of routes in the easier grades, and pretty dam stiff ones at the top end.

Access & Erosion: Go up to the right, then turn L and follow main gully up and around - taking a shortcut is awkward with ropes and stuff. You will need a static rope in addition to long slings for many of the belays. There are bolts however at the top of Easy Crack.

Local chat for left page (Swing Face–Sequins Wall): This end face to Hut Boulder goes by the name of Swing Face, by virtue of its well undercut base - catching many out who lower down and swing in - or fall off and swing out. Around the back of the boulder in the passage - it is dark, damp, chilly and frigid - the wind howls through here - duvet jacket for belaying compulsory. However, the aforementioned breeze certainly picks up on a hot summers afternoon, making it an ideal spot on those 30 degree days.

Crag layout map - page 148
Graded list - page 150

Chimaera   Chimneys   Infidel   Krait Arête   Crypt   Darth Vader   Hut Boulder   Honeycomb   Matterhorn
Anaconda   Judy   Dragon   Canyon   Advertisment   Kinda Lingers   Nemesis   Odin's Wall   Isolated Boulder   Maze

HARRISON'S ROCKS

BOWLES ROCKS

HIGH ROCKS

HIGH ROCKS ANNEXE

HAPPY VALLEY

BULLS HOLLOW

ERIDGE GREEN

UNDER ROCKS

STONE FARM

UK Trad	Fontainebleau colour (font grade)	Ticked		UK Trad	Fontainebleau colour (font grade)	Ticked

1a ① Green Ernie (f 2a)   S   TR
Not a very big route but very green.
Solo: 1960's

3a ② Silly Corner☆ (f 3a)   S   TR
The dry dog leg crack beneath the bridge.
Solo: 1960's

3b ③ Rhododendron Route☆ (f 3a)   S   TR
Lives up to its name.
Solo: Pre 1960's

4b ④ Bush Arête☆ (f 3b)   S   TR
Rather a lot of bush.
Solo: 1960's

5a ⑤ Spoon☆ (f 4a)   S   TR
A short arête.
Solo: 2005 Robin Mazinke

5a ⑥ Helyotosis☆ (f 4a)   S   TR
Reasonable.
TR: 2005 Hely Boylan

5b ⑦ Open Groove☆ (f 4b)   S   TR
Awkward with undergrowth.
Solo: 1960's

5c ⑧ Hornet☆ (f 5a)   S   TR
A short arête.
TR: 2005 Tim Skinner

5c ⑨ Seaman's Wall☆ (f 5b)   S   TR
The short wall.
Solo: 2005 Tim Skinner   *TR: 1970*

6a ⑩ Hull Motors☆ (f 5c)   S   TR
Many different ways - all awkward.
TR: 200

6a ⑪ Step On☆ (f 6a)   S   TR
A boulder problem.
Solo: 2005 Robin Mazinke

6b ⑫ Elysium☆ (f 6c)   S   TR
A boulder problem.
Solo: 2005

6c ⑬ Sinbad☆ (f 7b)   S   TR
A very flexible mantle is required.
Solo: 2009 Giles Taylor

Local chat: This section in the passage leading to the top is periodically cleared of Rhodies, whilst adding routes – it does not significantly add quality climbing though. Generally rather too green for comfort.

Top access & erosion beta: Go up the main gully to the left. Mass of rhodies on top so you will need a short static rope, plus machete and jungle warfare kit.

[UK 6c] SINBAD (font 7b), Giles Taylor ▷

HARRISON'S ROCKS

BOWLES ROCKS

HIGH ROCKS

HIGH ROCKS ANNEXE

HAPPY VALLEY

BULLS HOLLOW

ERIDGE GREEN

UNDER ROCKS

STONE FARM

Outside the Secret Garden →

↖ To Secret Garden

Trad	Fontainebleau colour (font grade)	Ticked		UK Trad	Fontainebleau colour (font grade)	Ticked

5a ① Bow Crack☆☆ (f **4a**) S TR
Not a very big route but worthwhile.
Solo: 1960's

5b ② Awkward Corner☆ (f **4b**) S TR
Small enough to boulder.
Solo: 1960's

5c ③ Orrer Crack☆☆ (f **5a**) S TR
Obvious main crack line.
Solo: 1960's

5c ④ Odin's Wall☆☆ (f **5b**) S TR
A superb wall climb on brittle rock - go carefully.
Solo: 1962 Martin Boysen   TR: 1959 Graeme Hughes

5c ⑤ Climber's Behaving Badly☆☆ (f **5b**) S TR
So named after several cars were completely trashed
during a climbing trip to Spain.
Solo: 2000 Mad Drivers   TR: 2000 Martin Randall

Local chat: A short wall of superb quality rock, very
similar to Fontainebleau with very fine grains of sand.
Always in the shade. Some of the top-outs remain
sandy and greasy – watch out.

> **Crag layout map - page 148**
> **Graded list - page 150**

5c ⑥ Navy Wall☆☆ (f **5b**) S TR
A short wall on superb crispy rock.
Solo: Pre 1960's

6a ⑦ The Ghost☆ (f **5c**) S TR
An eliminate on crimps.
Solo: 1980's

6a ⑧ Bow Spirit☆☆ (f **6a**) S TR
Topping out direct is somewhat airy.
Solo: 1979 David Atchison-Jones

6a ⑨ Rum, Bum & Biscuits☆☆ (f **6a**) S TR
The short technical wall.
Solo: 1980's

6a ⑩ Something Crack☆ (f **6a**) S TR
Often greasy unfortunately, (originally aid climbed).
Solo: 1995 Tim Skinner   TR: 1990's

6b ⑪ Whiff Whaff☆ (f **6c**) S TR
A technical wall on crimps.
TR: 1989 Paul Hayes

*Access & Erosion: Go up to the left under the bridge,
then left and around over the bridge. You will need a
static rope to extend belay karabiner down to the edge,
make sure it is hanging free.* ⚙

[UK 5c] NAVY WALL (font 5b), Steve Glennie

△ *EXTENDER (font 6c), Mark Croxall*

Gemstone - Above the Secret Garden

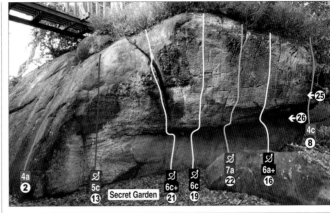

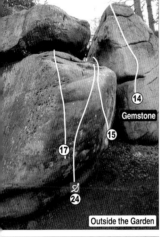

Outside the Garden

Inside the Garden

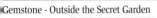

Gemstone - Outside the Secret Garden

		Problem				Problem
S	(1)	Yellimo (f 3b)		S	(15)	Thrust (f 6a)
S	(2)	Holly Slab (f 4a)		S	(16)	✍ Moss Side Story (f 6a+)
S	(3)	Windy Corner ↖← (f 4a)		S	(17)	Village Life (f 6b)
S	(4)	Testimony (f 4a)		S	(18)	Extender (f 6c)
S	(5)	Degenerate (f 4b)		S	(19)	✍ Carbon Fibre (f 6c)
S	(6)	Tricky Dicky (f 4b)		S	(20)	Barbed Wire Kiss (f 6c)
S	(7)	✍ Nose Grime (f 4c)		S	(21)	✍ Can Opener (f 6c+)
S	(8)	Scrap Arête (f 4c)		S	(22)	✍ Going Going (f 7a)
S	(9)	Barbed Wire Fence (f 4c)		S	(23)	A Bridge Too Far ♘ (f 7a+)
S	(10)	Delirium (f 5a)		S	(24)	✍ Slick City (f 7a+)
S	(11)	Profiterole (f 5a)		S	(25)	Crosstown Traffic ← (f 7c)
S	(12)	Cumberland (f 5c)				Traverse with hands above roof.
S	(13)	✍ Slap Happy (f 5c)		S	(26)	✍ Bum Dragon ← (f 7c+)
S	(14)	Vingt-et-Un (f 6a)				Traverse with hands below roof.

Local chat: This little bouldering area is tucked up and away from the main outcrop behind Odin's Wall. The Gemstone Block gives some very good mid level problems, go carefully – it looks small but several injuries have been sustained from miscalculated flying leaps! You can traverse the complete way around the giant Odin's Block, crimpy and good fun to give a full on warm up to Crosstown Traffic.

Crag layout map - page 148
Graded list - page 150

HARRISON'S ROCKS · BOWLES ROCKS · HIGH ROCKS · HIGH ROCKS ANNEXE · HAPPY VALLEY · BULLS HOLLOW · ERIDGE GREEN · UNDER ROCKS · STONE FARM

Anaconda   Judy   Dragon   Canyon   Advertisement   Kinda Lingers   Nemesis   Odin's Wall   Isolated Boulder   Maze
Chimaera   Chimneys   Infidel   Krait Arête   Crypt   Darth Vader   Hut Boulder   Honeycomb   Matterhorn

HARRISON'S ROCKS

BOWLES ROCKS

HIGH ROCKS

HIGH ROCKS ANNEXE

HAPPY VALLEY

BULLS HOLLOW

ERIDGE GREEN

UNDER ROCKS

STONE FARM

UK Trad	Fontainebleau colour (font grade)	Ticked		UK Trad	Fontainebleau colour (font grade)	Ticked

5a **(1) Degenerate**☆☆ (f **4b**) — S TR
A classic arête climb.

5c **(2) Profiterole**☆ (f **5a**) — S TR
Not completely straightforward.

6a **(3) Vingt-et-Un**☆ (f **6a**) — S TR
A tricky little arête.

6b **(4) Craig-Y-Blanco**☆☆☆ (f **6a+**) — S TR
A few holds have come off over the years, cute top out!
Solo: 1976 Mick Fowler   TR: 1960's Phil Maher

6b **(5) Honeycomb**☆☆ (f **6b**) — S TR
The original way up the Honeycomb area of rock.
Solo: 1983 Dan Wajzner   TR: 1980 Mick Fowler

6b **(6) Barracuda**☆☆☆ (f **6b+**) — S TR
The more direct & popular line up the Honeycomb Wall.
Solo: 1983 David Atchison-Jones   TR: 1981 David A-Jones

6b **(7) Honeypot**☆☆ (f **6c+**) — S TR
Going left into the scoop and up.
TR: 1994 Luc Percival

6c **(8) Honeycomb Direct**☆☆ (f **7a**) — S TR
A technical wall climb on small holds.
TR: 1986 Dave Turner

6c **(9) The Gob**☆☆ (f **7b**) — S TR
Following the left arête, often green unfortunately.
TR: 1994 Luc Percival

Local chat: This Honeycomb Wall is one of the natural marvels of sandstone in the South East of England. When the light glances the wall, you get a superb mottled effect - but only in the winter months. In summer, it is deep in shade and thankfully cool - to roast your fingers. All of the routes could be finger tendon snappers, but fortunately the pockets aren't big enough to do much damage - uncurling is more common. A slight bit too high for most boulderers, especially as the feet tend to pop off at the top when the body is askew. Knowing the numbers is par for the course, and taken into consideration for the Fontainebleau grades given.

Access & Erosion: Go along to the right and up the steps that lead to the top and bridges. Make sure to protect the top edge for these routes please, and have the belay karabiner below the edge - use a static rope or about 6 slings.

Crag layout map - page 148
Graded list - page 150

↖ [UK 6b] BARRACUDA (font 6b+), Nathalie Welch

HARRISON'S ROCKS

BOWLES ROCKS

HIGH ROCKS

HIGH ROCKS ANNEXE

HAPPY VALLEY

BULLS HOLLOW

ERIDGE GREEN

UNDER ROCKS

STONE FARM

UK Trad	Fontainebleau colour (font grade)	Ticked

4c ① Puzzle Corner (f 3c)   S TR
Struggle up and around the bridge.
Solo: 1960's

5a ② Greasy Crack (f 4a)   🗑 S TR
A squeezy little number.
Solo: 1960's

5b ③ Wishful Thinking ✭ (f 4b)   S TR
A running jump, or 6b pull on crimps.
Solo: 1981 Guy McLelland

6a ④ Woofus Weejects ✭ (f 6a)   S TR
The often greasy crack.
TR: 1993 Chris Arnold

Local chat: This sector is a very poor neighbour to Honeycomb, but still offers some pretty difficult problems and routes. Many will prefer a top rope, but an assortment of pads and spotters should easily suffice.

Access & Erosion: Go along to the right past the next buttress and up the steps that lead to the top and bridges. A short static rope is needed for most of the routes.

UK Trad	Fontainebleau colour (font grade)	Ticked

6a ⑤ Lunge'n'Shelf ✭ (f 6a)   S TR
Dynamic.
TR: 1983 Guy McLellan

6a ⑥ Ides of March ✭ (f 6a)   S TR
Overhanging wall.
TR: 1983 Guy McLellan

6a ⑦ Dagger Crack ✭✭ (f 6a)   🖐 S TR
A powerful move for most.
Solo: 1981 David Atchison-Jones   TR: 1980 Mick Fowle

6b ⑧ Craig-Y-Blanco ✭✭✭ (f 6a+)   S TR
A few holds have come off over the years, cute top out!
Solo: 1976 Mick Fowler   TR: 1960's Phil Mahe

7a ⑨ Final Destination ⬆ ✭✭ (f 7c+)   S TR
A technical dyno with difficulty holding the slap.
Solo: 2004 Ian Hufton

Crag layout map - page 148
Graded list - page 150

Chimaera   Chimneys   Infidel   Krait Arête   Crypt   Darth Vader   Hut Boulder   Honeycomb   Matterhorn
Anaconda   Judy   Dragon   Canyon   Advertisement   Kinda Lingers   Nemesis   Odin's Wall   Isolated Boulder   Maze

HARRISON'S ROCKS

BOWLES ROCKS

HIGH ROCKS

HIGH ROCKS ANNEXE

HAPPY VALLEY

BULLS HOLLOW

ERIDGE GREEN

UNDER ROCKS

STONE FARM

UK Trad	Fontainebleau colour (font grade)		Ticked	
6a	(1) **Marathon Man**☆☆ (f **6a**)		S	TR

Fun and damm awkward.

Solo: 1983 Guy McLelland   TR: 1982 David Atchison-Jones

UK Trad	Fontainebleau colour (font grade)		Ticked	
6b	(3) **Beer Gut Shuffle**☆☆ (f **6b**)		S	TR

Rather difficult top out.

Solo: 2005 Tim Skinner   TR: 1982 Barry Knight

6a	(2) **The Diver**☆ (f **6a**)		S	TR

A squeezy little number.

TR: 1992 Alan Grigg

Local chat: Even though these routes were done prior to bouldering mats, they are awkward and you are advised to have some good spotters to hand. The tree canopy tends to keep this area a bit green unfortunately.

ISOLATED BOULDER:

Access & Erosion: This majestic boulder is situated at the top end of High Rocks, next to what was once a serene bowling green. This area is still grassy enough to laze about in the sun, but not quite a fabo velvet carpet. The giant block is some 8m (32ft) high, and is completely free standing - like a very very mini version of the Falkenstein in the Elbsandstein. The giant boulder has a north wall of really hard sandstone, but the rest is quite soft and should be treated with care if soloing.

Ascent: There is no simple path to the top, you have to solo one of the routes. There are 3 usual options. Those with high skill level will solo [UK 5c] Dinner Plate (page 213), since the hard moves are low down and the top is not too frightening! Mid level climbers often prefer to solo [UK 5a] Simian Progress (page 214), this again has the benefit of a low down crux and the top overhang is pretty solid when you know the beta. The lower grade climbers usually tackle [UK 4a] Ordinary Route (page 211), this is by far the easiest route, but has some quite unnerving balance moves high up - and with no positive incuts.

Descent: The most popular way is to set up a free hanging abseil from the big Oak tree next to Tool Wall (page 213). This way the abseil can be left in place throughout your time on the boulder, and you will not damage the rock in descent. Remember to bring a spare rope with you for this abseil.

Chimaera   Chimneys   Infidel   Krait Arête   Crypt   Darth Vader   Hut Boulder   Honeycomb   Matterhorn
Anaconda   Judy   Dragon   Canyon   Advertisment   Kinda Lingers   Nemesis   Odin's Wall   Isolated Boulder   Maze

HARRISON'S ROCKS

BOWLES ROCKS

HIGH ROCKS

HIGH ROCKS ANNEXE

HAPPY VALLEY

BULLS HOLLOW

ERIDGE GREEN

UNDER ROCKS

STONE FARM

8m

UK Trad	Fontainebleau colour (font grade)	Ticked

5a ① North Wall☆☆☆ ☻☻(f **4a**) ☐S ☐TR

Bottom half is a sinch - though still fun. The swing left onto the overhanging wall is peanuts, then the difficulties start and the ground is exceptionally nasty to fall onto.
Solo: Pre 1960's

5c ② Simian Mistake☆☆☆ (f **5b**) ☐S ☐TR

Reasonably technical with a tricky finish.
Solo: Late 1950's　　　　　　*TR: Pre 1960's*

5c ③ Monkey Nut☆☆☆ (f **5b**) ☐S ☐TR

Brutish and very steep - a stamina test. Should feel very easy for an indoor wall trained monkey.
Solo: 1970's　　　　　　*TR: 1965 H. Barnes*

6a ④ Sputnik☆☆☆ (f **5c**) 〰 ☐S ☐TR

Climb up the edge of the arête.
Solo: 1992 Tim Skinner　　　*TR: 1956 John Smoker*

6a ⑤ Monkey Business☆☆ (f **5c**) ☐S ☐TR

Nice climbing and far easier than the direct version.
Solo: 1983 David Atchison-Jones　*TR: 1981 David A-Jones*

6a ⑥ The Sphinx☆☆☆ (f **6a**) ☐S ☐TR

Technical and steep - often damp unfortunately.
Solo: 1990's　　　　　　*TR: 1959 John Smoker*

6a ⑦ Oven Ready Freddy☆ (f **6a**) ☐S ☐TR

A boulder problem high up.
　　　　　　　　TR: 1989 Gary Wickham

6b ⑧ Simian Crimp☆☆ (f **6a+**) 〰 ☐S ☐TR

Crimps to start for those who like crimps.
Solo: 1981 Dan Wazjner

6b ⑨ Monkey Sphincter☆☆☆(f **6b+**) ☐S ☐TR

A great line but not that easy.
　　　　　　　　TR: 1981 Barry Knight

Local chat: The overhanging lower part stays dry all year, but the upper critical part gets very green and greasy over winter, drying out in late spring. Bad landings make soloing on this wall very nasty. New crimpy problem below Oven Ready Freddy – grade not sure, but quite hard.

Top access & erosion beta: See page 207

[UK 5c] SIMIAN MISTAKE (font 5b), Catherine Gallagher ▷

Crag layout map - page 148
Graded list - page 150

Anaconda　Judy　Dragon　Canyon　Advertisement　Kinda Lingers　Nemesis　Odin's Wall　Isolated Boulder　Maze
Chimaera　Chimneys　Infidel　Krait Arête　Crypt　Darth Vader　Hut Boulder　Honeycomb　Matterhorn

△△ *THE BLUES (font 6c), Danie Rushmer*   △ *THE MOJO (font 7b), Ben Read*

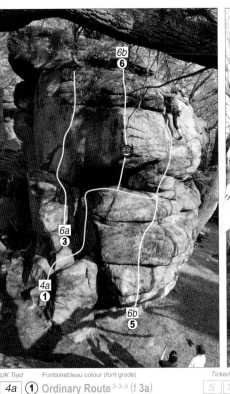

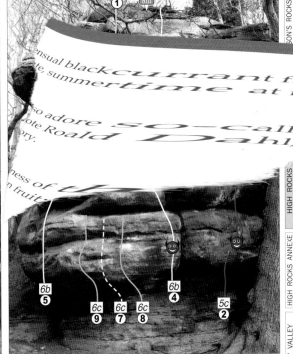

UK Trad　Fontainebleau colour (font grade)　Ticked

4a (1) **Ordinary Route**★★★ (f 3a) ── S TR

A very easy first section under the big roof. There are no positive holds in the upper groove, but with careful balance - it is ok. Requires cool.
Solo: Pre 1950's

5c (2) **Graveyard Groove**★★★ (f 5b) ── S TR

Grade assumes that you avoid the tree completely.
Solo: 1980 David Atchison-Jones　TR: 1958 John Smoker

6a (3) **Oven Ready Freddy**★ (f 6a) ── S TR

A boulder problem high up.
TR: 1989 Gary Wickham

6b (4) **Devastator**★★ (f 6a+) ── S TR

The original hard route of the block.
Solo: 1980's　TR: 1960's

6b (5) **Mysteries of the Orgasm**★★ (f 6c) ── S TR

Easiest way up this bulging piece of sandstone.
TR: 1992 Alan Grigg

6b (6) **Plantaganet**★★ (f 6c) ── S TR

The top nose provides an elevated boulder problem.
TR: 1992 Paul Widdowson

Local chat: A good area offering some lovely long routes, in addition to some powerful boulder problems mainly on slopers. Rock is soft at the bottom so grades may change considerably.

Top access & erosion beta: See page 207

UK Trad　Fontainebleau colour (font grade)　Ticked

6b (7) **The Blues**★ (f 6c) ── S TR

All holds allowed on Return of the Mojo line.

6c (8) **Return of the Mojo**★ (f 7a) ── S TR

Coming in from the right without the slots in the break.
Solo: 2002 Chez George

6c (9) **The Mojo**★ (f 7b) ── S TR

The roof problem from the left only on slopers.
Solo: 2003 Chez George

HARRISON'S ROCKS

BOWLES ROCKS

HIGH ROCKS

HIGH ROCKS ANNEXE

HAPPY VALLEY

BULLS HOLLOW

ERIDGE GREEN

UNDER ROCKS

STONE FARM

UK Trad	Fontainebleau colour (font grade)	Ticked

5c ① **Knife**☆☆☆ (f **5b**)   S TR
The easiest crack, but still can easily draw blood.
Solo: 1960's   *TR: 1960's*

5c ② **Fork**☆☆☆ (f **5b**)   S TR
Slightly steeper and seems a bit harder.
Solo: 1960's   *TR: 1960's*

5c ③ **Dinner Plate**☆☆☆ (f **5b**)   S TR
The difficulty is much more concentrated.
Solo: 1970's   *TR: 1960's*

6a ④ **Tool Wall**☆☆ (f **6a**)   S TR
An eliminate without touching the tree.
   TR: 1992 Alan Grigg

6a ⑤ **Temple of Doom**☆☆☆ (f **6a**)   S TR
Originally named "David Jones and the Temple of Doom."
   TR: 1987 David Atchison-Jones

UK Trad	Fontainebleau colour (font grade)	Ticked

6a ⑥ **Toothpick**☆☆☆ (f **6a**)   S TR
A good eliminate
   TR: 1999 Mike Eden

6b ⑦ **Early Breakfast**☆☆ (f **6c**)   S TR
The arête direct from the right.
Solo: 1990's   *TR: 1980 David Atchison-Jones*

6b ⑧ **The Full Monty**☆ (f **6c**)   S TR
The arête from the left.
Solo: 1989 M. Lewis

Local chat: An excellent wall covered in hand width cracks and small pockets for the fingers. You can climb almost anywhere here, but it's quite steep and most mid level climbers tend to get pumped silly. The main crack lines can either be jammed - or used as layaways with pockets. All of the eliminate lines are worth doing as is usual for sandstone. Gets sun in winter mornings, and nice shade on summer afternoons. A nice spot to chill out.

Top access & erosion beta: See page 207

◁ *[UK 5c] DINNER PLATE (font 5b), Catherine Gallagher*

HARRISON'S ROCKS

BOWLES ROCKS

HIGH ROCKS

HIGH ROCKS ANNEXE

HAPPY VALLEY

BULLS HOLLOW

ERIDGE GREEN

UNDER ROCKS

STONE FARM

Local chat: The main wall of Simian Face give very nice fingery climbing at a reasonable grade. The undercut start gives very fierce starts to the routes. Many bouldering possibilities exist on the juggy nature of this sector, holds change over the years with wear. Please go careful with your footwork.

Crag layout map - page 148
Graded list - page 150

UK Trad   Fontainebleau colour (font grade)   Ticked

5a ① **Simian Progress**☆☆☆ (f **4a**)   S | TR
Bridge very wide to reach the starting jugs, sprint left to the crack, easy thereafter - top overhang is awkward.
Solo: 1940's   TR: 1940's

5b ② **Simian Face**☆☆☆ (f **4c**)   S | TR
Start as for Simian Progress but continue up the very sustained wall, draining for the grade.
Solo: 1970's   TR: 1954 Derek Salter

5c ③ **Monkey Nut**☆☆☆ (f **5b**)   S | TR
Brutish and very steep - a stamina test. Should feel very easy for an indoor beastie climber. (M-Nutter - no feet)
Solo: 1970's   TR: 1965 H. Barnes

5c ④ **Simian Face Direct**☆☆ (f **5b**)   S | TR
Face feels harder after this start.
Solo: 1970's   TR: 1970's

6a ⑤ **Simian Crack Direct**☆ (f **5c**)   S | TR
Awkward finger locks, one move wonder.
Solo: 1959 Martin Boysen

6a ⑥ **Breakfast**☆☆ (f **5c**)   S | TR
Continue up the sandy arête from Simian Crack Direct.
Solo: 1970's   TR: 1959 Martin Boysen

6b ⑦ **Early Breakfast**☆☆ (f **6c**)   S | TR
The arête direct from the right.
Solo: 1990's   TR: 1980 David Atchison-Jones

6c ⑧ ⚹ **Happy Days**☆☆ (f **7a+**)   S | TR
Sit start on low break, up into thumb sprags, and then to the top and finish on the jugs.
Solo: Early 2000 Chez George

[UK 6a] MONKEY NUTTER (font 6a - without feet), Dave Potts ➢

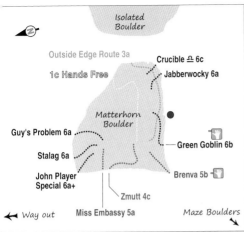

Isolated Boulder

Outside Edge Route 3a

Crucible ⚎ 6c

1c Hands Free

Jabberwocky 6a

Matterhorn Boulder

Guy's Problem 6a

Green Goblin 6b

Stalag 6a

John Player Special 6a+

Brenva 5b

Zmutt 4c

← Way out

Miss Embassy 5a

Maze Boulders

6m

6

6a+ 6b+ 5a 4c
⑩ ⑫ ④ ③ 🟑 7a ⑭ 5b ⑤

HARRISON'S ROCKS

BOWLES ROCKS

HIGH ROCKS

HIGH ROCKS ANNEXE

HAPPY VALLEY

BULLS HOLLOW

ERIDGE GREEN

UNDER ROCKS

STONE FARM

S ① **Hands Free (f 1c)** Slab to the top - no hands.

S ② **Outside Edge Route (f 3a)** Fun and simple.

S ③ **Zmutt (f 4c)** Assumes you know the rockover.

S ④ **Miss Embassy (f 5a)** Gentle and flexible.

S ⑤ **Brenva ☂ (f 5b)** Start with good pinch/dyno for right.

S ⑥ **Mayfair (f 5c)** A lowball excursion from Brenva.

S ⑦ **Guy's Problem (f 6a)** Often green unfortunately.

S ⑧ **Stalag (f 6a)** Tricky semi highball on face.

S ⑨ **Jabberwocky ⚎ (f 6a)** Slopers then mantle.

S ⑩ **John Player Special (f 6a+)** Pulling around arête.

S ⑪ **Green Goblin (f 6b)** Wall, up and right morpho.

S ⑫ **Tom's Mantle ⚎ (f 6b+)** Reverse hands mantle.

S ⑬ **Crucible ⚎ (f 6c)** Snubby arête with mantle.

S ⑭ **Old Kent Road (f 7a)** Using big flake (f 6b+).

S ⑮ **Brenva (f 7a)** Right heel hook, slap up right.

S ⑯ **Acid Test ≈ (f 7a+)** Toe-pocket, then 'only' crimps.

S ⑰ **The Wish ≈ (f 7c+)** Pull on with undercuts.

S ⑱ **The Slow Pull ≈ (f 7c+)** A mean traverse via Brenva.

S ⑲ **Dont Pierdol ≈ (f 8a+)** Foot used out right on prow.

Local chat: This boulder has the best rock on S-East Sandstone - it's as if one bloc got secretly stolen from Fontainebleau and put here - shush don't tell. 3 sides are indifferent, but the overhanging face is magical, a fine textured climbing paradise. There are simply hundreds of variations to all of the problems - make up your own at will. Listed here are the benchmark problems to show you how you are going. Get ticking those little solo boxes next to the numbers. The wall is covered in holds - do not create any more please!

Green Goblin - Barry Knight
Tom's Mantle - Ian Butler
Crucible - Chez George
Old Kent Road - Guy McLelland
Brenva.ss - Pete Ziegenfuss
Acid Test - Ian Stronghill
The Wish - Marek Migdal
The Slow Pull - Paul Ziegenfuss
Dont Pierdol - Peter Wycislik

Erosion beta: Please use a crash pad at all times on this boulder to protect the ground - and yourself perhaps. Also please remove tick marks and only clean holds very gently.

Crag layout map - page 148
Graded list - page 150

Not in

7c+
⑰

⑱

7a+ 8a+ 7a 7c+
⑯ ⑲ ⑮ ⑱

◁ *JOHN PLAYER SPECIAL (font 6a+), Matt Rogers*

Chimaera Chimneys Infidel Krait Arête Crypt Darth Vader Hut Boulder Honeycomb **Matterhorn**
Anaconda Judy Dragon Canyon Advertisement Kinda Lingers Nemesis Odin's Wall Isolated Boulder Maze

HARRISON'S ROCKS

BOWLES ROCKS

HIGH ROCKS

HIGH ROCKS ANNEXE

HAPPY VALLEY

BULLS HOLLOW

ERIDGE GREEN

UNDER ROCKS

STONE FARM

The Maze Boulders

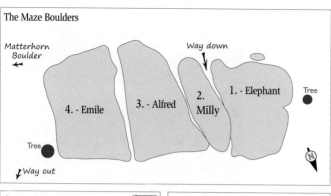

Matterhorn Boulder

Way down

4. - Emile   3. - Alfred   2. Milly   1. - Elephant

Tree

Tree

Way out

N

1. - Elephant

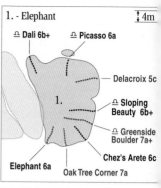

‡4m

Dali 6b+   Picasso 6a

Delacroix 5c

1.

Sloping Beauty 6b+

Greenside Boulder 7a+

Chez's Arete 6c

Elephant 6a   Oak Tree Corner 7a

4. - Emile

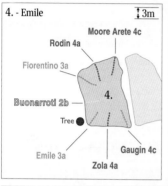

‡3m

Moore Arete 4c

Rodin 4a

Florentino 3a

Buonarroti 2b

4.

Tree

Emile 3a   Zola 4a   Gaugin 4c

3. - Alfred

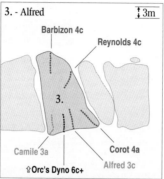

‡3m

Barbizon 4c

Reynolds 4c

3.

Camile 3a   Corot 4a

Orc's Dyno 6c+   Alfred 3c

2. - Milly

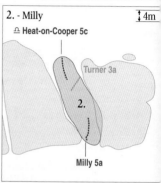

‡4m

Heat-on-Cooper 5c

Turner 3a

2.

Milly 5a

3a Emile   4a   4c   3a   6c+ Orc's Dyno   3c   4b   5a Milly   6a Elephant   7a   6c

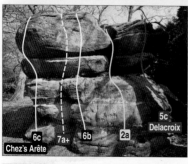

6c   7a+   6b   2a   5c Delacroix
Chez's Arête

Picasso 6a   Dali 6b+   Heat-On 5c

Local chat: 3 small boulders with a 4th resting on top. Some very nice stuff for warming up and having a fun play – great in the lower grades with tricky finishes. The Elephant Block tends to stay damp, so please don't climb it until the rock has dried out and gained some strength. Some really nasty mantleshelf problems on the Elephant Block.

ALFRED (font 3c), Kari Landen ▷

HARRISON'S ROCKS | BOWLES ROCKS | HIGH ROCKS | HIGH ROCKS ANNEXE | HAPPY VALLEY | BULLS HOLLOW | ERIDGE GREEN | UNDER ROCKS | STONE FARM

UK Trad	Fontainebleau colour (font grade)	Ticked

3a **(1)** **Fir Tree Wall** (f **3a**)   S TR
A bit balancy, can stay green & gooey.
Solo: Pre 1950's

4b **(2)** **Fir Tree Crack** ☆ (f **3b**)   S TR
Slightly technical - may be damp inside.
Solo: Pre 1950's

4b **(3)** **Annexe Slab** (f **3c**)   S TR
A very nice easy slab, neat footwork is the order.
Solo: Pre 1960's

5c **(4)** **Letter Box Wall** ☆☆ (f **5a**)   S TR
Trying to go right on good holds is powerful.
Solo: 1960's   *TR: 1957 Paul Lebars*

6a **(5)** **It's Only Natural** ☆☆ (f **5c**)   S TR
A blank wall, start using the left edge of the crack.
Solo: 1999 Tim Skinner

UK Trad	Fontainebleau colour (font grade)	Ticked

6a **(6)** **Titch Arête** ☆ (f **6a**)   S TR
Sometimes called Barefoot Arête, very technical.
Solo: 1960's   *TR: 1957 Chris Morle*

6a **(7)** **Shidid** ☆☆☆ (f **6a**)   S TR
Technical.
Solo: 1970's

6b **(8)** **Arnold Thesaanigger** ☆ (f **6a+**)   S TR
The short wall but powerful.
Solo: 1990 Matt Smith

6b **(9)** **Twitch** ☆☆☆ (f **6b**)   S TR
Originally at UK 5b, now hard with worn sandy holds.
Solo: 1960's

6c **(10)** **Southern Softie** ☆☆ (f **7a**)   S TR
Very morpho, 7b for short climbers like Johnny Dawes.
Solo: 1997 Johnny Dawes

Location: See page 148 High Rocks - for location map and parking. This outcrop is on private land, but is open access ground. Please give the greatest respect to the surroundings.

Access & Erosion: Please don't climb here when the ground is damp since the soil at the base is very likely to slide down the hill pretty fast. You will need a short static for a top rope set up on the nose-slab routes

K Trad	Fontainebleau colour (font grade)	Ticked

2a (1) Chimney One (f 2a)   S TR
A bit graunchy.
Solo: Pre 1940's

4b (2) Chimney Wall ☆ (f 3b)   S TR
A good short climb.
Solo: Pre 1940's

5b (3) Nose One ☆☆☆ (f 4b)   S TR
A lovely arête, straight up.
Solo: Pre 1940's

6a (4) Rupert and his Chums ☆ (f 5c)   S TR
Slabby and slippery.
TR: 1992 Mike Vetterlein

6b (5) Double Top ☆☆☆ (f 6b)   S TR
A technical and frictionless slab.
Solo: 1993 Doug Reid   TR: 1984 Guy McLelland

6c (6) Boogie Woogie Walk ☆☆ (f 7a+)   S TR
Sketchy slabwork, technical and difficult from the start.
TR: 1998 Luc Percival

Local chat: This western end of the Annexe is heavily shaded by Yew Trees. They unfortunately drip in winter keeping the rock green and damp. In April they dry out and often stay dry all summer. Even though south facing - stays in the shade.

Access & Erosion: The gully provides a good way up with less ground slip. Slings on the tree should be ample for a belay.

HARRISON'S ROCKS | BOWLES ROCKS | HIGH ROCKS | HIGH ROCKS ANNEXE | HAPPY VALLEY | BULLS HOLLOW | ERIDGE GREEN | UNDER ROCKS | STONE FARM

HARRISON'S ROCKS

BOWLES ROCKS

HIGH ROCKS

HIGH ROCKS ANNEXE

HAPPY VALLEY

BULLS HOLLOW

ERIDGE GREEN

UNDER ROCKS

STONE FARM

UK Trad	Fontainebleau colour (font grade)		Ticked
2a	**(1) Chimney One** (f 2a)		S TR

A bit graunchy.
Solo: Pre 1940's

| 4a | **(2) Nose Two** (f 3a) | | S   TR |

Short and very often very greasy - not nice.
Solo: Pre 1940's

| 5a | **(3) Spleen Slab**☆☆☆ (f 4a) | | S   TR |

An excellent slab route.
Solo: Pre 1960's

UK Trad	Fontainebleau colour (font grade)		Ticked
5b	**(4) Brain's Missing**☆ (f 4b)		S TR

Quite powerful - hence no brain required.
Solo: 1981 David Atchison-Jones

| 6c | **(5) Change in the Weather**☆☆ (f 7a) | | S   TR |

A slab with a good long reach. Gets a hefty grade and
defeats many that try it. A direct finish going up and left
remains a good possibility.
Solo: 2006 James Pearson   *TR: 1998 Luc Perciva*

Local chat: One of the best slabs at the Annexe,
offering a lovely couple of grade 5 problems, and
the classic Change in the Weather.

*Access & Erosion: The gully beneath Boogie Woogie
provides a good way up with less ground slip. Good
trees at the top of this wall.*

HARRISON'S ROCKS

BOWLES ROCKS

HIGH ROCKS

HIGH ROCKS ANNEXE

HAPPY VALLEY

BULLS HOLLOW

ERIDGE GREEN

UNDER ROCKS

STONE FARM

UK Trad		Fontainebleau colour (font grade)	Ticked

3b **(1)** **Chute and Chimney (f 3a)** 🗑 S TR

A dirty chimney.
Solo: Pre 1940's

2a **(2)** **Chimney Two (f 2a)** 🗑 S TR

Indifferent.
Solo: Pre 1940's

3a **(3)** **Nose Three**☆☆ **(f 2a)** S TR

A bit beefy.
Solo: Pre 1940's

4a **(4)** **Green Slab (Thinner)**☆ **(f 3a)** S TR

Mostly climbed without the hands, a doddle.
Solo: 1970's   *TR: 1957 Salt Sullivan*

5a **(5)** **Gorilla Wall**☆☆ **(f 4a)** S TR

Slightly technical.
Solo: Pre 1960's

5c **(6)** **Valkyrie Wall**☆☆ **(f 5a)** S TR

Good technical wall climbing.
Solo: 1970's   *TR: 1953 Ned Cordery*

*Local chat: A mixed bunch of routes here offering a
lot of good climbing in a short distance.*

*Access & Erosion: The gully at Boogie Woogie provides
a good way up with less ground slip. Good trees above
the Green Slab but you need a short static to set the
belay at the top of the rock edge for many of the routes.
Ground above is very steep and sketchy - bad when
wet underfoot.*

UK Trad		Fontainebleau colour (font grade)	Ticked

5c **(7)** **Didshi (f 5a)** S TR

Technical and crimpy.
Solo: 1970's

5c **(8)** **Fahrenheit**☆☆ **(f 5a)** S TR

Stand up very easily in balance, use pockets thereafter.
Solo: 1996 Tim Skinner   *TR: 1992 Paul Widdowson*

6a **(9)** **Thug**☆ **(f 6a)** S TR

The short bulge.
Solo: 1992 Paul Widdowson

HARRISON'S ROCKS

BOWLES ROCKS

HIGH ROCKS

HIGH ROCKS ANNEXE

HAPPY VALLEY

BULLS HOLLOW

ERIDGE GREEN

UNDER ROCKS

STONE FARM

UK Trad	Fontainebleau colour (font grade)	Ticked

4c **(1) Valhalla Wall**☆☆☆ (f 3c)   S   TR
A pretty good wall with chunky moves.
Solo: Pre 1960's   *TR: Pre 1950's*

5a **(2) Dumpy** (f 4a)   S   TR
Hmm.
Solo: Pre 1960's

5a **(3) Fig Roll**☆ (f 4a)   S   TR
A slab with a bit of a reach
Solo: 2005 Tim Skinner

5b **(4) Purgatory**☆☆ (f 4b)   S   TR
A nice pocketed wall.
Solo: Pre 1960's

UK Trad	Fontainebleau colour (font grade)	Ticked

5b **(5) Patrick's Wall**☆ (f 4b)   S   TR
Steep with an awkward mantle.
Solo: Pre 1960's

5b **(6) Agustus**☆ (f 4c)   S   TR
A slight touch of the technical.
Solo: 1981 David Atchison-Jones   *TR: 1970*

6a **(7) Billy the Bong**☆☆☆ (f 5c)   S   TR
Do not use the right arête.
     TR: 1990 Matt Sm

6b **(8) The Entertainer**☆☆☆ (f 6a+)   〰   S   TR
An excellent crimpy wall.
Solo: 1981 David Atchison-Jones   *TR: 1980 David A-Jone*

Local chat: These few buttresses give some very good short routes. It is a bit too high for comfortable bouldering, and the ground seems to be subsiding away beneath – so you may need to elevate soon in order to reach the starting holds (best not to boulder in this case). The rock is soft in parts, and hard and crimpy at other times. Worth the effort to set up a belay.

Access & Erosion: Shortest way to the top is going right, but it is a bit of a bushwack. Top belay trees are another 3m back, and you need a short static rope to set up a good belay.

HARRISON'S ROCKS

BOWLES ROCKS

HIGH ROCKS

HIGH ROCKS ANNEXE

HAPPY VALLEY

BULLS HOLLOW

ERIDGE GREEN

UNDER ROCKS

STONE FARM

3a **(1)** Horizon Crack ⋆ (f **3a**) S TR
Short but good.
Solo: Pre 1950's

3b **(2)** Horizon Wall ⋆ (f **3a**) S TR
Many variants and different holds possible.
Solo: Pre 1950's

Local chat: Horizon Wall is a tiny green lump of rock set up in the trees. Excellent quality rock but damm small. Monolith Buttress is pretty soft rock that offers some good eliminates to the standard ways up.

Access & Erosion: Either way up, 4 slings are ample for a belay using the tree.

UK Trad   Fontainebleau colour (font grade)   Ticked

3b **(3)** Monolith Crack (f **3a**) S TR
Nothing special.
Solo: Pre 1950's

4a **(4)** Monolith Right Buttress ⋆ (f **3b**) S TR
A better excursion.
Solo: 1960's   TR: Pre 1950's

5a **(5)** Monolith Left Buttress ⋆ (f **4a**) S TR
A nice buttress that often gets the spring sun. Originally the route escaped left at the top at UK 4a. Good eliminate lines - UK 5b to the left and UK 5a to the right.
Solo: Pre 1950's

5b **(6)** Monolith Left Hand ⋆ (f **4b**) S TR
A good excursion.
Solo: Pre 1960's

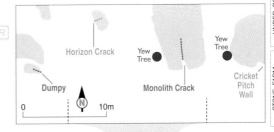

HARRISON'S ROCKS

BOWLES ROCKS

HIGH ROCKS

HIGH ROCKS ANNEXE

HAPPY VALLEY

BULLS HOLLOW

ERIDGE GREEN

UNDER ROCKS

STONE FARM

UK Trad		Fontainebleau colour (font grade)	Ticked		UK Trad		Fontainebleau colour (font grade)	Ticked
2b	①	**Boundary Gully (f 2a)**	S TR		5a	⑥	**Leg Break** (f 4a)	S TR
		A bit brambly usually. *Solo: Pre 1950's*					Up and around the tree. *Solo: 1960's*	
3a	②	**The Googly**☆ (f 3a)	S TR		5a	⑦	**Leg Stump**☆☆☆ (f 4a)	S TR
		The natural easiest way up this part. *Solo: Pre 1950's*					Short but excellent. *Solo: Pre 1960's*	
4a	③	**Out**☆☆ (f 3b)	S TR		5a	⑧	**Middle and Off**☆☆☆ (f 4a)	S TR
		The obvious nose line with a powerful move. *Solo: Pre 1960's*					A good line. *Solo: 1960's*	TR: 1957 Salt Sullivan
4a	④	**The Yorker**☆ (f 3b)	S TR		5b	⑨	**Middle Stump**☆☆☆ (f 4c)	S TR
		A direct start to the Googly. *Solo: Pre 1960's*					A good move in the middle. *Solo: 1960's*	TR: Pre 1960's (5c)
4c	⑤	**Off Stump**☆☆☆ (f 3c)	S TR		5b	⑩	**Wicked Maiden**☆ (f 4c)	S TR
		Easiest line up the fine top wall. *Solo: Pre 1960's*					Originally called Nob Nose; this name seemed much more fun and in keeping with the cricket tradition. *Solo: 1981 David Atchison-Jones*	TR:198

Local chat: This sector has a lovely shield of rock that offers enjoyable climbing in the mid to lower grades. Not too high but of good quality and worth a visit (wall is very shaded). There is a low traverse of the wall called – A line of Coke (perhaps in memory of the 1990's England cricket tours). There are a few more scrappy rocks further on but seem pointless to include.

Access & Erosion: Go up and around to the left. Even though there is a good Yew Tree at the top to hang a belay sling off, many routes are better protected with a belay karabiner actually at the top of the route. You will need a short static to reach the other trees set back from the top.

HAPPY VALLEY ROCKS

Happy Valley Rocks is one of those tiny outcrops that I could easily omit from this guidebook, but considering that it's only a few hundred yards from a spiffing good drinking house, it certainly warrants inclusion. It's just around the corner from Bulls Hollow, but is completely different in character, being smaller drier and with a very natural feel. Happy Valley Rocks is a series of small buttresses that give very good short routes, and faces South West to catch whatever evening sun is going. The sandstone is pretty soft, hardly making it ideal for hardcore bouldering, plus the holds are far too big for finely honed athletes. The surrounding land is part of Rusthall Common and gets various horticultural attention from year to year. Sometimes the undergrowth grows to jungle status, but at the time of writing (2010), there has been a massive clearance on the top plateau to make it grassy and open. (If you want to top rope - the trees are quite a long way back now.) The large block you generally first come across is called the Cheeswring, and must have been looking very suspect at some stage, since it now has blocks to support its base from wear and natural erosion. This lump gives some pretty fierce routes, bearing in mind the softness of the rock. Nearly all of the routes have been soloed - quite remarkable (read suicidal). It's a lot quieter here than the Toad Rock area, so if you are looking for a quiet evening of fun climbing before a pint or two, it might be just the ticket.

Location: Happy Valley Rocks **SAT NAV info**
P1 - Parking Grid reference: **TQ 567 393**
P1 - Postcode **TN4 8XD**
Rocks Grid reference: **TQ 565 391**

There is parking just outside St. Pauls Church, but please do not block the turning area. Continue going west on the footpath (in the same direction as the approach road), passing St. Pauls School House on your left. Follow this for 1 min, then branch left keeping the wall close to your left. Path starts to descend slowly. After another min, do not go straight ahead through the bike speed railings, instead fork right on track-path, the rocks are then reached in another 45 seconds. Easy recognised by the large lump of the Cheeswring.

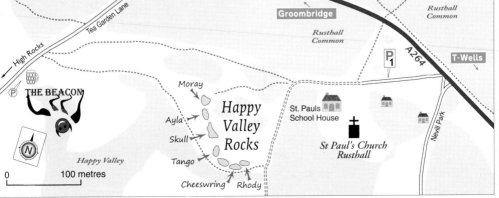

HARRISON'S ROCKS

BOWLES ROCKS

HIGH ROCKS

HIGH ROCKS ANNEXE

HAPPY VALLEY

BULLS HOLLOW

ERIDGE GREEN

UNDER ROCKS

STONE FARM

UK Trad		Fontainebleau colour (font grade)	Ticked	

| 2a | (1) | **Ever so Minnow Minnow** (f 1a) | S | TR |

Try this no hands.

| 3a | (2) | **Kippers**☆ (f 3a) | S | TR |

A good problem for smokers.

| 4a | (3) | **Moray**☆☆ (f 3b) | S | TR |

Good holds and nice climbing.

| 4b | (4) | **Stonefish**☆ (f 3b) | S | TR |

Slightly powerful.

| 4c | (5) | **Flying Trout**☆ (f 3c) | S | TR |

The arête.

| 4c | (6) | **Minnow**☆ (f 3c) | S | TR |

Not completely straightforward - crackline.

| 5a | (7) | **Sushi**☆ (f 4a) | S | TR |

Slightly technical.

| 5a | (8) | **Going Turbot**☆ (f 4a) | S | TR |

Steep but with good holds.

| 5b | (9) | ◿ **Red Snapper**☆ (f 4c) | S | TR |

Sit start down to the left, then direct through overhang.

Local chat: A lovely little overhanging prow gives a few classic top out struggles. Quite soft rock so have a good spotter in case a hold snaps off.

Access & Erosion: Trees are 14 metres back, so you will need a long static rope if you want to set up a top rope.

BOREAL

[UK 5b] RED SNAPPER (font 4c), David Atchison-Jones.

UK Trad	Fontainebleau colour (font grade)	Ticked

2a ① Mist (f 2a) · S · TR
The centre corner.

2a ② Ayla (f 2a) · S · TR
Not so easy for the short.

2b ③ Cleft (f 2a) · S · TR
Poor.

2b ④ Festive (f 2a) · S · TR
Slightly powerful.

3a ⑤ November Rain (f 3a) · S · TR
Quite tall.

3b ⑥ Master of Muck ⭐ (f 3a) · S · TR
A big highball for kids.

4b ⑦ Pot Belly ⭐ (f 3b) · S · TR
Short.

4b ⑧ Cornocopica ⭐ (f 3b) · S · TR
Short.

Local chat: A good buttress for the lower grade climber – however, feels pretty highball.

Access & Erosion: Trees are 10 metres back, so you will need a short static rope if you want to set up a top rope.

UK Trad		Fontainebleau colour (font grade)	Ticked	
1a	①	Wonderful Wizzard (f 2a)	S	TR
		Any route up here.		
3a	②	Deadly Lampshade★ (f 2b)	S	TR
		Nice climbing.		
4a	③	Corner Crack★★ (f 3a)	S	TR
		Not bad.		
4a	④	The Buzzard Years★ (f 3a)	S	TR
		Mantle top out.		

UK Trad		Fontainebleau colour (font grade)	Ticked	
4b	⑤	And Tigger Too★ (f 3b)	S	TR
		Good fun.		
4c	⑥	Home to Roost (f 3c)	S	TR
		Beefy.		
5a	⑦	Rotpunkt★ (f 4a)	S	TR
		Mediocre.		
6a	⑧	Pooh's Route★ (f 5c)	S	TR
		Hard mantle to finish.		

Local chat: A nice couple of small buttresses that are popular for an easy summers evening entertainment. Nothing too high or difficult.

4c	①	Tango★ ☠ (f 3c)	S	TR
		The obvious large arête.		
5c	②	Two Step★ ☠ (f 5a)	S	TR
		Nice climbing.		
5c	③	Pogo★ ☠ (f 5b)	S	TR
		Dodgy top out.		

Local chat: An awkward piece of rock, slightly too high to solo in comfort, slightly too grotty for the effort of setting up a top rope.

≪ [UK 3a] DEADLY LAMPSHADE (font 2b), Ollie Faber

HARRISON'S ROCKS

BOWLES ROCKS

HIGH ROCKS

HIGH ROCKS ANNEXE

HAPPY VALLEY

BULLS HOLLOW

ERIDGE GREEN

UNDER ROCKS

STONE FARM

UK Trad	Fontainebleau colour (font grade)	Ticked
3a	① **The Chimney** ☆ (f 3a)	S TR
	The easy way up and down.	
	Solo: Pre 1960's	
5b	② **From Behind** (f 4b)	S TR
	Tough little route.	
	Solo: 1980's	
5c	③ **Chalybeate** ☆☆☆ (f 5b)	S TR
	Harder than it looks.	
	Solo: Pre 1960's	
5c	④ **Thoroughly Kentish** ☆☆☆ (f 5b)	S TR
	The fine front face of the pinnacle.	
	Solo: 1960-70's	TR: Pre 1960's
6a	⑤ **Brouillard** ☆☆ (f 5c)	S TR
	Powerful moves for a while (also eliminate to the left).	
	Solo: 1996 John Patterson	TR: Pre 1960's
6a	⑥ **Freney** ☆☆ (f 5c)	S TR
	Steep and a bit sandy unfortunately.	
	Solo: 1996 John Patterson	TR: Pre 1960's

UK Trad	Fontainebleau colour (font grade)	Ticked
6a	⑦ **Eckpfeiler** ☆ (f 6a)	S TR
	Steep and a bit sandy also.	
	Solo: 1996 John Patterson	TR: 1980's
6a	⑧ **Sandstone Safari** ☆ (f 6a)	S TR
	Many different ways - all awkward.	
		TR: 1991 Tim Skinner
6b	⑨ **Harveys** ☆☆ (f 6b)	S TR
	Can be a bit green.	
		TR: 1999 Robin Mazinke
6b	⑩ **Colour of the Sun** ☆☆ (f 6b)	S TR
	The obvious arête.	
		TR: 1996 Ian Stronghil
6b	⑪ **Nightrain** ☆ (f 6b)	S TR
	Sandy and friable.	
		TR: 1996 Robin Mazinke

Local chat: The Cheesewring Rock is a free standing pinnacle at the side of the path, supported by a sandstone wall at the bottom. The rock quality is poor, so grades may well change - it is way too high and freaky for bouldering. This pinnacle tends to get enshrouded by bushes unfortunately - and usually stays greenish. Fun to visit - once in a lifetime.

Access & Erosion: You can reach the top plateau from the path approaching the rocks from the church. A careful stride gets you across onto the Pinnacle. A tree has fallen across to the top and provides easy belays for many of the routes. For routes such as Colour of the Sun, the belay karabiner would roll off the top of the pinnacle - the only other trees are 25 metres back, bring a very long static rope.

7m

HARRISON'S ROCKS

BOWLES ROCKS

HIGH ROCKS

HIGH ROCKS ANNEXE

HAPPY VALLEY

BULLS HOLLOW

ERIDGE GREEN

UNDER ROCKS

STONE FARM

UK Trad		Fontainebleau colour (font grade)	Ticked						
1b	①	The Race Home (f 2a)		S	TR
		Simple.			
4a	②	Grimace (f 3a)		S	TR
		Simple.			
4b	③	Undercut Rib (f 3b)		S	TR
		Often Green.			

UK Trad		Fontainebleau colour (font grade)	Ticked		
4c	④	Route Minor ⚝ (f 3c)		S	TR
		Often Green.			
5c	⑤	Rhody-O ⚝ (f 5c)		S	TR
		Often Green.			

Access & Erosion: Trees are 25 metres back, bring a very long static rope.

Local chat: This block to the side of the Cheeswring is fun on a hot summers day, after it has dried out and the green dust is easily brushed off. Otherwise forget it.

HARRISON'S ROCKS

BOWLES ROCKS

HIGH ROCKS

HIGH ROCKS ANNEXE

HAPPY VALLEY

BULLS HOLLOW

ERIDGE GREEN

UNDER ROCKS

STONE FARM

Bulls Hollow was a sandstone quarry during Victorian times, but shut up shop around 100 years ago. As a result of the quarrying, you don't tend to find any of the typical sandstone rock formations such as rounded breaks or honeycomb structures. Cleaving excavation has left assorted vertical walls that are interspersed by natural crack lines, and bounded to the edge by yellow putty. The surface of the rock has hardened over time, but in many areas it is still very soft and has a distinctly yellow-orange hue. The Hollow is situated on top of a substantial sandstone ridge that runs West from Tunbridge Wells to Groombridge. Surprisingly, the Hollow seems to be a natural drainage pit and water finds it difficult to escape from the central area at the bottom. Even in a good summer, you can see what looks like a water table seeping from the rock, keeping it damp to about 8 feet high. Aquaness and mosquitos apart, the climbing 'when' relatively dry, is very good indeed and really worth the trip out. Most of the routes feel more like climbing limestone than sandstone because of the flat vertical nature. The harder routes are usually technically difficult, but don't demand the raw power that severe overhanging rock demands. Indoor wall climbers will find it a bit tricky since many of the holds are a bit damp and greasy, even to the extent of being unobvious. Climbing here is not everybodys cup of tea, but to come here on a good day when you are going well is very rewarding, and perhaps even enjoyable.

Location: Bulls Hollow   **SAT NAV info**
P1 - Parking Grid reference: **TQ 568 396**
P1 - Postcode **TN4 8NS**
Rocks Grid reference: **TQ 568 396**

There is no specific car park for Bulls Hollow. The road that runs down to Denny Bottom has no parking restrictions at present. It does get quite chocker with folks picnicing at Toad Rock and visiting the Pub, so it's a bit hit and miss how far you will have to walk. P1 is a sandstone slabby area overlooking Toad Rock and is pretty handy to park at. From P1 follow the road down to the bend, where a small road goes ahead between 2 rocks. Turn R and drop down the path in the trees to Avalanche Arête area. (The outcrop is only a 1-2 min walk from the Pub - The Toad Rock Retreat.

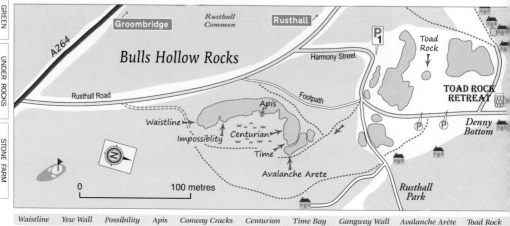

Waistline   Yew Wall   Possibility   Apis   Conway Cracks   Centurion   Time Bay   Gangway Wall   Avalanche Arête   Toad Rock

HARRISON'S ROCKS

BOWLES ROCKS

HIGH ROCKS

HIGH ROCKS ANNEXE

HAPPY VALLEY

BULLS HOLLOW

ERIDGE GREEN

UNDER ROCKS

STONE FARM

Trad   Fontainebleau colour (font grade)   Ticked

2a **①** Tree Climb ☆ (f 2a)   S   TR
A fun route up beside the old tree - or up the tree.
Solo: Pre 1960's

3a **②** Broken Crack ☆ (f 3a)   S   TR
Not too bad.
Solo: Pre 1950's

3b **③** The Chasm (f 3a)   🗑 S   TR
Not very inviting
Solo: Pre 1950's

5a **④** Waistline ☆☆ (f 4a)   S   TR
Very short but a good little outing.
Solo: 1980's

5b **⑤** Ferne ☆ (f 4b)   S   TR
Not too bad.
TR: 2005 Mark Brewster

5c **⑥** Uncertainty (f 5a)   🗑 S   TR
More of a dead cert - don't bother.
Solo: 1975 Mick Fowler

5c **⑦** Sandcastle ☆ (f 5a)   S   TR
The impending nose - sandy but ok.
Solo: 1980's   *TR: 1960's Gordon DeLacy*

6a **⑧** Bulging Waistline ☆ (f 5c)   S   TR
Direct start with lower traverse line.
Solo: 1980's

6a **⑨** Callum (f 6a)   S   TR
Sandy and steep (tree stump is not in at this grade).
TR: 2005 Mark Brewster

Local chat: The far end of Bulls Hollow gets very overgrown during summer - not a good time to try these routes - if there ever is a good time. Very poor rock unfortunately - and mostly stays damp except for Waistline.

Access & Erosion: Go up the easy gully to the left. Routes on the waistline face require 2 static ropes to form a yoke. Otherwise a short static rope should suffice. The tree growing on the rockface looks a trifle top heavy for the visible root structure, beware.

HARRISON'S ROCKS
BOWLES ROCKS
HIGH ROCKS
HIGH ROCKS ANNEXE
HAPPY VALLEY
BULLS HOLLOW
ERIDGE GREEN
UNDER ROCKS
STONE FARM

UK Trad	Fontainebleau colour (font grade)	Ticked	UK Trad	Fontainebleau colour (font grade)	Ticked

3a ① **Yellowstone Wall** (f 3a)   Grim S TR
Not a very good route.
Solo: Pre 1950's

4b ② **Yellowstone Crack** (f 3b)   Grim S TR
Another not a very good route.
Solo: Pre 1950's

5b ③ **Taurus** ☆ (f 4b)   Grim S TR
Another mediocre route.
Solo: 1960's

Local chat: This sector varies from reasonably poor to completely disgusting. A few climbers like it – but you are well advised that this is one of the worst sections of rock in the South East – you have been warned!

Access & Erosion: Go to the left and up around the Waistline sector. Trees are a good 15m back from the top edge, you will need a long static rope for the belays.

5b ④ **Yew Wall** ☆☆ (f 4c)   S TR
Soft rock but quite good climbing.
Solo: 1980's   TR: 1972 Nigel Hea

5c ⑤ **Poltergeist** ☆☆ (f 5a)   S TF
Only good if dry.
Solo: 1980's   TR: 1975 Nigel Hea

5c ⑥ **Sandcastle** ☆ (f 5a)   S TF
The impending nose - sandy but ok.
Solo: 1980's   TR: 1960's Gordon DeLae

6a ⑦ **Minotaur** ☆☆ (f 6a)   S TF
Technical but not often in condition - poor rock also.
TR: 1975 Mick Fowle

HARRISON'S ROCKS

BOWLES ROCKS

HIGH ROCKS

HIGH ROCKS ANNEXE

HAPPY VALLEY

BULLS HOLLOW

ERIDGE GREEN

UNDER ROCKS

STONE FARM

UK Trad	Fontainebleau colour (font grade)		Ticked
4b	**①** **Sentry Box** ☆ (f 3b)		S TR

Not a brilliant route unfortunately.
Solo: Pre 1950's

| **4b** | **②** **Possibility Wall** ☆☆ (f 3b) | | S TR |

A fine little slab when dry and not green - rarely.
Solo: Pre 1960's

| **5a** | **③** **Achtung** (f 4a) | Grim 🗑 S TR |

A really dreadful route.
Solo: Perhaps!   TR: 1980's

UK Trad	Fontainebleau colour (font grade)		Ticked
5b	**④** **Sentry Box Arête** ☆ (f 4b)		S TR

A good line on poor rock.
Solo: 1960's   TR: 1960's

| **5b** | **⑤** **Impossibility** ☆☆ (f 4b) | | S TR |

Shock - quite a good little slab if not slimey.
Solo: 1970's   TR: 1970's

| **6a** | **⑥** **The Scoop** ☆ (f 6a+) | | S TR |

Rarely dry, but Mick reckons its a classic!
                                          TR: 1974 Mick Fowler

Local chat: This is one of the more popular areas of Bulls Hollow. The slab/wall does dry out and becomes worth climbing on. Get this slab at the wrong time and you are best off going for an early drink.

Access & Erosion: You can enter the narrowing chimney to the left. This is dark and dank, but can be quite easily climbed at 2a - with a very useful tree root. If you have plenty of ropes and belay gear, it is better to go all the way around to the left end past Waistline Buttress. There are bolts at the top of Possibility Wall, plus the big trees for the routes on the right topo. For routes on the left you need to use a 15-20m static rope.

Getting to the Rocks by Train: Top Tip - put your mountain bike on the train.

Option 1: Tunbridge Wells Main Line Station: From Charing Cross to Hastings:
This is a good regular service. See the small map on page 234. Head S on the main road, then soon pick up a bridleway that links to Cabbage Patch Lane, and then onto High Rocks Lane. You can also cut South to the footpath that runs alongside the fun tourist railway. High Rocks - 35 mins nice walk.
Option 2: Eridge Station: Branch line from Oxted-Uckfield, [Victoria & London Bridge]. With a pub next to the Eridge Station, you can plan to catch the train back with pretty good accuracy. Harrison's, Eridge and Bowles - all around 25 mins walk. Harrison's - go along Forge Road, then cross over at the level crossing, turn L and follow public footpath below rocks. Bowles - a nice cross country path leads to the outcrop. Eridge - Turn L out of station, passing pub, then follow b/w that runs beside busy main road. Doing a circular route of Eridge-Harrison's is a fun day out.

Waistline   Yew Wall   Possibility   Apis   Conway Cracks   Centurion   Time Bay   Gangway Wall   Avalanche Arête   Toad Rock

HARRISON'S ROCKS

BOWLES ROCKS

HIGH ROCKS

HIGH ROCKS ANNEXE

HAPPY VALLEY

BULLS HOLLOW

ERIDGE GREEN

UNDER ROCKS

STONE FARM

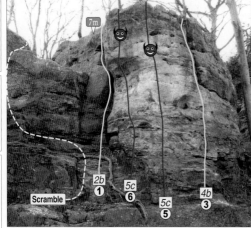

UK Trad	Fontainebleau colour (font grade)	Ticked

2b ① Trident Chimney (f 2a) `S` `TR`
Nothing special to say the least.
Solo: Pre 1950's

3a ② Cellar Wall (f 2a) 🗑 `S` `TR`
Awful.
Solo: Pre 1950's

4b ③ Apis ⋆ (f 4b) `S` `TR`
Usually green - quite exposed.
Solo: 1960's

UK Trad	Fontainebleau colour (font grade)	Ticked

5b ④ Moss (f 4b) 🗑 `S` `TR`
Very well named.
Solo: 1970's

5c ⑤ Apis Variation ⋆ (f 5a) `S` `TR`
Poor rock and usually damp.
Solo: 1980's   *TR: 1960's Nigel Hea*

5c ⑥ Apis Poor Variation ⋆ (f 5a) `S` `TR`
Go left onto more poor rock.
TR: 1996 Robin Mazink

Local chat: The Apis arete has quite an impressive appearance, and feels pretty high and exposed for a tiny quarry. Soft rock is the big disappointment unfortunately.

Access & Erosion: With gear it is best to go to the far left end of the outcrop, up and around. You can scramble up the wall in a zig zag manner, but this is often green, greasy, and positively hazardous. To the right of Apis area is a chute called the Coal Bunker. Whilst ascent isn't too difficult, it is much easier in descent - and rather dirty. There are bolts on the top of Apis, but you will need a short static rope for the other belays.

HARRISON'S ROCKS

BOWLES ROCKS

HIGH ROCKS

HIGH ROCKS ANNEXE

HAPPY VALLEY

BULLS HOLLOW

ERIDGE GREEN

UNDER ROCKS

STONE FARM

UK Trad	Fontainebleau colour (font grade)	Ticked
3b	**(1)** Conway's Variation ☆☆ (f 3a)	S TR
	The practical and easy way up this buttress.	
	Solo: Pre 1960's	
3b	**(2)** Conway's Buttress ☆☆ (f 3a)	S TR
	A good route for once - escaping left gives you a rest.	
	Solo: Pre 1960's	TR: Pre 1950's
3c	**(3)** Conway's Direct ☆☆ (f 3b)	S TR
	A little more sustained finish.	
	Solo: Pre 1960's	
4a	**(4)** Blasphemy (f 3b)	S TR
	The damp and green corner.	
	Solo: 1960's	
4b	**(5)** Solo (f 3b)	S TR
	Very soft and sandy rock.	
	Solo: 1960's	
4b	**(6)** Conway's Crack ☆☆ (f 3c)	S TR
	Very steep for the grade, beginners will be challenged.	
	Solo: 1960's	TR: Pre 1950's

UK Trad	Fontainebleau colour (font grade)	Ticked
4b	**(7)** Bramble Corner ☆☆☆ (f 4b)	S TR
	Usually very dark and damp, good climbing.	
	Solo: 1960's	
4c	**(8)** Solo Right Hand ☆ (f 4c)	S TR
	Slightly harder start. Nose to the left is UK 6a.	
	Solo: 1960's	
5c	**(9)** Knott ☆☆ (f 5a)	S TR
	Steep but with good bridging rests.	
	Solo: 1960's	
5c	**(10)** Yellow Tube (f 5b)	S TR
	Originally an aid route known as Hanging Crack.	
	Solo: 1970's	TR: 1974 Mick Fowler
6b	**(11)** The Shield ☆☆☆ (f 6b)	S TR
	A very rare excellent route. Needs to be bone dry in a heatwave. Very tricky route finding with lots of on-off moves, highly sustained.	
		TR: 1975 Mick Fowler

Local chat: This bay offers a good selection of routes in the lower grades. The technical difficulty is not high, but the steepness and odd nature of the rock will surprise those only used to climbing on an indoor wall. Most routes feel pretty sustained.

Access & Erosion: Go direct to the top of this sector on the way into the Hollow to set up a belay. Descend by the Coal Chute to the left. Bolts on top but a good 4 metres back, make sure to extend and set belay karabiner over the edge. No close belay for The Shield, you need a long 15 static rope.

Warning: The large block at the top of route 5 - Solo, looks highly unstable and undercut. △

HARRISON'S ROCKS

BOWLES ROCKS

HIGH ROCKS

HIGH ROCKS ANNEXE

HAPPY VALLEY

BULLS HOLLOW

ERIDGE GREEN

UNDER ROCKS

STONE FARM

UK Trad	Fontainebleau colour (font grade)	Ticked		UK Trad	Fontainebleau colour (font grade)	Ticked

4c **① Centurion's Groove** ✵✵✵ (f **3c**) `S` `TR`
A fine high diedre.
Solo: Pre 1960's   *TR: Pre 1950's*

5c **② Broken Nose** ✵✵ (f **5a**) `S` `TR`
Soft rock with holds wearing away.
Solo: 1960's   *TR: Pre 1950's*

5c **③ Knott** ✵✵ (f **5a**) `S` `TR`
Steep but with good bridging rests.
Solo: 1960's

5c **④ Caesar** ✵✵ (f **5b**) `S` `TR`
A good few moves on this steep arête.
Solo: 1980's   *TR: 1974 Nigel Head*

6a **⑤ The Wall** ✵✵✵ (f **5c**) `S` `TR`
A sustained excellent route.
Solo: 1996 John Patterson   *TR: 1960'*

6a **⑥ Pseudonym** ✵ (f **6a**) `S` `TR`
A technical wall climb on small holds.
Solo: 1982 David Atchison-Jones   *TR: 1960'*

6b **⑦ The Shield** ✵✵✵ (f **6a+**) `S` `TR`
A very rare excellent route. Needs to be bone dry in a heatwave. Very tricky route finding with lots of on-off moves, highly sustained.
TR: 1975 Mick Fowle

6b **⑧ Squeak ya Heel Cups** (f **6b**) `S` `TR`
Short but not easy.
TR: 1993 James Dunlop

Local chat: This central wall is the showpiece for Bulls Hollow. The main Centurion's Groove is an excellent classic line and well worth doing. The other routes are considerably harder, and are increasingly difficult to onsight. This is made even more so because they are rarely climbed and don't have chalk on them, plus wandering around a bit. In a good early spring before the leaves come on the trees, this sector can be good, or in a very hot summer when everything dries out anyway.

Access & Erosion: Go to the top on the way in from Toad Rock. Bolt belays at the top of The Wall and Centurion's Groove. Other routes you will need a long 15m static rope to reach substantial trees.

HARRISON'S ROCKS
BOWLES ROCKS
HIGH ROCKS
HIGH ROCKS ANNEXE
HIGH ROCKS
HAPPY VALLEY
BULLS HOLLOW
ERIDGE GREEN
UNDER ROCKS
STONE FARM

UK Trad	Fontainebleau colour (font grade)		Ticked		UK Trad	Fontainebleau colour (font grade)		Ticked
3a	(1) **Slab Chimney**☆ (f **3a**)		S TR		5b	(5) **Eyewash** (f **4b**)	🗑	S TR
	Moderately uninteresting. *Solo: Pre 1950's*					A dank wall. *Solo: 1981 David Atchison-Jones* TR:1970's		
4c	(2) **Slab Variant**☆☆ (f **3c**)		S TR		5c	(6) **Broken Nose**☆☆ (f **5a**)		S TR
	A fun little number. *Solo: Pre 1950's*					Soft rock with holds wearing away. *Solo: 1960's* TR: Pre 1960's		
5a	(3) **Full Moon** (f **4a**)	🗑	S TR		5c	(7) **Cauliflower Ear**☆ (f **5b**)		S TR
	Crackline past the Yew Stump. *Solo: 1960's*					Climb the upper wall without the left arête. *TR: 2005 Graham Adcock*		
5b	(4) **Triangle Arête** (f **4b**)	🗑	S TR		6c	(8) **Time Waits for No One**☆☆ (f **7a**)		S TR
	Usually damp. *Solo: Pre 1950's*					A highly technical wall where time certainly doesn't wait. *TR: 1982 David Atchison-Jones*		

Local chat: A very mixed sector where you have complete rubbish next to excellent routes. Catches the sun in the early summer morning giving it a nice aspect - plus some prospect of drying out. During summer becomes damper and damper. Time Waits for No One is the hardest route at this outcrop - and very much in character with the early 1980's - a technical testpiece without modern power.

Access & Erosion: Go to the top on the way in from Toad Rock. You can follow the twisting chimney on the right, but this can be awkward with a big sac. A short static rope is needed for some of the belays.

HARRISON'S ROCKS

BOWLES ROCKS

HIGH ROCKS

HIGH ROCKS ANNEXE

HAPPY VALLEY

BULLS HOLLOW

ERIDGE GREEN

UNDER ROCKS

STONE FARM

UK Trad	Fontainebleau colour (font grade)		Ticked
3a	**①** Gangway Wall☆☆ (f 3a)		S TR

The obvious line on the buttress.
Solo: Pre 1960's

UK Trad	Fontainebleau colour (font grade)		Ticked
5b	**②** Crossply☆☆ (f 4c)		S TR

Quite sandy unfortunately.
Solo: 1981 Guy McLelland   *TR: 1970's*

5c	**③** The Bitch and the Meal Ticket☆ (f 5a)	S TR

A bit of a power move.
TR: 1994 Chris Tullis

> *Local chat: This buttress is neither small or big,
> however, the tops of the routes feel very exposed.
> The rock is quite poor yellow, but still manages to
> stay together in the upper parts of the buttress.*

UK Trad	Fontainebleau colour (font grade)		Ticked
5c	**④** Square Cut☆ (f 5a)		S TR

A rising line - mediocre.
Solo: 1982 David Atchison-Jones   *TR: 1975 John Stevenson*

6a	**⑤** Handle With Care☆ (f 5c)	S TR

Harder than it looks.
Solo: 1980's   *TR: 1960's*

6a	**⑥** Too Hot to Handle☆ (f 6a)	S TR

A tricky wee start to Handle With Care.
Solo: 1980's   *TR: 1982 David Atchison-Jones*

*Access & Erosion: Go to the top on the way in from
Toad Rock. You can follow the twisting chimney on the
left, but this can be awkward with a big sac. There are
a couple of good trees at the top, and 4-5 slings should
sort you out. You will need an extra short static rope for
route 4 - Square Cut, in order to keep it secure on the
arête.*

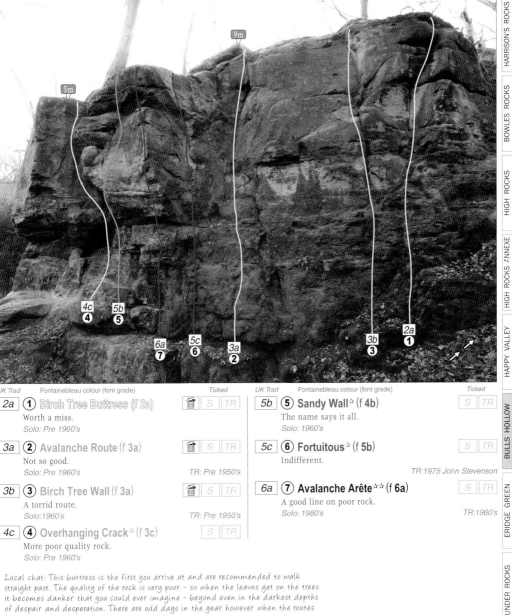

UK Trad	Fontainebleau colour (font grade)	Ticked		UK Trad	Fontainebleau colour (font grade)	Ticked
2a	① Birch Tree Buttress (f 2a)	🗑 S TR		5b	⑤ Sandy Wall☆ (f 4b)	S TR
	Worth a miss.				The name says it all.	
	Solo: Pre 1960's				*Solo: 1960's*	
3a	② Avalanche Route (f 3a)	🗑 S TR		5c	⑥ Fortuitous☆ (f 5b)	S TR
	Not so good.				Indifferent.	
	Solo: Pre 1960's	*TR: Pre 1950's*				*TR:1975 John Stevenson*
3b	③ Birch Tree Wall (f 3a)	🗑 S TR		6a	⑦ Avalanche Arête☆☆ (f 6a)	S TR
	A torrid route.				A good line on poor rock.	
	Solo:1960's	*TR: Pre 1950's*			*Solo: 1980's*	*TR:1960's*
4c	④ Overhanging Crack☆ (f 3c)	S TR				
	More poor quality rock.					
	Solo: Pre 1960's					

Local chat: This buttress is the first you arrive at and are recommended to walk straight past. The quality of the rock is very poor – so when the leaves get on the trees it becomes danker that you could ever imagine – beyond even in the darkest depths of despair and desperation. There are odd days in the year however when the routes are just worth doing – hmmm, perhaps not!

Top access & erosion beta: Best erosion stuff here is to avoid the place completely, go to the top on the way in from Toad Rock and keep going. All routes generally require a long static rope to reach substantial trees.

HARRISON'S ROCKS | BOWLES ROCKS | HIGH ROCKS | HIGH ROCKS ANNEXE | HIGH ROCKS | HAPPY VALLEY | BULLS HOLLOW | ERIDGE GREEN | UNDER ROCKS | STONE FARM

Waistline   Yew Wall   Possibility   Apis   Conway Cracks   Centurion   Time Bay   Gangway Wall   Avalanche Arête   Toad Rock

HARRISON'S ROCKS

BOWLES ROCKS

HIGH ROCKS

HIGH ROCKS ANNEXE

HAPPY VALLEY

BULLS HOLLOW

ERIDGE GREEN

UNDER ROCKS

STONE FARM

Toad Rock bouldering is mostly good fun and a laugh, rather than high-tension state of the art stuff. The Toad Rock itself is very fragile and hence is surrounded by iron railings to prevent oyks from trashing it completely. There is another giant pinnacle, but amusingly too intimidating to need fencing off. The rock is fairly soft so watch it when attempting high balls - of which there are a good many. It's not worth naming or grading the problems here because the rock wears so quickly that after a while, the grade changes and it becomes a different problem. There must be over a hundred different problems, ranging from diabolical mantles, to fun little traverses, and scary high walls.

The spot is very popular with families; kiddies just love playing in the sand.

△ *Jingo in the Chaos - [UK-2a]*

▽ *Toad Rock in the centre*

Waistline   Yew Wall   Possibility   Apis   Conway Cracks   Centurion   Time Bay   Gangway Wall   Avalanche Arête   Toad Rock

▽ Ollie Faber on the Mushroom Stone

△ Jingo playing on a Mantle

HARRISON'S ROCKS

BOWLES ROCKS

HIGH ROCKS

HIGH ROCKS ANNEXE

HAPPY VALLEY

BULLS HOLLOW

ERIDGE GREEN

UNDER ROCKS

STONE FARM

Eridge Green Rocks are usually referred to simply as Eridge. It's a broken outcrop of sandstone that is of variable height and quality, and is generally softer than at the other outcrops. It has a smoother texture which offers fewer holds, so the routes tend to be harder with a significant number in the 6a grades and above. The rocks mostly face east, which is fairly uncommon in this area. They are perhaps at their best on a spring morning when the ferns are low, and the sun filters through the barren trees to warm the rock. In a hot summer, the afternoon shade and plentiful tree canopy provides a good place to climb on cool rock and picnic in warm shade. In late summer, the undergrowth then gets a bit carried away and you may well have to thwack down ferns and brambles to reach some of the routes or top belays. The painful downside for Eridge, is that during the long summer evenings, it is sheltered from any westerly wind. This makes it an ideal spot for midges & mosquitoes to exercise their gnashers, nothing can prepare you for this onslaught. This area is both an SSSI and a nature reserve, and consequently there are many special plants growing in and around the rocks. It has been agreed locally that certain parts of the rocks should not be climbed on, so lichens can grow in peace. Therefore, these sectors are not included in this guidebook. Should this change, topos will be available on our website. There are often signposts to illustrate where not to climb.

Location: Eridge Green Rocks **SAT NAV info**
P1 - Parking Grid reference: **TQ 555 355**
P1 - Postcode **TN3 9JU**
Rocks Grid reference: **TQ 555 355**

There are 3 separate parking areas. For P1; Turn off the A26 on small road with the church on your right. At P1 - there is room for about 8 cars, make sure not to block the small road, or the entrance to the field. If P1 is full or closed, please park near the village hall (Eridge Parish Room). From P2, cross the busy main road and follow the footpath in the woods, 5 mins walk to Innominate sector. The Mammoth area is separated from the main outcrop, it is quickest to park at P3 then enter the woods at the large gate opposite.

[UK 6c] NON PAREIL (font 7b), Barnaby Ventham ▷

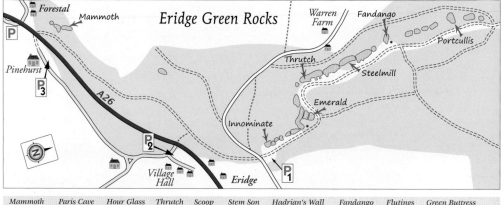

HARRISON'S ROCKS
BOWLES ROCKS
HIGH ROCKS
HIGH ROCKS ANNEXE
HAPPY VALLEY
BULLS HOLLOW
ERIDGE GREEN
UNDER ROCKS
STONE FARM

1b
- ☐ Boxing Day Crack(f 2a) p67
- ☐ Fingernail Crack (f 2a) p28
- ☐ Isometric Ch. (f 2a) p102
- ☐ Snake's 1b
- ☐ Keystone Crack (f 2a) p278
- ☐ Bivouac Chimney (f 2a) p254

2a
- ☐ Giant step-Man (f 2a) p250
- ☐ Easy Gully (f 2a) p260

2b
- ☐ Green Bollard Ch. (f 2a) p271
- ☐ Truncate (f 3a) p254
- ☐ Flake Crack (f 3a) p254
- ☐ Boulder Chimney (f 3a) p252

3a
- ☐ Keystone Wall (f 3a) p278

3b
- ☐ Elephant's Tail (f 3a) p250
- ☐ Embarkation Ck. (f 3a) p261
- ☐ Yew Crack (f 3a) p261

4a
- ☐ Heffalump (f 3b) p250
- ☐ Capstan Wall (f 3a) p276
- ☐ Slanting Crack (f 3a) p263
- ☐ Geronimo (f 3b) p254
- ☐ Hartleys (f 3a) p279
- ☐ Toadstool Crack (f 3b) p267

4b
- ☐ Mamba C-Home (f 3b) p267
- ☐ Pedestal Wall (f 3b) p282
- ☐ Spot the Dog (f 3b) p261
- ☐ Six in the Morning (f 3b) p254
- ☐ Just Cause (f 3b) p268
- ☐ Flutings (f 3b) p279
- ☐ Barbican Buttress (f 3c) p285

4c
- ☐ Keystone Face (f 3c) p278
- ☐ Arete (f 3c) p260
- ☐ Remus (f 3c) p274
- ☐ Dusk Crack (f 3c) p258
- ☐ Backyard (f 3c) p268
- ☐ Tree Root (f 3c) p283
- ☐ Fluted Fancy (f 3c) p279

5a
- ☐ Still-C-b Worse (f 5a) p283
- ☐ Eridge Tower R. (f 4a) p285
- ☐ Shanty Wall (f 4a) p276
- ☐ Roman Nose (f 4a) p274
- ☐ Hanging Crack (f 4a) p253
- ☐ Y Crack (f 4a) p250
- ☐ More Ticks-Tim (f 4a) p281
- ☐ Equilibrium Wall (f 4a) p252
- ☐ Battlements C. (f 4b) p285

5b
- ☐ Scooped Slab (f 4b) p263
- ☐ Oh-er Missus (f 4b) p283
- ☐ Hadrian's Wall (f 4b) p273
- ☐ Misty Wall (f 4b) p276

- ☐ Layaway (f 4b) p274
- ☐ Tweedle Dee (f 4b) p267
- ☐ Hour Glass (f 4c) p258
- ☐ Just CIA (f 4c) p268
- ☐ Keystone Kops (f 4c) p278
- ☐ Elastic Head (f 4c) p282
- ☐ Wobble (f 4c) p282
- ☐ The P-Pengster (f 4c) p267
- ☐ Hipposuction (f 4c) p274
- ☐ Optical Racer (f 4c) p285
- ☐ Just Ice (f 4c) p268
- ☐ Romulus (f 4c) p274
- ☐ Paisley (f 4c) p279
- ☐ Eric (f 4c) p277
- ☐ Sonny Dribble (f 4c) p281
- ☐ Innominate C. (f 4c) p252
- ☐ Tusk (f 4c) p251
- ☐ Concorde (f 4c) p276
- ☐ Fernkop Crack (f 4c) p281
- ☐ Siesta Wall (f 4c) p252
- ☐ Mammoth Wall (f 4c) p251

5c
- ☐ Boulancourt (f 5a) p281
- ☐ Libra (f 5a) p253
- ☐ Nuthin'Fancy (f 5a) p253
- ☐ Fruits (f 5a) p277
- ☐ Good R.G-Line (f 5a) p274
- ☐ Elephant's Head (f 5b) p250
- ☐ Brian's Corner (f 5b) p262
- ☐ Wet Bank Hol. (f 5b) p282
- ☐ Too Short (f 5b) p253
- ☐ Viking Line (f 5b) p276
- ☐ Short Work (f 5b) p281
- ☐ Tweedle Dum (f 5b) p267
- ☐ Trainer Drainer (f 5b) p253
- ☐ Last - S-Wine (f 5b) p252
- ☐ Middleclass P (f 5b) p261
- ☐ Antoninus (f 5b) p273
- ☐ Polly Ticks (f 5b) p264
- ☐ Big Fat Tart (f 5b) p252
- ☐ Wall-Extinct M (f 5b) p251
- ☐ Communist (f 5b) p264
- ☐ Splendeedo (f 5b) p260
- ☐ Bald Turkey (f 5b) p273
- ☐ Asterix (f 5b) p273
- ☐ Impacted Stool (f 5b) p262
- ☐ Tusk Direct Start (f 5b) p251
- ☐ Portcullis (f 5b) p285
- ☐ The Pillar (f 5b) p262
- ☐ Fandango (f 5b) p277
- ☐ Fontainebleau (f 5b) p281

6a
- ☐ I'm a Tractor (f 5c) p283
- ☐ Hazel (f 5c) p282
- ☐ Genesis (f 5c) p268
- ☐ Stirling Moss (f 5c) p263
- ☐ Obelisk (f 5c) p263
- ☐ Claudius (f 5c) p273
- ☐ Elephant's Arse (f 5c) p250

- ☐ Dilemma (f 5c) p264
- ☐ Cracking Up (f 5c) p254
- ☐ Thrutch (f 5c) p261
- ☐ Steelmill (f 5c) p268
- ☐ Thrupenny Bit (f 6a) p285
- ☐ Parisian Affair (f 6a) p255
- ☐ Empty Vee (f 6a) p262
- ☐ Too Short Direct (f 6a) p255
- ☐ In-Beginning (f 6a) p268
- ☐ Even Shorter Men. (f 6a) p255
- ☐ Hyphenated Jones (f 6a) p281
- ☐ Dr. Kemp's Cure (f 6a) p255
- ☐ Safe Sex (f 6a) p255
- ☐ Earthrise (f 6a) p262
- ☐ Life - Old Dog (f 6a) p277
- ☐ Afterburner (f 6a) p263
- ☐ Aero (f 6a) p285
- ☐ Good R-Poor L. (f 6a) p273
- ☐ Mein Herr (f 6a) p263
- ☐ Emerald (f 6a) p260
- ☐ Close to You (f 6a) p252
- ☐ Appetite for Dest. (f 6a) p273
- ☐ Revelations (f 6a) p271
- ☐ Stem Son (f 6a) p267
- ☐ Local Vigilantes (f 6a) p283
- ☐ Mellow Toot (f 6a) p264
- ☐ Iron Man Tyson (f 6a) p264
- ☐ Fly by Knight (f 6a) p273
- ☐ Poofy Finger (f 6a) p271
- ☐ Sandstone Hell (f 6a) p260
- ☐ Snap, Crackle (f 6a) p263
- ☐ 5.11 Crack (f 6a) p260
- ☐ Nododedendron (f 6a) p260

6b
- ☐ Innominate Buttress (f 6a+) p252
- ☐ Brighton Rock (f 6a+) p281
- ☐ More Monkey-Funky (f 6a+) p261
- ☐ Yellow Soot (f 6a+) p264
- ☐ Steamroller (f 6a+) p285
- ☐ Touchdown (f 6a+) p268
- ☐ Nigel Mantel (f 6a+) p263
- ☐ Triceratops (f 6a+) p262
- ☐ Scorpion (f 6a+) p271
- ☐ Sandstorm (f 6a+) p257
- ☐ Prowess (f 6a+) p254
- ☐ Hottie (f 6a+) p252
- ☐ Condom Corner (f 6a+) p254
- ☐ Big Boss (f 6b) p264
- ☐ More Cake for Me (f 6b) p257
- ☐ Waffer Thin (f 6b) p263
- ☐ Roman Nose Direct (f 6b) p273
- ☐ Achilles Last Stand (f 6b) p273
- ☐ Snail Trail (f 6b) p258
- ☐ Milly-la-Foret (f 6b) p281
- ☐ Kinetix (f 6b) p262
- ☐ Cosmo Irrazionale (f 6b+) p262
- ☐ Tortoise on a Spin (f 6b+) p261
- ☐ The Nail (f 6b+) p263
- ☐ Scirocco (f 6b+) p257

- ☐ Ken Clean Air (f 6b+) p264
- ☐ Lazy Chive (f 6b+) p271
- ☐ Lou (f 6b+) p267
- ☐ Amazing Oliver (f 6b+) p281
- ☐ Higher Purchase (f 6c) p258
- ☐ 1664 (f 6c) p283
- ☐ Diagonal (f 6c) p251
- ☐ The Beguiled (f 6c) p258
- ☐ Evoloution (f 6c) p267
- ☐ Meaty Thighs (f 6c) p258
- ☐ Velcro Arete (f 6c) p261
- ☐ Zugswang (f 6c+) p258

6c
- ☐ The Crunch (f 7a) p257
- ☐ Indian Traverse (f 7a) p271
- ☐ Azazel (f 7a) p271
- ☐ Yankee Affair (f 7a) p255
- ☐ Sansara (f 7a+) p255
- ☐ Turning the Leaf (f 7a+) p261
- ☐ The Crunch Direct (f 7b) p257
- ☐ Watchtower (f 7b) p253
- ☐ Jude's Wall (f 7b) p267
- ☐ Nonpareil (f 7b) p254

7a
- ☐ Tusky (f 7b+) p264
- ☐ Hypersonic (f 7b+) p262
- ☐ Nightfall (f 7c) p264
- ☐ Judamondo (f 7c) p258
- ☐ The Read Line (f 7c) p271

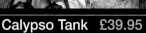

HARRISON'S ROCKS

BOWLES ROCKS

HIGH ROCKS

HIGH ROCKS ANNEXE

HAPPY VALLEY

BULLS HOLLOW

ERIDGE GREEN

UNDER ROCKS

STONE FARM

UK Trad   Fontainebleau colour (font grade)   Ticked

2a ① A Giant Step for Mankind (f 2a) | S | TR |
A little problem.
Solo: Pre 1960's

3b ② Elephant's Tail (f 3a) | S | TR |
Backside of the Elephant.
Solo: Pre 1960's

4a ③ Heffalump (f 3b) | S | TR |
A very diddy route.
Solo: 1984 Ben Bevan-Pritchard   TR: 1984 Geoff Pearson

5a ④ Y Crack☆ (f 4a) | S | TR |
Not a route for a day when you're going badly.
Solo: Pre 1960's

5c ⑤ Elephant's Head☆ (f 5b) | S | TR |
The nose, awkward high up.
Solo: 1980's   TR: Pre 1960's

6a ⑥ Elephant's Arse (f 5c) | S | TR |
A very Fontainebleau style route, crimps but no pain.
Solo: 1997 Robin Mazinke   TR: 1997 Robin Mazinke

Local chat: This buttress is hidden for most of the year
in the woods and remains unclimbed (very noisy from the
close proximity of the road). It was more popular when
the normal parking was at the village hall in Eridge, but
during 2000-2010 it has remained somewhat esoteric.
Best on a sunny day in early spring.

*Access & Erosion: Go up to the left of the rock. Setting
up a belay is quite complicated - in order to stop the
top rope from rolling off the Elephant. You will need 2
static ropes. Set the karabiner low down, and set up a
quickdraw to clip for topping out on the slab - it is bigger
and scarier than you think.*

HARRISON'S ROCKS

BOWLES ROCKS

HIGH ROCKS

HIGH ROCKS ANNEXE

HAPPY VALLEY

BULLS HOLLOW

ERIDGE GREEN

UNDER ROCKS

STONE FARM

UK Trad	Fontainebleau colour (font grade)	Ticked

5b ① **Tusk** (f **4c**) S TR

Drifting right.

TR: 1991 Tim Skinner

5b ② **Mammoth Wall**☆☆ (f **4c**) S TR

The imposing centre route.

Solo: 1980's   TR: 1971 Nigel Head

5c ③ **Wall of the Extinct Mammoth**☆ (f **5b**) S TR

Direct finish.

TR: 1990 Tim Skinner

UK Trad	Fontainebleau colour (font grade)	Ticked

5c ④ **Tusk Direct** (f **5b**) S TR

Direct.

TR: 1996 Robin Mazinke

6b ⑤ **Diagonal**☆☆ (f **6c**) S TR

The long rampline.

Solo: 1994 John Patterson   TR: 1984 Guy McLelland

Local chat: The main Mammoth Wall gives some pretty rigorous climbs. The rock is on the soft side so the grades may change as traffic either wears away the holds - or makes them bigger. Not often done so you will have to clean the holds usually. Wait for a good dry spell so that the green dust is fully dry.

Access & Erosion: Go to the top as for the Elephant, but continue around the back of the holly trees to find a cut tunnel that leads to the top. A short static is needed for the belay set up.

Crag layout map - page 246
Graded tick list - page 248

HARRISON'S ROCKS

BOWLES ROCKS

HIGH ROCKS

HIGH ROCKS ANNEXE

HAPPY VALLEY

BULLS HOLLOW

ERIDGE GREEN

UNDER ROCKS

STONE FARM

UK Trad	Fontainebleau colour (font grade)	Ticked

2b ① Boulder Chimney (f 3a)   🗑 S TR
Awkward and of little interest.
Solo: Pre 1950's

5a ② Equilibrium Wall☆☆ (f 4a)   S TR
Much harder than it looks.
Solo: Pre 1960's   *TR: Pre 1950's*

5b ③ Innominate Crack☆☆☆ (f 4c)   S TR
Lovely climbing on dry rock.
Solo: Pre 1950's

5b ④ Siesta Wall☆☆ (f 4c)   S TR
Problematic in parts.
Solo: Pre 1960's

5c ⑤ Last of the Summer Wine☆ (f 5b)   S TR
A nice route up the front.
Solo: 1993 R. Darnell   *TR:1993 Steve Durkin*

UK Trad	Fontainebleau colour (font grade)	Ticked

5c ⑥ Big Fat Tart☆☆ (f 5b)   S TR
A lovely wall.
Solo: 1992 Matt Smith   *TR:1992 Andy Hughe*

6a ⑦ Close to You (f 6a)   S TR
In the trees starting on the two iron holds.
Solo: 2006 John Patterson   *TR:1994 Mike Vetterle*

6b ⑧ Innominate Buttress☆☆ (f 6a+)   S TR
A fun eliminate but a bit difficult low down.
Solo: 2000

6b ⑨ Hottie☆ (f 6a+)   S TR
Not an easy finish.
        TR:1980

Local chat: A very popular spot opposite the usual parking area. Rock is quite soft so the holds wear away and grades may easily change. Gets the full blast of the sun in the day - especially morning, so keep clear in summer.

Top access & erosion beta: This is a very difficult place to set up the belays, and you will need a long 15 metre static rope, plus good protection for the soft top edge of the rocks here. Please do not climb without protecting the edge.

Crag layout map - page 246
Graded tick list - page 248

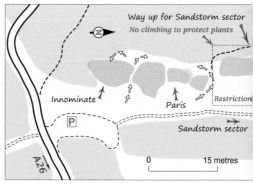

Way up for Sandstorm sector
No climbing to protect plants

Innominate
Paris
Restriction
Sandstorm sector

P

A26

0   15 metres

Note: Parking is usually possible in the small layby above. If this is closed or full up, alternative parking (P2) can be found opposite the village hall (or on the side of the minor roads), as shown on the intro map - page 246.

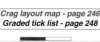

| Innominate | Sandstorm | Emerald | Pillar | Big Boss | Steelmill | Roman Nose | Keystone | Brighton Rock | Portcullis |
| Mammoth | Paris Cave | Hour Glass | Thrutch | Scoop | Stem Son | Hadrian's Wall | Fandango | Flutings | Green Buttress |

HARRISON'S ROCKS

BOWLES ROCKS

HIGH ROCKS

HIGH ROCKS ANNEXE

HAPPY VALLEY

BULLS HOLLOW

ERIDGE GREEN

UNDER ROCKS

STONE FARM

K Trad   Fontainebleau colour (font grade)   Ticked

5a   **(1)** **Hanging Crack** ☆☆☆ (f **4a**)   S   TR
Sandy but good.
Solo: Pre 1950's

5c   **(2)** **Libra** ☆☆ (f **5a**)   S   TR
Tricky bit is high up.
Solo: 1970's

5c   **(3)** **Nuthin' Fancy** ☆ (f **5a**)   S   TR
Soon gets tiring if you hang around.
Solo: 1992 Tim Skinner

5c   **(4)** **Too Short** ☆☆ (f **5b**)   S   TR
Name gives it away somewhat.
Solo: 1993 Matt Smith   *TR: 1991 Robin Mazinke*

5c   **(5)** **Trainer Drainer** ☆ (f **5b**)   S   TR
Keeps going all the way.
Solo: 1993 Matt Smith   *TR: 1990 Andy Hughes*

6b   **(6)** **Prowess** ☆☆☆ (f **6a+**)   S   TR
Starts around the corner then up the arête.
Solo: 1997 Robin Mazinke   *TR: 1991 Mike Vetterlein*

6c   **(7)** **The Watchtower** ☆☆ ☠ (f **7b**)   S   TR
The steep wall then pockets up to the flake.
Solo: 2003 Ian Stronghill

HARRISON'S ROCKS

BOWLES ROCKS

HIGH ROCKS

HIGH ROCKS ANNEXE

HAPPY VALLEY

BULLS HOLLOW

ERIDGE GREEN

UNDER ROCKS

STONE FARM

UK Trad		Fontainebleau colour (font grade)	Ticked	
1b	① Bivouac Chimney (f 2a)		S	TR
	Not the place to bivouac.			
3a	② Truncate☆ (f 3a)		S	TR
	Nice easy way up here.			
3a	③ Flake Crack☆☆ (f 3a)		S	TR
	Nothing too taxing.			
4a	④ Geronimo (f 3b)		S	TR
	A pleasant buttress.			
4b	⑤ Six in the Morning☆ (f 3b)		S	TR
	A gnarly crack.			
6a	⑥ Cracking Up☆ (f 5c)		S	TR
	Climb the arête on the right side.			
6a	⑦ Parisian Affair☆☆ (f 6a)		S	TR
	Direct up above overhang.			
6a	⑧ Too Short to Mention☆☆ (f 6a)		S	TR
	Start left and drift right.			
6a	⑨ Even Shorter Mention☆☆ (f 6a)		S	TR
	A pleasant buttress.			
6a	⑩ Dr. Kemp's Cure☆ ☠(f 6a)		S	TR
	The arête before turning left up the bank.			

BOREAL

◁ [UK 6a] PARISIAN AFFAIR (font 6a), Mark Glennie

Mammoth   Paris Cave   Hour Glass   Thrutch   Scoop   Stem Son   Hadrian's Wall   Fandango   Flutings   Green Buttress
Innominate   Sandstorm   Emerald   Pillar   Big Boss   Steelmill   Roman Nose   Keystone   Brighton Rock   Portcullis

HARRISON'S ROCKS

BOWLES ROCKS

HIGH ROCKS

HIGH ROCKS ANNEXE

HAPPY VALLEY

BULLS HOLLOW

ERIDGE GREEN

UNDER ROCKS

STONE FARM

K Trad   Fontainebleau colour (font grade)   Ticked

6a (11) **Safe Sex**☆ ☠(f **6a**)   S   TR

Wall with few pockets.

6b (12) **Prowess**☆☆☆ ☠☠(f **6a+**)   S   TR

Normally done with a top rope - but easy if you are tall.
Solo: 1997 Robin Mazinke   *TR: 1991 Mike Vetterlein*

6b (13) **Condom Corner**☆ ☠(f **6a+**)   S   TR

Start on flake and finish direct.

6c (14) **Yankee Affair**☆ (f **7a**)   S   TR

Start in the back, no left wall allowed - finish direct.
Solo: Pete Zeigenfuss

6c (15) **Sansara**☆ (f **7a+**)   S   TR

A dynamic approach is the norm.
Solo: 2003 Ian Stronghill

6c (16) **Nonpareil**☆☆ ☠☠(f **7b**)   S   TR

Technical and full of awkwardness.
     TR: 1992 Paul Widdowson

*Local chat: This is a small bay set up above the path, and
in summer is hidden by the undergrowth. A popular little
bouldering area with some good problems. Bit of a suntrap in
the morning. A couple of highballs for the adventurous.*

*Access & Erosion: Please always use a crash pad here
to protect the ground. No belay points on top, so you
need 2 static ropes to set up a belay, plus good edge
protection. Tying down to the ground-tree stump behind
the prow, keeps the top belay from moving.*

*Access: The next few buttresses are presently not used
for climbing, and left for the natural habitat to evolve.
Please read signs in place.*

HARRISON'S ROCKS

BOWLES ROCKS

HIGH ROCKS

HIGH ROCKS ANNEXE

HAPPY VALLEY

BULLS HOLLOW

ERIDGE GREEN

UNDER ROCKS

STONE FARM

9m

UK Trad	Fontainebleau colour (font grade)		Ticked
6b	**(1) Sandstorm** ☆☆☆ (f 6a+)		S TR

A steep and quite complicated climb.
Solo: 1995 John Patterson   *TR: 1979 Mick Fowler*

| 6b | **(2) More Cake for Me** ☆☆☆ (f 6b) | | S TR |

A steep and impressive wall.
TR: 1989 Paul Hayes

| 6b | **(3) Scirocco** ☆☆ (f 6b+) | | S TR |

On the edge of the no climbing zone - best left alone.
Solo: 1991 Matt Smith

UK Trad	Fontainebleau colour (font grade)		Ticked
6c	**(4) The Crunch** ☆☆☆ (f 7a)		S TR

Original start by traverse in, and finish left up Sandstorm.
TR: 1981 Mick Fowler

| 6c | **(5) The Crunch Direct** ☆☆ (f 7b) | | S TR |

A direct start, but finish may be impossible now.
TR: 1980's

Local chat: The Sandstorm Buttress is the large lump of rock that you can actually touch whilst still on the track. The sectors to its left are not climbed on although they often look clean and spankingly good quality. The bay formed to the right of this buttress is less appealing and is also given up to moss growing lichens. The handful of routes on this buttress are all long and demanding. The rock is always green and often greasy – par for the course. This said, you will need pretty dry conditions to succeed here, suggest you pick a hot spell in summer after a long dry period.

Top access & erosion beta: Best to access by the path going up to the right of Paris Cave, then follow trail along the top. Long static rope for belays essential.

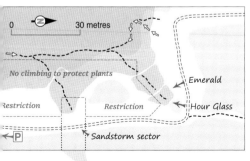

0   30 metres

No climbing to protect plants

← Emerald

Restriction   Restriction

← Hour Glass

←P

↑ Sandstorm sector

[UK 6b] MORE CAKE FOR ME (font 6b), Steve Glennie

Crag layout map - page 246
Graded tick list - page 248

HARRISON'S ROCKS
BOWLES ROCKS
HIGH ROCKS
HIGH ROCKS ANNEXE
HAPPY VALLEY
BULLS HOLLOW
ERIDGE GREEN
UNDER ROCKS
STONE FARM

UK Trad   Fontainebleau colour (font grade)   Ticked

4c ① **Dusk Crack** ✶✶ (f **3b**)   S TR
A route with surprisingly few holds.
Solo: Pre 1960's

5b ② **Hour Glass** (f **4c**)   S TR
The obvious shape in the rock.
Solo: 1978 Mick Fowler

6b ③ **Snail Trail** ✶✶✶ (f **6b**)   S TR
Finding the sequence of undercuts is the trick.
TR: 1980's Ed Sto...

6b ④ **The Beguiled** ✶✶ (f **6c**)   S TR
A line of fingertip slots.
Solo: 1991 John Patterson   TR: 1984 Guy McLellan

6b ⑤ **Meaty Thighs** ✶✶ (f **6c**)   S TR
The difficult arête mainly on the left.
TR: 1992 Alan Grig...

7a ⑥ **Judamondo** ✶✶✶ (f **7c**)   S TR
A superb line of widely spaced pockets.
TR: 2010 Ben Rea...

Local chat: This wall is usually hidden by a Yew Tree in front, with a very spread out canopy that edges up to the wall. Nearly always in the shade and dark. Stays cool in summer, but the holds can sometimes be a bit greasy.

Top access & erosion beta: Go around to the right until you find a pretty obvious easy-gully. Trees set back - you will need a long static rope to extend belay karabiner over the edge.

[UK 7a] JUDAMONDO (font 7c), Ben Read ...

No climbing to protect plants

Locust 5b
Finance 5c
Higher Purchase 6c
Dusk Crack

Hour Glass

Emerald
Zugswang

Snail Trail

Judamondo

Meaty Thighs   The Beguiled   Yew Tree

P

Crag layout map - page 246
Graded tick list - page 248

Mammoth   Paris Cave   Hour Glass   Thrutch   Scoop   Stem Son   Hadrian's Wall   Fandango   Flutings   Green Buttress
   Innominate   Sandstorm   Emerald   Pillar   Big Boss   Steelmill   Roman Nose   Keystone   Brighton Rock   Portcullis

HARRISON'S ROCKS

BOWLES ROCKS

HIGH ROCKS

HIGH ROCKS ANNEXE

HAPPY VALLEY

BULLS HOLLOW

ERIDGE GREEN

UNDER ROCKS

STONE FARM

UK Trad		Fontainebleau colour (font grade)	Ticked		
2a	(1)	Easy Gully (f 2a)		S	TR

Perhaps called easy, but not that straightforward.
Solo: Pre 1960's

| 4c | (2) | Arête (f 3c) | | S | TR |

Mediocre to poor.
Solo: Pre 1960's

| 5c | (3) | Splendeedo☆ (f 5b) | | S | TR |

The wall using the arête also (to right of main photo).
TR: 2009 Barnaby Ventham

| 6a | (4) | Emerald☆☆ (f 6a) | | S | TR |

The obvious ramp line.
Solo: 1996 Tim Skinner   *TR: 1990*

UK Trad		Fontainebleau colour (font grade)	Ticked		
6a	(5)	Sandstone Hell (f 6a)		S	TR

Poor rock and usually greasy.
TR: 1990 Mike Vetterle

| 6a | (6) | 5.11 Crack☆☆ (f 6a) | | S | TR |

Crack around the corner to the right of main photo.
Solo: 1990's   *TR: 1990 Oliver H*

| 6a | (7) | Nododendron☆ (f 6a) | | S | TR |

Left of wall.
TR: 1998 Mike Ede

| 6b | (8) | Zugswang☆☆ (f 6c+) | | S | TR |

Topping out direct is somewhat difficult.
TR: 1992 Paul Widdowse

Local chat: This is a north facing sector, don't expect dry routes here in anything other than a miraculous heatwave. Then there are usually plenty of mosquitos to keep you company. Not a terrific amount to recommend this sector unfortunately.

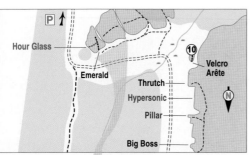

Access & Erosion: Use the easy gully going right to get to the top. Long static rope is needed for the belays.

HARRISON'S ROCKS

BOWLES ROCKS

HIGH ROCKS

HIGH ROCKS ANNEXE

HAPPY VALLEY

BULLS HOLLOW

ERIDGE GREEN

UNDER ROCKS

STONE FARM

Trad	Fontainebleau colour (font grade)	Ticked	UK Trad	Fontainebleau colour (font grade)	Ticked

3b (1) Yew Crack (f 3a) — S TR
A very poor route.
Solo: Pre 1950's

4b (2) Spot the Dog ✩✩ (f 3b) — S TR
Originally - Spot the Dog and the Breath of Death.
Solo: 1992 Doug Reid

5c (3) Middleclass Ponce ✩✩ (f 5b) — S TR
Sneaking in.
Solo: 1997 Henry Widd   *TR: 1992 Doug Reid*

6a (4) Thrutch ✩✩ (f 5c) — S TR
A fine climb in a good position.
Solo: 1960's

6a (5) Empty Vee (f 6a) — S TR
A wide crack of very limited appeal.
TR: 1990 Mike Vetterlein

6a (6) Earthrise ✩✩✩ (f 6a) — S TR
A good route up the front buttress.
Solo: 1998 John Patterson   *TR: 1994*

6b (7) More Monkey than Funky ✩ (f 6a+) — S TR
Not straightforward.
Solo: 1993 Tim Skinner   *TR: 1990 Oliver Hill*

6b (8) Cosmo Irrazionale ✩ (f 6b+) — S TR
Good dynamic wall climbing.
TR: 2005 Chris Gibson

6b (9) Tortoise on a Spin Out ✩ (f 6b+) — S TR
Not straightforward.
Solo: 1990 Paul Stone

6b (10) Velcro Arete ✩ (f ☝ 6c) — S TR
The right arête of the boulder (See the plan on p260)
Solo: 2003 Ian Hufton

6c (11) Turning the Leaf ✩ (f 7a+) — S TR
Low level traverse, too sandy and has fallen off in parts.
Solo: 2004 Ian Stronghill

Local chat: This is the first area at the end of the bend in the track. Quite nice climbing but softish rock, making some of the starts a bit harder in the future perhaps.

Access & Erosion: Go along to the gully right of Big Boss area, then follow bushwack trail along the top of the outcrop back to this sector. Short static rope needed.

Crag layout map - page 246
Graded tick list - page 248

HARRISON'S ROCKS

BOWLES ROCKS

HIGH ROCKS

HIGH ROCKS ANNEXE

HAPPY VALLEY

BULLS HOLLOW

ERIDGE GREEN

UNDER ROCKS

STONE FARM

UK Trad   Fontainebleau colour (font grade)   Ticked

5c ① **Brian's Corner**☆☆ (f **5b**)   S TR
Quite a good little corner - when dry.
Solo: 1995 John Patterson   TR: 1990 Brian Kavanagh

5c ② **Impacted Stool** (f **5b**)   🗑 S TR
Going via the oval pocket then exit up and right.
Solo: 1995 John Patterson   TR: 1992 Paul Widdowson

5c ③ **Pillar**☆☆☆ (f **5b**)   S TR
A superb white piece of rock - tricky finish.
Solo: 1991 John Patterson   TR: 1960's

6a ④ **Obelisk**☆☆ (f **5c**)   ✋ S TR
Another fine arête.
Solo: 1991 John Patterson   TR: 1979 Mick Fowler

6a ⑤ **Empty Vee** (f **6a**)   🗑 S TR
A wide crack of very limited appeal.
TR: 1990 Mike Vetterlein

Local chat: A mixed bunch. The Pillar is very much the classic route with a tricky finish to get onsight – for the grade. The other parts are a natural drainage area and the tops are rather disgusting at present. The wall left of Hypersonic may well give a rather hard route in the future!

Top access & erosion beta: Go right to the gully just past Big Boss, then follow bushwack path back along the top. Hypersonic area has no belay points - long static rope required - and is generally used to top out, very sandy.

UK Trad   Fontainebleau colour (font grade)   Ticked

6b ⑥ **Triceratops**☆ (f **6a+**)   S TR
Quite strenuous.
TR: 1980

6b ⑦ **Waffer Thin**☆ (f **6b**)   S TR
A full on wall.
Solo: 1991 John Patterson   TR: 1980

6b ⑧ **Kinetix**☆☆ (f **6b**)   S TR
Climbing the wall without the arête.
Solo: 1998 John Patterson   TR: 1980

7a ⑨ **Hypersonic**☆🏃 (f **7b+**)   S TR
The obvious highball line up the centre of the wall.
Solo: 2003 Ian Stronghill

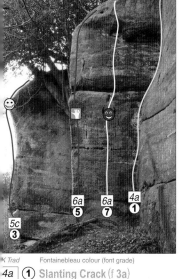

Trad   Fontainebleau colour (font grade)   *Ticked*   **UK Trad**   Fontainebleau colour (font grade)   *Ticked*

4a (1) **Slanting Crack** (f 3a)   S   TR
Difficult to top out.
Solo: Pre 1950's

5b (2) **Scooped Slab**✩✩ (f 4b)   S   TR
A few worn holds but a nice small wall (UK 5c direct).
Solo: 1960's

5c (3) **Pillar**✩✩✩ (f 5b)   S   TR
A superb white piece of rock - tricky finish.
Solo: 1991 John Patterson   *TR: 1960's*

6a (4) **Stirling Moss**✩✩ (f 5c)   S   TR
Directly up the wall on small holds.
Solo: 1991 John Patterson   *TR: 1980's*

6a (5) **Obelisk**✩✩ (f 5c)   S   TR
Another fine arête.
Solo: 1991 John Patterson   *TR: 1979 Mick Fowler*

6a (6) **Afterburner**✩✩ (f 6a)   S   TR
Another more difficult fine arête.
Solo: 1991 Matt Smith

6a (7) **Mein Herr** (f 6a)   S   TR
A rather difficult fine wall.
Solo: 2006 John Patterson   *TR: 1992 Alan Grigg*

6a (8) **Snap, Crackle and Pop**✩ (f 6a)   S   TR
Going direct from the start of Scooped Slab.
Solo: 1992 John Patterson   *TR: 1980's*

6b (9) **Nigel Mantel**✩ (f 6a+)   S   TR
No surprise in the finishing move.
    TR: 1990 Matt Smith

6b (10) **The Nail**✩ (f 6b+)   S   TR
The obvious crack around the right arête.
    TR: 1992 Alan Grigg

Local chat: The 5b route up the centre of the slab is popular - being one of the few easier routes at Eridge (can be climbed direct also). The wall is not that big, so it is hardly surprising that most of the routes have been soloed - however, don't let this lead you into thinking that they are easy - John Patterson is somewhat of fairly lean climbing machine.

Access & Erosion: Go to the right and up the gully beyond Big Boss. Follow the bushwack trail back along the top. Slings are adequate for a belay on Scooped Slab, but you will need a short static for the other routes.

Crag layout map - page 246
Graded tick list - page 248

Mammoth   Paris Cave   Hour Glass   Thrutch   *Scoop*   Stem Son   Hadrian's Wall   Fandango   Flutings   Green Buttress
Innominate   Sandstorm   Emerald   Pillar   Big Boss   Steelmill   Roman Nose   Keystone   Brighton Rock   Portcullis

HARRISON'S ROCKS
BOWLES ROCKS
HIGH ROCKS
HIGH ROCKS ANNEXE
HAPPY VALLEY
BULLS HOLLOW
ERIDGE GREEN
UNDER ROCKS
STONE FARM

UK Trad	Fontainebleau colour (font grade)		Ticked

5c (**1**) **Polly Ticks** (f **5b**)   S   TR
Hardly a classic.
TR: 1990 Oliver Hill

5c (**2**) **Communist**⭑ (f **5b**)   S   TR
Technical wall climbing.
TR: 1990 Oliver Hill

6a (**3**) **Dilemma**⭑⭑⭑ (f **5c**)   S   TR
Easy to the thumping overhang above.
Solo: 1960's

6a (**4**) **Mellow Toot**⭑ (f **6a**)   S   TR
Usually green and greasy.
Solo: 1998 John Patterson   *TR: 1991 Andy Hughes*

6a (**5**) **Iron Man Tyson**⭑ (f **6a**)   S   TR
Wall climbing on good pockets.
Solo: 1998 John Patterson   *TR: 1980's*

6b (**6**) **Yellow Soot**⭑⭑ (f **6a+**)   S   TR
Easy until the finish.
TR: 1984 Guy McLella

6b (**7**) **Big Boss**⭑⭑ (f **6b**)   S   TR
A tricky high move with an awkward finish.
TR: 1999 David Atchison-Jon

6b (**8**) **Ken Clean Air System**⭑⭑ (f **6b+**)   S   TR
Standing start to climb the impending arête.
TR: 1990 Mike Ed

7a (**9**) **Tusky**⭑ (f **7b+**)   S   TR
A head height traverse into Nightfall.
Solo: 2003 Ian Stronghill

7a (**10**) **Nightfall**⭑ (∅ f **7c**)   S   TR
A sit start to Ken.... to the pocket high on the arête.
Solo: 2003 Ian Stronghill

Local chat: This is a fine looking and impending buttress. The rock is slightly soft - so many pockets are likely to crumble or wear away - grades may change therefore. Routes feel quite long and are well known for their pretty stiff finishes.

Top access & erosion beta: Go up the esoteric gully on the right which leads to the top. A short static rope is needed for most of the belays.

Crag layout map - page 246
Graded tick list - page 248

[UK 6b] BIG BOSS (font 6b), Matt Tullis

Innominate   Sandstorm   Emerald   Pillar   Big Boss   Steelmill   Roman Nose   Keystone   Brighton Rock   Portcullis
Mammoth   Paris Cave   Hour Glass   Thrutch   Scoop   Stem Son   Hadrian's Wall   Fandango   Flutings   Green Buttress

HARRISON'S ROCKS
BOWLES ROCKS
HIGH ROCKS
HIGH ROCKS ANNEXE
HIGH VALLEY
HAPPY VALLEY
BULLS HOLLOW
ERIDGE GREEN
UNDER ROCKS
STONE FARM

UK Trad				Ticked

4a (1) **Toadstool Crack** (f 3b)   S   TR
A ghastly corner crack.
Solo: Pre 1950's

4b (2) **Mamba's Come Home to Roost** (f 3b)   S   TR
A little wall, usually disgustingly green.
Solo: Pre 1960's

5b (3) **Tweedle Dee** (f 4b)   S   TR
Quite a pleasant wall.
Solo: 1992   *TR: 1990 Oliver Hill*

5b (4) **The Pink Pengster** (f 4c)   S   TR
Technical wall climbing.
TR: 1994 Doug Reid

5c (5) **Tweedle Dum** (f 5b)   S   TR
Climb the arête, starting on the left side.
TR: 1990 Oliver Hill

UK Trad				Ticked

6a (6) **Stem Son** ☆ (f 6a)   S   TR
A technical groove.
Solo: 1998 John Patterson   *TR: 1990 Oliver Hill*

6b (7) **Lou** ☆☆ (f 6b+)   S   TR
Pockets and good quality climbing.
Solo: 1995 John Patterson   *TR: 1990 Paul Widdowson*

6b (8) **Evolution** ☆ (f 6c)   S   TR
Technical wall climbing.
TR: 1997 Daimon Beail

6c (9) **Jude's Wall** ☆☆ (f 7b)   S   TR
Technical and reachy wall climbing.
TR: 2009 Ben Read

Local chat: This small wall before the intimidating Steelmill sector is often overlooked. Good quality routes - but on the short side, slightly too high for simple anxiety free bouldering. Does clean up well in a dry spell.

Top access & erosion beta: Not always the most popular of spots - so don't expect a good trail leading to the top. Bushwacking up to the left is shortest by distance, but Jude's Wall can easily be reached from the top of Steelmill Wall - so you might want to use the longer and easier way up. Short static rope needed for all of the belays.

Crag layout map - page 246
Graded tick list - page 248

◁ [UK 6c] JUDE'S WALL (font 7b), Ben Read

Mammoth   Paris Cave   Hour Glass   Thrutch   Scoop   Stem Son   Hadrian's Wall   Fandango   Flutings   Green Buttress
Innominate   Sandstorm   Emerald   Pillar   Big Boss   Steelmill   Roman Nose   Keystone   Brighton Rock   Portcullis

HARRISON'S ROCKS

BOWLES ROCKS

HIGH ROCKS

HIGH ROCKS ANNEXE

HAPPY VALLEY

BULLS HOLLOW

ERIDGE GREEN

UNDER ROCKS

STONE FARM

Indian Trav 7a

UK Trad	Fontainebleau colour (font grade)	Ticked		UK Trad	Fontainebleau colour (font grade)	Ticked

4a **(1) Toadstool Crack** (f 3b)   S TR

The rather ghastly corner crack.

Solo: Pre 1950's

4b **(2) Just Cause** (f 3b)   🗑 S TR

Technical with balance required.

Solo: 1994 Tim Skinner   *TR: 1990 Oliver Hill*

4c **(3) Backyard** (f 3b)   S TR

A crack line - and not a good one at that.

Solo: 1994 Tim Skinner   *TR: 1990 Oliver Hill*

5b **(4) Just CIA** (f 4c)   S TR

A short wall climb.

Solo: 1992 Tim Skinner   *TR: 1990 Oliver Hill*

5b **(5) Just Ice** (f 4c)   S TR

Another short wall climb.

TR: 1990 Oliver Hill

6a **(6) Genesis**☆☆ (f 5c)   S TR

Only a couple of actually hard moves.

Solo: 1991 John Patterson   *TR: 1989 G. Hill*

6a **(7) Steelmill**☆☆☆ (f 6a)   S TR

More of a pump than hard moves.

Solo: 1991 John Patterson   *TR: 1979 Mick Fowle*

6a **(8) In The Beginning**☆☆ (f 6a)   S TR

.... there was Barnaby ☺. A good direct line to the top.

TR: 2009 Barnaby Ventham

6b **(9) Touchdown**☆☆☆ (f 6a+)   S TR

Hard start, hard middle and hard finish.

TR: 1982 Mick Fowler

Local chat: The Steelmill wall is enshrouded by a giant Yew tree, keeping it in shade all year round. In summer the entire wall dries out to give excellent long and pumpy routes. In winter it remains green and slimey. The smaller buttress to the left is usually overgrown and the routes are seldom done!

Access & Erosion: Go right - 70 yds and up the gully past Roman Nose (Concorde) sector. Short static rope needed for some belays to get belay karabiner in the best place to prevent erosion.

BOREAL

[UK 6a] STEELMILL (font 6a), Rachel Hoyland ▷

9m

HARRISON'S ROCKS

BOWLES ROCKS

HIGH ROCKS

HIGH ROCKS ANNEXE

HAPPY VALLEY

BULLS HOLLOW

ERIDGE GREEN

UNDER ROCKS

STONE FARM

UK Trad			Ticked		UK Trad			Ticked

2a **(1)** Green Bollard Chimney* (f 2a) — S TR
Sometimes used as a way to the top - but not ideal.
Solo: Pre 1950's

6b **(5)** Scorpion★★★ (f 6a+) — S TR
Steep and on pockets.
TR: 1990 G. Hill

6a **(2)** Revelations★★★ (f 6a) — S TR
A surprisingly good climb when in condition.
Solo: 1996 Robin Mazinke   TR: 1989 Oliver Hill

6b **(6)** Lazy Chive★★ (f 6b+) — S TR
A gruesome move to finish.
TR: 1990 Paul Widdowson

6a **(3)** Poofy Finger's Revenge★★ (f 6a) — S TR
Climbing the wall without using the crack up right.
TR: 1989 G. Hill

6c **(7)** Indian Traverse★ (f 7a) — S TR
The curving traverse line of good-ish holds.
Solo: 2008 Peter Wycislik

6b **(4)** Touchdown★★★ (f 6a+) — S TR
Hard start, hard middle and hard finish.
TR: 1982 Mick Fowler

6c **(8)** Azazel★ (f 7a) — S TR
No footlocks out right allowed (6c if used).
Solo: 2003 Ian Hufton

Local chat: This is one of the best pieces of rock at Eridge and has a lovely small bay of grass at its base. The rock is not so strong - so be very careful with your cranking. Very steep for sandstone - routes are all very different in style.

7a **(9)** The Read Line★ (f 7c) — S TR
The long line of sandy rails - right to left.
Solo: 2009 Ben Read

Access & Erosion: Go right and up the gully past Roman Nose (Concorde) sector. Short static rope needed for most belays to get belay karabiner in the best place to prevent erosion.

 BOREAL

 BEAL

◁ [UK 6b] LAZY CHIVE (font 6b+), Steve Glennie

Crag layout map - page 246
Graded tick list - page 248

HARRISON'S ROCKS

BOWLES ROCKS

HIGH ROCKS

HIGH ROCKS ANNEXE

HAPPY VALLEY

BULLS HOLLOW

ERIDGE GREEN

UNDER ROCKS

STONE FARM

UK Trad	Fontainebleau colour (font grade)	Ticked

2a **(1) Green Bollard Chimney**☆ (f 2a) S TR
Sometimes used as a way to the top - but not ideal.
Solo: Pre 1950's

5b **(2) Hadrian's Wall**☆☆☆ (f 4b) S TR
Few incut holds makes this a rather sketchy solo.
Solo: 1950's Frank Elliot

5c **(3) Antoninus**☆ (f 5b) S TR
A bunched up awkward route.
Solo: 1993 Tim Skinner   *TR: 1990 Mike Vetterlein*

Local chat: Hadrian's Wall faces you directly as you approach on the main track, with the nose of Asterix being very prominent and appealing. The wall is usually overhung by branches that tend to drip after rain unfortunately, making it greener than would be desired. In a dry spell, this wall gives short but intense routes; most are tricky in the wrong place for soloing without getting the heebeegeebies.

UK Trad	Fontainebleau colour (font grade)	Ticked

5c **(4) Bald Turkey**☆ (f 5b) S TR
Originally called 'The Great Bald Turkey meets a Dwarf with a Problem.' Difficult to top out.
TR: 1990 Paul Stone

5c **(5) Asterix**☆☆☆ (f 5b) S TR
Hard if you don't do it correctly.
Solo: 1981 David Atchison-Jones   *TR: 1978 Mick Fowler*

6a **(6) Claudius Drops a Clanger**☆☆☆ (f 5c) S TR
Technical wall climbing.
Solo: 1980's Various Centurions

Access & Erosion: Go right and up the gully past Roman Nose (Concorde) sector. There are thin trees above the wall for slings (4 are adequate), I generally use a back up static rope to more substantial trees further back.

◁ *[UK 5c] ASTERIX (font 5b), Rob Davies*

HARRISON'S ROCKS

BOWLES ROCKS

HIGH ROCKS

HIGH ROCKS ANNEXE

HAPPY VALLEY

BULLS HOLLOW

ERIDGE GREEN

UNDER ROCKS

STONE FARM

4c	**① Remus**✩✩ (f 3c)	S TR	**5c**	**⑦ Asterix**✩✩✩ (f 5b)	S TR

A fine route up this open book groove.
Solo: Pre 1960's

Hard if you don't do it correctly.
Solo: 1981 David Atchison-Jones   *TR: 1978 Mick Fowle*

5a **② Roman Nose**✩✩ (f 4a)   S TR

A nice variation to Remus, step onto the nose.
Solo: 1981 David Atchison-Jones   *TR: 1950's Frank Elliot*

6a **⑧ Good Route, Poor Line**✩✩ (f 6a)   S TR

Poorly wanders around.
TR: 1984 Paul Haye

5b **③ Layaway**✩ (f 4b)   S TR

Not so good friction may be a problem.
Solo: 1970's

6a **⑨ Appetite for Destruction** (f 6a)   S TR

Hardly appetising.
TR: 1996 Robin Mazink

5b **④ Hipposuction**✩ (f 4c)   S TR

A delicate groove.
Solo: 1993 Tim Skinner   *TR: 1991 Doug Reid*

6a **⑩ Fly by Knight**✩✩✩ (f 6a)   S TR

Technical wall climbing.
Solo: 1992 Tim Skinner   *TR: 1984 Guy McLellan*

5b **⑤ Romulus**✩ (f 4c)   S TR

A crack to thwart those who don't get on with cracks.
Solo: Pre 1960's   *TR: Pre 1950's*

6b **⑪ Roman Nose Direct**✩ (f 6b)   S TR

May get harder with holds wearing away.
Solo: 1992 Tim Skinner   *TR: 1982 Mick Fowle*

5c **⑥ Good Route, Good Line**✩✩ (f 5a)   S TR

Good technical good climbing.
Solo: 1993 Chris Murray   *TR: 1984 Tim Daniells*

6b **⑫ Achilles Last Stand**✩✩ (f 6b)   S TR

May get harder with holds wearing away.
TR: 1991 Theseus Gerrard

Local chat: This sector is without doubt the most accessible area at Eridge for climbers in the mid grades, and with routes short enough that climbing them onsight is highly possible. The sector gets early morning sun and dries out pretty quickly – so long as the holly trees above the routes remain trimmed.

Access & Erosion: Go right and up the gully past Roman Nose (Concorde) sector. There are thin trees above the wall for slings (4 are adequate), I generally use a back up static rope to more substantial trees further back.

Crag layout map - page 246
Graded tick list - page 248

[UK 4c] REMUS (font 3c), Tracey Lintern ➤

HARRISON'S ROCKS

BOWLES ROCKS

HIGH ROCKS

HIGH ROCKS ANNEXE

HAPPY VALLEY

BULLS HOLLOW

ERIDGE GREEN

UNDER ROCKS

STONE FARM

UK Trad	Fontainebleau colour (font grade)	Ticked		UK Trad	Fontainebleau colour (font grade)	Ticked

4a **① Capstan Wall**☆☆ (f 3a)   S   TR

A cracking little number.
Solo: Pre 1950's

5a **② Shanty Wall** (f 4a)   S   TR

A groove to nowhere.
Solo: Pre 1960's   *TR: Pre 1950's*

5b **③ Misty Wall**☆ (f 4b)   S   TR

A short wall before entertaining cracks.
TR: 1996 Robin Mazinke

5b **④ Concorde**☆☆☆ (f 4c)   S   TR

A superb little arête with a good landing.
Solo: 1975 Mick Fowler

5c **⑤ Viking Line**☆☆ (f 5b)   S   TR

A technical wall climb on small holds.
Solo: 1996 Tim Skinner   *TR: 1996 Robin Mazinke*

Local chat: A very good little tower offering some short routes in easier grades. The right wall tends to get minimal traffic, and as such is usually moss covered. The whole area gets a bit engulfed with ferns in late summer.

Top access & erosion beta: Go up just to the right of this sector. It is a popular way up for quite a few of the buttresses, so should be well worn through the top jungle of undergrowth.

8m

7m

HARRISON'S ROCKS

BOWLES ROCKS

HIGH ROCKS

HIGH ROCKS ANNEXE

HAPPY VALLEY

BULLS HOLLOW

ERIDGE GREEN

UNDER ROCKS

STONE FARM

JK Trad | Fontainebleau colour (font grade) | Ticked

5b **①** **Eric**☆☆ (f **4c**) | S | TR

The easiest way up the centre of the wall.
Solo: 1950's Frank Elliot

5c **②** **Fruits** (f **5a**) | S | TR

The line up the left side of the wall avoiding Eric.
TR: 1991 Robin Mazinke

UK Trad | Fontainebleau colour (font grade) | Ticked

5c **③** **Fandango**☆☆☆ ⚑ (f **5b**) | S | TR

An excellent highball.
Solo: 1981 David Atchison-Jones | *TR: 1960's*

6a **④** **Life in the Old Dog Yet**☆☆☆ (f **6a**) | S | TR

A seemingly unattractive highball.
TR: 1993 Chris Arnold

Roman Nose

Keystone Cop

Fandango

P

Concorde

Life in the Old dog Yet

0   70 metres

Local chat: This is one of the more recognisable parts of Eridge, since the large boulder is very close to the path and easy to spot. There is currently a large pine tree just behind the block; there were many more before the great storm in the 1980's when a lot of the massive old trees got blown over. Only a handful of routes on this block - with Fandango being the most outstanding by far. Shade on this for most of the day - and sun straight in your eyes as you fumble to top out - climbing in shades for once may be quite sensible.

Access & Erosion: Go to the right of the Fandango wall, then locate the obvious large gully trending up. A trail leads off to the top of the rocks on your left. You need to make 2 easy leaps across the gaps to get onto the final Fandango Block. Take up 2 static ropes to ensure belay does not roll off the top of the block.

Crag layout map - page 246
Graded tick list - page 248

HARRISON'S ROCKS

BOWLES ROCKS

HIGH ROCKS

HIGH ROCKS ANNEXE

HAPPY VALLEY

BULLS HOLLOW

ERIDGE GREEN

UNDER ROCKS

STONE FARM

5m

5b ④   4c ③   1b ①   3a ②

UK Trad	Fontainebleau colour (font grade)	Ticked		UK Trad	Fontainebleau colour (font grade)	Ticked	
1b	① **Keystone Crack** (f 2a)	S	TR	4c	③ **Keystone Face** (f 3c)	S	TR

1b ① **Keystone Crack** (f 2a)
The obvious crack.
Solo: Pre 1950's

3a ② **Keystone Wall** (f 3a)
A pretty short wall.
Solo: Pre 1960's

4c ③ **Keystone Face** (f 3c)
Another short wall.
Solo: Pre 1960's

5b ④ **Keystone Kops** (f 4c)
Beefy at the top.

TR: 1996 Robin Mazinke

Local chat: A small wall just above the path. It suffers from overhanging foliage. Would be fun little routes if they were cleaned up. Note The top block is balanced on the lower – these sort of blocks undoubtedly decay over time and collapse.

Top access & erosion beta: Go up to the left of the block, 4 slings should be enough to set up a belay.

[UK 6c] (font 7a) page 271
INDIAN TRAVERSE,
Barnaby Ventham ➢

Crag layout map - page 246
Graded tick list - page 248

HARRISON'S ROCKS
BOWLES ROCKS
HIGH ROCKS
HIGH ROCKS ANNEXE
HAPPY VALLEY
BULLS HOLLOW
ERIDGE GREEN
UNDER ROCKS
STONE FARM

JK Trad   Fontainebleau colour (font grade)   *Ticked*   *UK Trad*   Fontainebleau colour (font grade)   *Ticked*

4a **(1) Hartleys** ☆ (f **3a**)   S TR

A nice short wall, beefy and use the tree.
Solo: 1950's

4c **(3) Fluted Fancy** ☆ (f **3c**)   Ω S TR

Start on front wall, then around (top block disintegrating).
Solo: Pre 1960's

4b **(2) Flutings** ☆☆ (f **3b**)   Ω S TR

Sway onto the arête but finish up the front with a mantle.
Solo: Pre 1950's

5b **(4) Paisley** ☆ (f **4c**)   S TR

Short and sharp.
Solo: 1993 Chris Murray

Local chat: Can stay green for quite a while, but is certainly good fun for the lower grade climber on pretty good rock – for Eridge.

Top access & erosion beta: Go up to the left very easily.
4 Slings should be adequate to set up a belay.

[UK 4a] (font 3a)
HARTLEYS,
James
Hargreaves ▷

HARRISON'S ROCKS

BOWLES ROCKS

HIGH ROCKS

HIGH ROCKS ANNEXE

HAPPY VALLEY

BULLS HOLLOW

ERIDGE GREEN

UNDER ROCKS

STONE FARM

UK Trad	Fontainebleau colour (font grade)		Ticked

5a **(1)** **More Ticks for Tim**⁎ (f **4a**)   S TR

A chimney.

Solo: 2005 Robin Mazinke

5b **(2)** **Sonny Dribble Chops**⁎⁎☠ (f **4c**)   S TR

Nice technical problem.

Solo: 1989 Paul Stone

5b **(3)** **Fernkop Crack**⁎ (f **4c**)   S TR

A wide crack, nasty to leave the ground.

Solo: Pre 1950's

5c **(4)** **Boulancourt**⁎ (f **5a**)   S TR

The rounded arête, short and sharp.

TR: 2007 Bob Russell

5c **(5)** **Short Work**⁎ (f **5b**)   S TR

A technical groove.

Solo: 1993 Tim Skinner

5c **(6)** **Fontainebleau**⁎ (f **5b**)   S TR

Very tiring and feels like 6a.

Solo: Pre 1960's

6a **(7)** **Hypenated Jones**⁎ (f **6a**)   S TR

Front of the buttress.

Solo: 2006 John Patterson   *TR: 1990's*

6b **(8)** **Brighton Rock**⁎ (f **6a+**)   S TR

Short wall with no crack allowed.

Solo: 1993 Chris Murray   *TR: Pre 1989 Paul Stone*

6b **(9)** **Milly-la-Forêt**⁎ (f **6b**)   S TR

As crimps brake off, this gets stiffer - and is now hard!

TR: 2007 Bob R, then Peri Cheale

6b **(10)** **Amazing Oliver**⁎ (f **6b+**)   S TR

Once called 'Oliver and his Amazing Underpants.'

Solo: 1991 Matt Smith

Local chat: A small bouldering area with some elephants arse's to cope with - spotters very useful with a selection of big pads.

◁ *[UK 5b] SONNY DRIBBLE CHOPS (font 4c), Mark Glennie*

Access & Erosion: The right buttress top is reached easier by going around to the right (Font to the left). 2 static ropes are needed for some of the belays.

HARRISON'S ROCKS

BOWLES ROCKS

HIGH ROCKS

HIGH ROCKS ANNEXE

HAPPY VALLEY

BULLS HOLLOW

ERIDGE GREEN

UNDER ROCKS

STONE FARM

UK Trad	Fontainebleau colour (font grade)		Ticked

4b   **①** **Pedestal Wall** ✷ (f 3b)   S   TR

Prepare for a sketchy finish.
Solo: Pre 1950's

5b   **②** **Elastic Headbands** ✷✷ (f 4c)   S   TR

This must be named after the famous Oliver Hill, surely.
Solo: 1990 Andy Hughes

5b   **③** **Wobble** ✷✷ (f 4c)   S   TR

A rounded prow.
Solo: 1993 Tim Skinner

Local chat: This wall continues along from the
Brighton Rock alcove and is slightly elevated. It
gives medium quality bouldering that gets pretty
overgrown during summer due to an infestation of
Holly Trees; as for the winter – it's green and dank
beyond belief. When kept clean, its ok-ish.

*Top access & erosion beta: Go around to the right
and easily to the top.*

UK Trad	Fontainebleau colour (font grade)		Ticked

5c   **④** **Another Wet Bank Holiday** ✷✷ (f 5b)   S   TR

Very often greasy and totally unpleasant.
Solo: 1994 Mike Vetterlein   TR: 1994 Robin Mazinke

6a   **⑤** **Hazel** ✷ (f 5c)   S   TR

An arête with a tricky finish.
Solo: 2003 Graham West

HARRISON'S ROCKS

BOWLES ROCKS

HIGH ROCKS

HIGH ROCKS ANN-EXE

HAPPY VALLEY

BULLS HOLLOW

ERIDGE GREEN

UNDER ROCKS

STONE FARM

UK Trad   Fontainebleau colour (font grade)   Ticked

4c ① **Tree Route** ⚬ (f 3c)   S   TR
The groove in the centre.
Solo: 1996 Robin Mazinke

5a ② **Still, It Could Be Worse** ⚬ (f 4a)   S   TR
Damp.
Solo: 1996 John Patterson   *TR: 1996 Robin Mazinke*

5b ③ **Ooh-er Missus** ⚬ (f 4b)   S   TR
Climb the corner, tricky finish.
Solo: 1996 John Patterson   *TR: 1996 Robin Mazinke*

UK Trad   Fontainebleau colour (font grade)   Ticked

6a ④ **I'm a Tractor** ⚬ (f 5c)   S   TR
Green - Originally 'I'm not worried, I'm a Tractor.'
Solo: 1996 Tim Skinner   *TR: 1996 Robin Mazinke*

6a ⑤ **Local Vigilantes** ⚬ (f 6a)   S   TR
Powerful route up the centre.
Solo: 1996 John Patterson   *TR: 1996 Robin Mazinke*

6b ⑥ **1664** ⚬ (f 6c)   S   TR
A long reach may be required - plus strength.
TR: 1996 John Patterson

Local chat: This Green Buttress at Eridge Green is generally very green - and gets even greener throughout the year when periods of dampness and greenness arrive and the green moss spreads. This buttress is beyond green - so be prepared. Not to everyone's cup of tea, however, good climbing during an extended dry spell.

Access & Erosion: Go up to the right of the buttress easily to the top. A short static plus slings are required for the belay set ups.

Crag layout map - page 246
Graded tick list - page 248

HARRISON'S ROCKS

BOWLES ROCKS

HIGH ROCKS

HIGH ROCKS ANNEXE

HAPPY VALLEY

BULLS HOLLOW

ERIDGE GREEN

UNDER ROCKS

STONE FARM

UK Trad	Fontainebleau colour (font grade)		Ticked

4b ① Barbican Buttress☆☆☆ (f **3c**) S TR

The classic groove in the corner.

Solo: Pre 1950's

5a ② Eridge Tower Route☆ (f **4a**) S TR

Stuck around the back and not over inspiring.

Solo: Pre 1950's

5a ③ Battlements Crack☆☆☆ (f **4b**) S TR

A fierce and impending line - easy moves but tough.

Solo: Pre 1950's

5b ④ Optical Racer☆☆☆ (f **4c**) S TR

Just one hard move.

Solo: 1990's   *TR: 1989 Matt Smith*

UK Trad	Fontainebleau colour (font grade)		Ticked

5c ⑤ Portcullis☆☆☆ (f **5b**) S TR

A lovely route up the front of Eridge Tower.

Solo: 1980's Mick Fowler   *TR: Pre 1960's*

6a ⑥ Thrupenny Bit☆☆☆ (f **6a**) S TR

A variation to the traditional Portcullis.

TR: 2003 Malcolm McPerson

6a ⑦ Aero☆☆☆ (f **6a**) S TR

Climb the wall direct.

Solo: 1998 John Patterson   *TR: 1979 Mick Fowler*

6b ⑧ Steamroller☆☆☆ (f **6a+**) S TR

Centre line.

Solo: 1994 John Patterson   *TR: 1978 Mike Morrison*

Local chat: Eventually after wandering down the main track you will arrive at Eridge Tower. In winter this is prominent, yet in summer it gets enshrouded by trees with a giant leafy canopy. After a damp spell it is not so good, but does stay drgish when there are only light summer showers. The rock is quite soft, and has a lovely pocketed characteristic that allows for a varied style on most of the routes. Top feels very exposed - and solo here at your peril. All of the routes are classics and are worth ticking.

Access & Erosion: Go up to the left of the tower for easy access - take a wide loop to minimise ground slip. There are no belay points on top so you need to use a tree set some way back. Even with a static rope, the tree moves and will make the rope saw through the top edge - this must be protected so that the rope slides on the protector as it is weighted.

Crag layout map - page 246
Graded tick list - page 248

◁ [UK 5a] BATTLEMENTS CRACK (font 4b), The Wizard

HARRISON'S ROCKS

BOWLES ROCKS

HIGH ROCKS

HIGH ROCKS ANNEXE

HAPPY VALLEY

BULLS HOLLOW

ERIDGE GREEN

UNDER ROCKS

STONE FARM

Under Rocks is a hidden outcrop that is rarely visited by most climbers. The rock in most parts is very soft and friable and there isn't really anything worthwhile for bouldering. The central large pot holed wall (Uganda Wall) gives a very good array of top end 5c and low end 6a routes. The other climbs thereabouts are mostly for the record and are rather poor neighbours. As a climbing outcrop, it doesn't suit a group of mixed standard climbers unfortunately. As a beauty spot, it's unrivalled in late spring when the surrounding woodland is carpeted with bluebells and the tree canopy is light and airy. During summer, the lack of wind and heavy foliage can trap in the moisture and keep the spot pretty dank. Conversely, during a heat wave it makes for a really good hideaway.

Under Rocks is not the easiest of outcrops to find and by comparison with all of the other areas, it's fiendishly difficult. The normal approach is by following a very old track between hedges. After the winter rains, this can be somewhat squishy underfoot and many climbers resort to crossing the grazing fields directly. Usually the gates are left open, but there are also cross country fences to easily leap over and therefore leave any fences undamaged. The outcrop would appear to be on private land, but ownership is generally unknown. Climbing here has been going on for 30 plus years with seemingly no ill effect, local farmers seem pretty content that climbers do their own thing. Please do not do anything that could endanger access to this lovely spot.

Location: Under Rocks **SAT NAV info**
P1 - Parking Grid reference: **TQ 563 264**
P1 - Postcode **TN20 6NH**
Under Rocks Grid reference: **TQ 556 263**

Park nearby to P1, taking full consideration for local residents please. From the junction head South with the house Twits Ghyll house to your L. After 15 seconds, leave the road and bear right to follow a footpath into bushes, passing services markers in the ground to your right. This path soon curves around into an old lane, enclosed on both sides with tree hedges. After 6 mins the lane curves around to the left. At 7 mins, you arrive at a low cross country horse jump, turn right to stay high in the field, then drop down. 8 mins enter woods. 9 mins to the rocks.

[UK 6a] PRESSURE (font 6a), Klára Vlčkova ▷

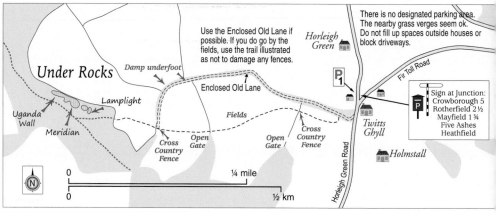

Uganda Wall   Evening Arête   Outfall   Meridian   Departure Slab   Lamplight

HARRISON'S ROCKS

BOWLES ROCKS

HIGH ROCKS

HIGH ROCKS ANNEXE

HAPPY VALLEY

BULLS HOLLOW

ERIDGE GREEN

UNDER ROCKS

STONE FARM

UK Trad	Fontainebleau colour (font grade)	Ticked		UK Trad	Fontainebleau colour (font grade)	Ticked

5c ① **Central Crack**☆☆☆ (f 5b) ✋ S TR
A classic corner that get progressively harder.
Solo: 1980's   *TR: 1960's*

5c ② **Uganda Wall**☆☆☆ (f 5b) S TR
Good holds arrive just in time.
Solo: 1983 David Atchison-Jones   *TR: 1960's*

5c ③ **Fireball**☆☆☆ (f 5b) S TR
Ironically, both Tim and David have been keen Fireball
sailors when not climbing or guidebook writing.
Solo: 1983 David Atchison-Jones   *TR: 1960's Tim Daniells*

6a ④ **Magic Pebble**☆☆☆ (f 5c) S TR
Shares a resting jug with Uganda Wall.
                    TR: 1970's

6a ⑤ **Dogs of War**☆☆☆ (f 5c) S TR
Angle of the wall allows resting - just!
                    TR: 1980's

6a ⑥ **Over the Hill**☆☆☆ (f 5c) S TR
A couple of pocket moves to thwart you.
                    TR: 1980's

6a ⑦ **Birthday Buttress**☆☆ (f 6a) S TR
Short and thin.
                    TR: 1995 Robin Mazinke

6a ⑧ **Pressure**☆☆☆ (f 6a) S TR
A cracker of a stopper move usually tests the belay.
                    TR: 1980's Climbers Various

6a ⑨ **The Thirteenth Light**☆☆☆ (f 6a) S TR
Intense wall climbing.
                    TR: 1970's

6b ⑩ **Lionheart**☆☆☆ (f 6a+) S TR
Hard bit is quite short - but intense, two ways possible.
                    TR: 1970's Tim Daniells

Local chat: This central wall is magical - a climbers playground. All of the routes are difficult, requiring a good use of sloping footholds combined with mono finger pockets. Those used to conglomerate rock should do ok here too. For the first visit - the grades seem tough, but after a while they seem reasonable - if not easy.

Access & Erosion: Go to the left when looking at the main wall, after 40 yards there is a gully to ascend - an old tree root provides adequate hand holds - if dry underfoot this is ok, going further along is easier. 4 slings should suffice if you don't mind taking a right swinger. A short static rope can be useful for belays at the top of some routes, and also backing up smaller trees near the top edge.

BOREAL

[UK 6a] MAGIC PEBBLE (font 5c), Klára Vlčkova ▷

HARRISON'S ROCKS

BOWLES ROCKS

HIGH ROCKS

HIGH ROCKS ANNEXE

HAPPY VALLEY

BULLS HOLLOW

ERIDGE GREEN

UNDER ROCKS

STONE FARM

◁ Trad   Fontainebleau colour (font grade)   *Ticked*

5b **(1) Evening Arête**☆☆☆ (f **4b**)   S TR

Climbing on the right side - top is the crux.
Solo: 1960's   *TR: 1960's*

5c **(2) Central Crack**☆☆☆ (f **5b**)   S TR

A classic corner that get progressively harder.
Solo: 1980's   *TR: 1960's*

*Local chat: This side wall is unfortunately blank
in the top section, but has plenty of poor holds in
the lower part which makes getting to the midway
break a real struggle - given such a short distance.*

UK Trad   Fontainebleau colour (font grade)   *Ticked*

5c **(3) The Touch**☆☆ (f **5b**)   S TR

A pretty stiff bottom wall using lower hold going up to a
right thumb press, then up to the rounded ledge.
Solo: 1983 Dan Wajzner   *TR: 1982 Barry Knight*

6a **(4) The Alien**☆☆☆ (f **5c**)   S TR

Originally named 'The alien succumbs to the intergalactic
funkativity of the funkblasters.' A fun eliminate.
Solo: 1990's   *TR: 1982 David Atchison-Jones*

*Access & Erosion: Go to the left when looking at
the main wall, after 40 yards there is a gully to
ascend - an old tree root provides adequate hand
holds - if dry underfoot this is ok, going further
along is easier. The fallen down tree at the top
gets in the way a bit, take an additional short
static rope to set up a suitable belay.*

◁ *[UK 5c] THE TOUCH (font 5b), Paul Robertson*

HARRISON'S ROCKS

BOWLES ROCKS

HIGH ROCKS

HIGH ROCKS ANNEXE

HAPPY VALLEY

BULLS HOLLOW

ERIDGE GREEN

UNDER ROCKS

STONE FARM

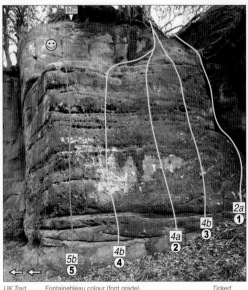

UK Trad   Fontainebleau colour (font grade)   Ticked

2a ① **Channelsea Crack** ✷ (f **2a**)   S TR
The easy grotty crack.
Solo: 1970's

4a ② **Speak No Evil** ✷✷ (f **3a**)   S TR
A mediocre short wall.
Solo: 1970's

4b ③ **See No Evil** ✷✷ (f **3b**)   S TR
Moss covered short wall.
Solo: 1970's

4b ④ **Hear No Evil** ✷✷ (f **3b**)   S TR
Another mediocre short wall.
Solo: 1970's

5b ⑤ **Evening Arête** ✷✷✷ (f **4b**)   S TR
Climbing on the right side - with some slopers to finish.
Solo: 1960's   *TR: 1960's*

Local chat: This prominent buttress offers some good routes up to the midway terrace, and are ideal for lower grade climbers - or even beginners. The outfall face to the right is nearly always manky and horrible. Only to be ever considered in the hottest of hot summers. (Don't be deceived by the relatively good looking appearance in the photo topo!)

UK Trad   Fontainebleau colour (font grade)   Ticked

5c ⑥ **Rapunzel** ✷ (f **5b**)   S TR
Flakey and soft rock, good when dry.
TR: 1970's George Hounson

5c ⑦ **Bow Locks** ✷✷ (f **5b**)   S TR
Steep and funky.
TR: 1994 Mike Vetterle

6a ⑧ **What the Buck** ✷ (f **6a**)   S TR
Very often "really" damp.
TR: 1990 Theseus Gerra

6a ⑨ **Outfall Crack** (f **6a**)   S TR
A diabolical, wet, skanky off width.
TR: 1993 Tim Skinne

Access & Erosion: Go past the main wall, then after 40 yards there is a gully to ascend - an old tree root provides adequate hand holds - if dry underfoot this is ok, going further along is easier. A few slings are good for this sector, but you may want to back up the edge belay so take an additional static rope.

K Trad	Fontainebleau colour (font grade)	Ticked

4a ① **Merlin** (f 3a)   `S` `TR`
A grotty wall.
Solo: 1995 Robin Mazinke   *TR: 1994 Mike Vetterlein*

5b ② **Peregrine**☆☆ (f 4b)   `S` `TR`
The easiest slanting line.
Solo: 1970's   *TR: 1970's*

5c ③ **Rapunzel**☆ (f 5a)   `S` `TR`
Flakey and soft rock, good when dry.
TR: 1970's George Hounsome

5c ④ **Dark Crack** (f 5b)   🗑 `S` `TR`
Dire and sandy.
Solo: 1983 David Atchison-Jones   *TR: 1970's Tim Daniells*

5c ⑤ **Bow Locks**☆☆ (f 5b)   `S` `TR`
Steep and funky.
TR: 1994 Mike Vetterlein

5c ⑥ **Kestrel**☆ (f 5b)   `S` `TR`
Overhanging and dirty.
TR: 1994 Mike Vetterlein

UK Trad	Fontainebleau colour (font grade)	Ticked

6b ⑦ **One Up**☆ (f 6a+)   `S` `TR`
Originally - 'One Up, All Up - Except Matt.'
TR: 1992 Paul Stone

6b ⑧ **Meridian**☆☆ (f 6b+)   `S` `TR`
Steep, but soft rock unfortunately.
Solo: 1995 Chris Murray   *TR: 1982 David Atchison-Jones*

6b ⑨ **Meridian Direct**☆☆ (f 6c)   `S` `TR`
Steep, but soft rock unfortunately.
Solo: 1995 Chris Murray   *TR: 1989 Paul Stone*

6b ⑩ **Mastercard**☆☆ (f 6c)   `S` `TR`
Steep and soft rock unfortunately.
TR: 1990 Paul Widdowson

6b ⑪ **Funnel Web**☆☆ (f 6c+)   `S` `TR`
Steep and even softer rock unfortunately.
TR: 1990 Paul Stone

Local chat: A very overhanging area. The rock has a dark brown crust which is only so hard, underneath it is very soft and sandy – hence the routes can easily change grade and will not be around for ever. Not often in condition. Quality of the climbing is excellent, but you do need to be a bit of a powerhouse.

Access & Erosion: Most people use the main access up the left side of the outcrop and go along the top to reach this sector.

HARRISON'S ROCKS | BOWLES ROCKS | HIGH ROCKS | HIGH ROCKS ANNEXE | HAPPY VALLEY | BULLS HOLLOW | ERIDGE GREEN | UNDER ROCKS | STONE FARM

Uganda Wall   Evening Arête   Outfall   Meridian   Departure Slab   Lamplight

HARRISON'S ROCKS
BOWLES ROCKS
HIGH ROCKS
HIGH ROCKS ANNEXE
HAPPY VALLEY
BULLS HOLLOW
ERIDGE GREEN
UNDER ROCKS
STONE FARM

UK Trad	Fontainebleau colour (font grade)		Ticked

1b ① Thorny Crack (f 2a)
Name says it all.
Solo: Pre 1960's

3a ② Roger's Wall (f 2a)
The short crackline to defeat most.
Solo: 1970's

4a ③ Departure Slab (f 3a)
Gets very overgrown in summer.
Solo: 1960's

5a ④ Lamplight☆ (f 4a)
Mediocre - but best of the bunch.
Solo: 1970's

5b ⑤ Magic Mushroom☆ (f 4b)
Very poor.
Solo: 1970's

UK Trad	Fontainebleau colour (font grade)		Ticked

5b ⑥ No Ghosts☆ (f 4b)
Not a bad small wall.
Solo: 1970's

5b ⑦ Trouble with the Rubble☆ (f 4c)
Friable rock, more difficult than it looks.
Solo: 1988 Andy Hughes

5c ⑧ The Waltzing Buzzard (f 5a)
A fair eliminate.
Solo: 1990 Mike Spencer   TR: 1992 Robin Mazin

5c ⑨ Manteloid (f 5b)
Very much a mantle.
Solo: 1993 Matt Smith   TR: 1990 Matt Sm

6a ⑩ Wind and Wuthering☆ (f 5c)
A fair eliminate.
Solo: 1990 Mike Spencer

Local chat: These are the firs two buttresses that you will see up on your right as you walk down the wooded dell. In late summer they can get almost overgrown, yet in winter and spring they are clearly seen. The rock is pretty soft – you certainly wouldn't be comfortable soloing any of these routes in the fear of the holds breaking off. Routes would no doubt be cleaner with traffic - but then again they would very likely to have completely worn away. Nothing brilliant, but worth doing once in a lifetime.

Access & Erosion: Don't expect a well worn trail to the top of these blocks. Access up either side, you will need a short static rope to reach the trees for a substantial belay. Also a static rope is handy to set up for the descent - which in rock shoes is rather sketchy.

tone Farm Rocks have a very different feel to the ain sandstone outcrops near Tunbridge Wells being smaller and set high on a hill with superb ews. The outcrop only just reaches 8 metres 24 feet) high - on top of the isolated Stone Farm boulder at the eastern end. For the most part, ne rock is generally about 6 metres high - but ease note, the topouts are never straightforward nd a top rope is advisable on most of the short imbs. There is good scope for bouldering here especially in the lower grades. The rock is soft owever, so even beginners should wipe their noes perfectly clean before bouldering. Use a rash pad to protect both the ground and yourself. here are some lovely grassy areas for a picnic, nd you only have to carry the champagne amper a short distance to the rocks.

The outcrop ownership is held in a charitable trust on behalf of the British Mountaineering Council and is managed by them. Various work is done to protect the habitat, so please take note of any signs that the BMC have put up. The site is also listed as a SSSI. All efforts must be made to ensure that minimal wear takes place due to the softness of the sandstone. Please do not scratch or deface the rock in any way at all, and only use a cloth rag to clean the rock if need be.
Belay bolts have been placed in the tops of many boulders, but climbers should be aware that unlike an indoor climbing centre, these are not checked regularly, and are not guaranteed. All climbers must judge for themselves if they are happy to use them. If in doubt, seek a strong tree to make an additional belay backup.

Location: Stone Farm Rocks **SAT NAV**
P1 - Parking Grid reference: **TQ 384 347**
P1 - Postcode **RH19 4HW**
Rocks Grid reference: **TQ 381 347**

Use big map on inside cover to arrive at parking. (Note: you sometimes get a long traffic tailback at Felbridge (jtn A264 & A22), a smart move is to approach East Grinstead on B2110 via Turners Hill.) There is room for about 4 cars at P1, if not - please do not block the small road.
P1: 2 mins walk, P2: 4 mins walk
To Rocks: From P1, go up the road for 50 yards (30 secs), then turn L at a rocky lump (opposite Stone Hill House), and follow a track-bridleway, rocks are in 200 yds on your left. From P2, use a concessionary footpath that leads up the hill to the rocks.

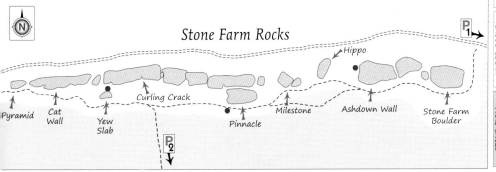

Stone Farm Rocks

Pyramid   Cat Wall   Yew Slab   Control   Curling Crack   Pinnacle   Milestone   Hippo   Ashdown Wall   Stone Farm Boulder

HARRISON'S ROCKS · BOWLES ROCKS · HIGH ROCKS · HIGH ROCKS ANNEXE · HIGH ROCKS ANNEXE · HAPPY VALLEY · BULLS HOLLOW · ERIDGE GREEN · UNDER ROCKS · STONE FARM

HARRISON'S ROCKS

BOWLES ROCKS

HIGH ROCKS

HIGH ROCKS ANNEXE

HAPPY VALLEY

BULLS HOLLOW

ERIDGE GREEN

UNDER ROCKS

STONE FARM

1b
- ☐ Pleasure Dome (f 1a) p311
- ☐ Root Chimney (f 2a) p300
- ☐ Choo Choo Mama (f 1c) p312
- ☐ Holly Leaf Crack (f 2a) p303

2a
- ☐ Yew Slab Arete (f 2a) p301
- ☐ Zog the Dog (f 1c) p312
- ☐ Step Up (f 2a) p311
- ☐ Inside or Out (f 2a) p304
- ☐ The Ramp (f 2a) p300
- ☐ Pinnacle Chimney (f 2a) p307
- ☐ Central Jordan (f 2a) p310
- ☐ Easy Crack (f 2a) p307

2b
- ☐ Bin the Trainers (f 2a) p311
- ☐ Intro Climb (f 2a) p312
- ☐ Medway Slab (f 2a) p299

3a
- ☐ Marmelade (f 2a) p312
- ☐ Tiger the Tiger (f 2b) p312
- ☐ Undercut Arete (f 2c) p304
- ☐ Dinosaurs don't Dyno (f 2b) p312
- ☐ Thomas the Tank (f 2b) p312
- ☐ Yew Left Me (f 2b) p301
- ☐ Garden Wall Crack (f 3a) p303

3b
- ☐ Obscene Gesture (f 2b) p298
- ☐ Pine Crack (f 2c) p300
- ☐ Bulging Corner (f 2c) p312
- ☐ Grooving Away (f 3a) p311

4a
- ☐ SE Corner Crack (f 3a) p317
- ☐ Open Chimney (f 3a) p312
- ☐ One Hold Route (f 3a) p298
- ☐ East Jordan (f 3a) p310
- ☐ Prelude (f 3a) p312
- ☐ Tiny Wall (f 3a) p312
- ☐ Pyramid Route (f 3a) p298
- ☐ The Face (f 3a) p300
- ☐ Pinnacle Buttress (f 3a) p307
- ☐ Milestone Arete (f 3a) p311
- ☐ Stone Farm Chimney (f 3a) p299

4b
- ☐ Epitaph (f 3b) p312
- ☐ Curling Crack (f 3b) p304
- ☐ Milestone Stride (f 3b) p311
- ☐ Kneeling Boulder (f 3b) p298
- ☐ Undercut Wall (f 3b) p304
- ☐ Stone Farm Crack (f 3b) p300
- ☐ Slab Buttress (f 3b) p300

4c
- ☐ Remote (f 3c) p303
- ☐ Yew Slab (f 3c) p301
- ☐ Ashdown Wall (f 3c) p312
- ☐ Primitive Groove (f 3c) p315
- ☐ Green Wall (f 3c) p317

5a
- ☐ Nobbly Knee (f 4a) p311
- ☐ Slab Buttress Left (f 4a) p300
- ☐ Hairy Scary (f 4a) p311
- ☐ Key Wall (f 4a) p308
- ☐ Green Face (f 4a) p317
- ☐ Pharoah's Curse (f 4a) p298
- ☐ North East Corner (f 4a) p317
- ☐ Slab Buttress Right (f 4a) p300
- ☐ SW Corner Scoop (f 4a) p314
- ☐ Key Wall RH (f 4a) p308
- ☐ Trans-A-Banana (f 4a) p312
- ☐ Leaning Crack (f 4a) p314
- ☐ Balham Boot Boys (f 4a) p317

5b
- ☐ Pincushion (f 4b) p307
- ☐ Pinnacle Arete (f 4b) p307
- ☐ Stepping Out (f 4b) p314
- ☐ Cheeky Little Number (f 4b) p307
- ☐ Diagonal Route (f 4b) p317
- ☐ Bulging Wall (f 4b) p312
- ☐ Kheop's Progress (f 4b) p298
- ☐ Jump Start (f 4b) p311
- ☐ Font Blue (f 4c) p311
- ☐ Praying Mantles (f 4c) p307
- ☐ Time Warp (f 4c) p315
- ☐ Front Face (f 4c) p304
- ☐ Sweet Carol (f 4c) p299
- ☐ Simpering Savage (f 4c) p317

5c
- ☐ Yew Wall Arete (f 5a) p301
- ☐ Clapham Common (f 5a) p317
- ☐ Pine Buttress (f 5b) p300
- ☐ Yew Just Crimp (f 5b) p301
- ☐ Mad as a Hatter (f 5b) p315
- ☐ Gus the Dog (f 5b) p304
- ☐ Thin (f 5b) p304
- ☐ Leisure Line (f 5b) p310
- ☐ Footie (f 5b) p299
- ☐ Bare Necessities (f 5b) p307
- ☐ Cat Wall (f 5b) p299
- ☐ Disillusion (f 5b) p304

6a
- ☐ Bulging Bastard (f 5c) p312
- ☐ Very Very Fat (f 5c) p304
- ☐ Backhander (f 5c) p311
- ☐ Belle Vue Terrace (f 5c) p308
- ☐ Wind Me Up (f 5c) p315
- ☐ Nose Direct (f 5c) p310
- ☐ Mania (f 5c) p304
- ☐ Ducking Fesperate (f 5c) p314
- ☐ Giza the Geezer (f 5c) p298
- ☐ Bare Essentials (f 6a) p307
- ☐ Illusion (f 6a) p304
- ☐ Boulder Wall (f 6a) p315
- ☐ Sticky Fingers (f 6a) p315
- ☐ Hungry Heart (f 6a) p314
- ☐ Absent Friends (f 6a) p310
- ☐ Poohped (f 6a) p312
- ☐ Barn Door Experience (f 6a) p307
- ☐ Concentration Cut (f 6a) p311
- ☐ Grave Digger (f 6a) p299
- ☐ Chalk and Cheese (f 6a) p299
- ☐ King Arthur (f 6a) p310
- ☐ Belly Up (f 6a) p307
- ☐ Control (f 6a) p303

6b
- ☐ Topcat (f 6a+) p299
- ☐ Control Freak (f 6a+) p303
- ☐ Chipperydoodah (f 6a+) p304
- ☐ Merton Mugger (f 6a+) p317
- ☐ Bellatissimo (f 6b) p308
- ☐ Excalibur (f 6b) p304
- ☐ Kathmandu (f 6b) p299
- ☐ Arthur's Little Problem (f 6b) p310
- ☐ More Footie Fun (f 6b+) p299
- ☐ Biometric Slab (f 6b+) p300
- ☐ Yew Wall (f 6b+) p301
- ☐ Milestone Mantle (f 6b+) p311
- ☐ Peter Pan (f 6b+) p315
- ☐ L'ottimista (f 6c) p308
- ☐ Fish and Chips (f 6c) p304

6c
- ☐ S-Nettle Var (f 7a) p315
- ☐ Birdie Num Nums (f 7a) p317
- ☐ Quoi Faire (f 7a) p308
- ☐ Stinging Nettle (f 7a+) p317
- ☐ Guy's Route (f 7a+) p314

BOREAL

THE ART OF CLIMBING

Tribal by

www.e-boreal.com

STONE FARM ROCKS - Pyramid

HARRISON'S ROCKS

BOWLES ROCKS

HIGH ROCKS

HIGH ROCKS ANNEXE

HAPPY VALLEY

BULLS HOLLOW

ERIDGE GREEN

UNDER ROCKS

STONE FARM

UK Trad		Fontainebleau colour (font grade)	Ticked			UK Trad		Fontainebleau colour (font grade)	Ticked	
3b	①	**Obscene Gesture** (f 2b)	S	TR		5a	⑤	**Pharoah's Curse** ☆☆ (f 4a)	S	TR

3b ① **Obscene Gesture** (f 2b)   S   TR
A simple fun route.
Solo: Pre 1960's

4a ② **One Hold Route** ☆ (f 3a)   S   TR
Topping out can prove awkward.
Solo: Pre 1960's

4a ③ **Pyramid Route** ☆☆ (f 3a)   S   TR
Awkward step up to start, sneaks off left.
Solo: Pre 1950's

4b ④ **Kneeling Boulder** ☆☆ (f 3b)   S   TR
Awkward step up to start, very good & airy finish.
Solo: Pre 1950's

5a ⑤ **Pharoah's Curse** ☆☆ (f 4a)   S   TR
A direct line with a beefy move.
Solo: 2000 Graham West

5b ⑥ **Kheops Progress** ☆ (f 4b)   S   TR
Fun.
Solo: 1970's

6a ⑦ **Giza the Geezer** ☆ (f 5c)   ⚖ S   TR
A good little mantleshelf problem - many solutions.
Solo: 1980 Guy McLelland

Local chat: This boulder marks the far end of the good climbing at Stone Farm Rocks. Beyond this, the rocks fizzle out and are not worth climbing on. This block offers some good bouldering - please use a crash pad - slightly too high for the comfort of many, but not that bad really since the top lump is not where the hardest climbing is.

Top access & erosion beta: Go up to the left or right. There are belay bolts for the central routes, but a sling - high in the tree is better for the left side routes - 4 slings should suffice.

Crag layout map - page 295
Graded tick list - page 296

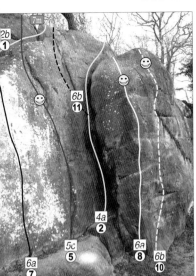

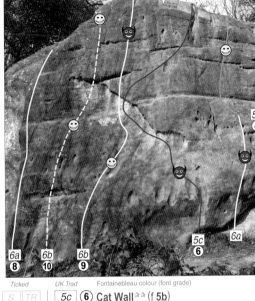

HARRISON'S ROCKS

BOWLES ROCKS

HIGH ROCKS

HIGH ROCKS ANNEXE

HAPPY VALLEY

BULLS HOLLOW

ERIDGE GREEN

UNDER ROCKS

STONE FARM

UK Trad	Fontainebleau colour (font grade)	Ticked

2b **(1) Medway Slab** (f 2a)
The easy groove starting bottom left.
Solo: Pre 1950's

4a **(2) Stone Farm Chimney*** (f 3a)
Awkward for beginners.
Solo: Pre 1950's

4b **(3) Stone Farm Crack**** (f 3b)
Technical and troublesome for beginners.
Solo: Pre 1950's

5b **(4) Sweet Carol*** (f 4c)
A very nice upper wall (tough font 6a lower section).
Solo: 1981 David Atchison-Jones

5c **(5) Footie**** (f 5b)
Climbing the wall without using the crack up right.
Solo: 1981 Gareth Harding   TR: 1970's

Local chat: Cat Wall got its name many years ago, because the climbers who frequented the area always used to visit The Cat Inn at West Hoathly afterwards, drinking 'Very pleasant draught Cider.' Unfortunately the ground below has subsided quite a bit, and a lot of the starting holds have worn away. Despite the wear, the climbs are still very good, many have highball cruxes.

Top access & erosion beta: Climb up the tree roots to the left of the buttress. There are some bolt belays for Footie and Cat Wall - 2 extension slings are a must. For Stone Farm Chimney - using a high sling on the tree is best. You will need a static extension for Kathmandu & Chalk.

UK Trad	Fontainebleau colour (font grade)	Ticked

5c **(6) Cat Wall**** (f 5b)
A difficult and powerful start (was once 5a).
Solo: Pre 1960's   TR: Pre 1950's

6a **(7) Grave Digger** (f 6a)
Boulder problem.
Solo: 1980's

6a **(8) Chalk and Cheese*** (f 6a)
The obvious arête.
Solo: 1983 Guy McLelland

6b **(9) Top Cat**** ☠ (f 6a+)
The good direct line.
Solo: 1990's   TR: 1980's

6b **(10) Kathmandu***** ☠ (f 6b)
The tricky direct line with an interesting finish.
Solo: 1990's   TR: 1981 David Atchison-Jones

6b **(11) More Footie Fun*** ☠ (f 6b+)
The tricky flake line going left.
    TR: 2008 Ian Bull

Note: The ground has subsided a good couple of feet here - please use crash pads at all times. Be very careful with placing your feet - do not scrabble with them, and make sure to step off a mat with very clean shoes.

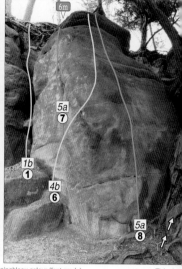

UK Trad	Fontainebleau colour (font grade)	Ticked		UK Trad	Fontainebleau colour (font grade)	Ticked

1b ① Root Chimney (f 2a)
Not good.
Solo: Pre 1950's

2a ② The Ramp (f 2a)
Fun without hands.
Solo: Pre 1950's

3b ③ Pine Crack (f 2c)
A classic beginners climb.
Solo: Pre 1950's

4a ④ The Face (f 3a)
Wall climb up past the old carved face.
Solo: Pre 1960's

4b ⑤ Stone Farm Crack (f 3b)
Technical and troublesome for beginners.
Solo: Pre 1960's

4b ⑥ Slab Buttress (f 3b)
A fun slab.
Solo: Pre 1950's

5a ⑦ Slab Buttress Left (f 4a)
Left of slab.
Solo: Pre 1960's

5a ⑧ Slab Buttress Right (f 4a)
Lower right of slab.
Solo: Pre 1960's

5c ⑨ Pine Buttress (f 5b)
Straight up the centre.
Solo: Pre 1960's

6b ⑩ Biometric Slab (f 6b+)
An eliminate.
Solo: 1980's Climbers various

Local chat: A popular spot down at the far end of Stone Farm. A couple of classic crack climbs that give a very good tussle for beginners. Some enjoyable harder routes that are surprisingly tricky. Slab Buttress remains in the shade all day and is a good place for a hot summer's afternoon.

Access & Erosion: Go up to the right clambering around the roots of the giant Yew Tree (or go left of Cat Wall). There are no bolt belays at present for Pine Buttress routes, and you will need a static rope, slings and edge protectors (bolt belays are planned). There is a holly tree at the top of Slab Buttress but you are advised to back up with a long static rope.

Pyramid Cat Wall Yew Slab Control Curling Crack Pinnacle Milestone Hippo Ashdown Wall Stone Farm Boulder

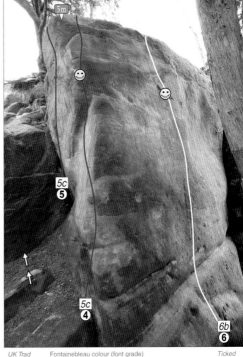

UK Trad	Fontainebleau colour (font grade)		Ticked

2a (1) Yew Slab Arête (f 2a)   S   TR

An arête, not quite hands free for most.
Solo: Pre 1950's

3a (2) Yew Left Me (f 2b)   S   TR

A good route short problem.
Solo: Pre 1950's

4c (3) Yew Slab * (f 3c)   S   TR

A lovely balance climb centre - can be done no hands.
Solo: Pre 1950's

Local chat: Yew Slab is a very good place for beginners to get used to the different friction of sandstone to that of an indoor climbing wall. There are many different problems that can be made up from the large selection of holds available.

Access & Erosion: Please do not attempt to climb anywhere on this block in trainers, normal shoes or boots. Clean your feet well first, and step off a clean piece of carpet. Definitely use a bouldering mat. A top rope can be set up using both trees to form a yoke above the centre of the slab.

UK Trad	Fontainebleau colour (font grade)		Ticked

5c (4) Yew Wall Arête * (f 5a)   S   TR

A tricky arête.
Solo: Pre 1960's

5c (5) Yew Just Crimp ** (f 5b)   S   TR

Left end of buttress.
Solo: 1999 A. Rowland

6b (6) Yew Wall * (f 6b+)   S   TR

The difficult slab.

TR: 2009 Barnaby Ventham

Local chat: Yew Wall is set up high above Yew Slab, and remains in the shade of the dense Yew Tree in front of it. The green dust on the routes soon dries out in summer and can be easily wiped off with a rag - please do not use a brush that may wear the fragile top protective skin of the sandstone rock.

Access & Erosion: You will need 4 slings and a back up static rope.

Crag layout map - page 295
Graded tick list - page 296

HARRISON'S ROCKS

BOWLES ROCKS

HIGH ROCKS

HIGH ROCKS ANNEXE

HAPPY VALLEY

BULLS HOLLOW

ERIDGE GREEN

UNDER ROCKS

STONE FARM

8m

6b ⑤

3a ②

4c ③

6a ④

1b ①

5a

6a

5a

HARRISON'S ROCKS

BOWLES ROCKS

HIGH ROCKS

HIGH ROCKS ANNEXE

HAPPY VALLEY

BULLS HOLLOW

ERIDGE GREEN

UNDER ROCKS

STONE FARM

UK Trad — Fontainebleau colour (font grade) — Ticked

1b ① Holly Leaf Crack (f 2a)
| S | TR |
A crack of little merit.
Solo: Pre 1960's — TR: Pre 1950's

3a ② Garden Wall Crack ☆ (f 3a)
| S | TR |
A good route.
Solo: Pre 1950's

4c ③ Remote ☆☆ (f 3c)
| S | TR |
A very easy start leads to an interesting top out.
Solo: 1960's

6a ④ Control ☆☆ (f 6a)
| S | TR |
More than just one move and poor footholds.
Solo: 1990's — TR: 1980's

6b ⑤ Control Freak ☆☆ (f 6a+)
| S | TR |
Finishing up the flake line.
Solo: 1980's — TR: 1993 Matt Smith

Local chat: Control Wall offers two very good easy routes, and two mid grade bastards. Nothing too hard – but no soft touches.

The small boulder bulge to the right may look attractive, but is very soft and sandy. Grades change with use so these - topo font grades are pretty academic.

Access & Erosion: Easiest up to the left beneath Yew Wall, but you can scramble up the right side fairly easily too. The top edge of Control must be protected, and since there are no ideal belays close - so you will need a static rope and edge protection. Set the belay karabiner quite low, then have a higher running belay karabiner to clip for the very hard move on the top slab.

BOREAL

◁ *[UK 6a] CONTROL (font 6a), The Wizard*

Crag layout map - page 295
Graded tick list - page 296

Pyramid   Cat Wall   Yew Slab   Control   Curling Crack   Pinnacle   Milestone   Hippo   Ashdown Wall   Stone Farm Boulder

HARRISON'S ROCKS
BOWLES ROCKS
HIGH ROCKS
HIGH ROCKS ANNEXE
HAPPY VALLEY
BULLS HOLLOW
ERIDGE GREEN
UNDER ROCKS
STONE FARM

UK Trad	Fontainebleau colour (font grade)	Ticked

2a **(1) Inside or Out**☆ (f 2a) — S TR
An awkward chimney.
Solo: Pre 1950's

3a **(2) Undercut Arête**☆ (f 2c) — S TR
Not too easy but pretty undercut.
Solo: Pre 1960's

4b **(3) Curling Crack**☆☆☆ (f 3b) — S TR
A jamming crack that will thwart beginners big time.
Solo: Pre 1950's

4b **(4) Undercut Wall**☆☆ (f 3b) — S TR
Pretty steep for most beginners.
Solo: Pre 1950's

5b **(5) Front Face**☆☆ (f 4c) — S TR
Very easy to fall off onsight, (harder on the left).
Solo: 1960's — *TR: Pre 1960's*

5c **(6) Gus the Dog** (f 5b) — S TR
A squeezed in eliminate scurrying off left.
TR: 2001 R. Hitchcock

5c **(7) Thin**☆☆ (f 5b) — S TR
Lives up to its name, quite off-on, easy to fall off.
Solo: 1970's — *TR: 1970's*

5c **(8) Disillusion**☆ (f 5b) — S TR
A very awkward excursion since the block is not allowed.
Solo: 1998 A. Smith — *TR: 1985 Barry Franklin*

6a **(9) Very Very Fat**☆☆ (f 5c) — S TR
Avoiding Thin.
Solo: 1970's — *TR: 1970's*

6a **(10) Mania**☆☆ (f 5c) — S TR
Steep and difficult to work out.
Solo: 1984 Paul Hayes

6a **(11) Illusion**☆☆ (f 6a) — S TR
It's all about technique.
Solo: 1980's — *TR: 1985 Barry Franklin*

6b **(12) Chipperydoodah**☆ (f 6a+) — S TR
Good start but poor finish.
Solo: 1980's — *TR: 1980's*

6b **(13) Excalibur**☆☆ (f 6b) — S TR
Powerful.
Solo: 1981 David Atchison-Jones

6b **(14) Fish & Chips**☆ (f 6c) — S TR
The short wall.
Solo: 1990's — *TR: 1980's*

Local chat: An excellent area with classic routes in just about all grades. Sunny and warm, the harder routes are not suited to hot sweaty conditions.

Access & Erosion: Go up either side. Some insitu bolts on top, but a static rope is needed for some routes.

[UK 4b] CURLING CRACK (font 3b), Sheena Murphy ≫

HARRISON'S ROCKS
BOWLES ROCKS
HIGH ROCKS
HIGH ROCKS ANNEXE
HAPPY VALLEY
BULLS HOLLOW
ERIDGE GREEN
UNDER ROCKS
STONE FARM

| UK Trad | | Fontainebleau colour (font grade) | Ticked | | UK Trad | | Fontainebleau colour (font grade) | Ticked |

2a ① Pinnacle Chimney (f 2a)   S TR
A simple excursion.
Solo: Pre 1950's

2a ② Easy Crack (f 2a)   S TR
Name is a giveaway.
Solo: Pre 1950's

4a ③ Pinnacle Buttress ✰✰✰ (f 3a)   S TR
Easiest way up this bit of rock.
Solo: Pre 1950's

5b ④ Pincushion ✰✰ (f 4b)   S TR
A difficult shortcut onto Pinnacle Buttress.
Solo: 1970's

5b ⑤ Pinnacle Arête ✰✰ (f 4b)   S TR
A good little route.
Solo: 1970's

5b ⑥ Cheeky Little Number (f 4b)   S TR
An eliminate avoiding the arête.
Solo: 2003 Robin Mazinke   *TR: 2002 Graham West*

5b ⑦ Praying Mantles ✰✰ (f 4c)   S TR
A very good eliminate.
Solo: 1980's   *TR: 1980's*

5c ⑧ Bare Necessities ✰✰ (f 5b)   S TR
Nothing too hard when you've got it wired.
Solo: 1984 Paul Hayes

6a ⑨ Bare Essentials ✰ (f 6a)   ♎ S TR
Going left at the top misses a good crux.
Solo: 1981 Gareth Harding   *TR: 1970's*

6a ⑩ Barn Door Experience ✰ (f 6a)   S TR
Interesting on-off moves staying on the right side.
Solo: 1980's Climbers various

6a ⑪ Belly Up ✰ (f 6a)   S TR
A somewhat awkward top out using rope grooves.
TR: 1995 Tim Skinner

Local chat: An area just a bit too high for relaxed fun bouldering. Some very good routes/highballs however.

Access & Erosion: Go up to the left via gully. Several insitu bolts on top - 2 slings needed.

◁ [UK 5c] BARE NECESSITIES (font 5b), Chez George

Crag layout map - page 295
Graded tick list - page 296

Pyramid   Cat Wall   Yew Slab   Control   Curling Crack   Pinnacle   Milestone   Hippo   Ashdown Wall   Stone Farm Boulder

HARRISON'S ROCKS

BOWLES ROCKS

HIGH ROCKS

HIGH ROCKS ANNEXE

HAPPY VALLEY

BULLS HOLLOW

ERIDGE GREEN

UNDER ROCKS

STONE FARM

UK Trad	Fontainebleau colour (font grade)	Ticked		UK Trad	Fontainebleau colour (font grade)	Ticked
5a	① **Key Wall**☆☆☆ ♀ (f 4a)	S TR		6b	④ **Bellatissimo**☆☆ (f 6b)	S TR

5a ① **Key Wall**☆☆☆ ♀ (f 4a)   S TR
Much more difficult than it looks.
Solo: Pre 1960's

5a ② **Key Wall-Right Hand**☆☆☆ ♀ (f 4a)   S TR
Drifting right is highball but good fun.
Solo: Pre 1960's

6a ③ **Belle Vue Terrace**☆ ♀ (f 5c)   S TR
Bold but not too tricky.
Solo: 1970's   TR: 1970's

6b ④ **Bellatissimo**☆☆ (f 6b)   S TR
A very good direct line - most jump off.
Solo: 1980's

6b ⑤ **L'ottimista**☆☆ ☠ (f 6c)   S TR
Low start and stay on the left side of the nose all the way
up. It has a long reach and a blind slap for the top out
sloper.
Solo: 2009 James O'neil

6c ⑥ **Quoi Faire**☆☆ ☠ (f 7a)   S TR
Quite a powerful move at mid height.
Solo: 1980's   TR: 1983 Guy McLelland

☐ ⑦ ....   S TR
Quite difficult.

*Local chat: At 8 metres high - and with some punchy
finishes, it makes for some dodgy high ball problems,
perhaps better attempted with a rope if you don't know
the numbers. A tree grows in front of the main south face,
keeping Quoi Faire a bit green during the summer months -
but with handy shade too. Not a huge number of routes, but
excellent ones at that. The big gap in the centre may yield
one day, very poor slopers.*

*Access & Erosion: A passage to the right leads up
behind the Pinnacle. A few 2a moves allow access to
the top. Bolts in the top of the pinnacle are used for the
belays. A few slings should be all that you need.*

*Note: The undercut nature of this block is very soft
sandstone, so please be careful with your feet and
wipe them clean before bouldering on the rock. Do
not boulder in trainers please, and use a crash pad to
protect the ground and limit erosion.*

Crag layout map - page 295
Graded tick list - page 296

[UK 6b] L'OTTIMISTA (font 6c), Chez George ▷

HARRISON'S ROCKS

BOWLES ROCKS

HIGH ROCKS

HIGH ROCKS ANNEXE

HAPPY VALLEY

BULLS HOLLOW

ERIDGE GREEN

UNDER ROCKS

STONE FARM

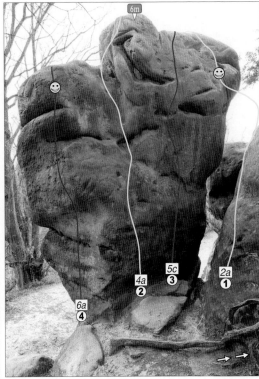

UK Trad	Fontainebleau colour (font grade)	Ticked

2a (1) Central Jordan ☆ ☠ (f 2a)   S   TR
Very straightforward.
Solo: Pre 1950's

4a (2) East Jordan ☆ ☠ (f 3a)   S   TR
Steady and good.
Solo: Pre 1950's

5c (3) Leisure Line ☆ ☠ (f 5b)   S   TR
Bold but not too tricky.
Solo: 1980's   *TR: 1980's*

6a (4) Nose Direct ☆☆ (f 5c)   S   TR
Top mantle is very awkward and has a nasty landing.
Solo: 1970's   *TR: 1970's*

Local chat: The back of the boulder remains shady and often damp. In a good dry period however, there are a couple of good mid grade routes. Nothing too special but fun anyway. There are a couple of short boulder problem routes on Arthur's Boulder – short and a bit bunched up.

Access & Erosion: Go up the passage to the right and then you have to solo the last few moves of Central Jordan. Incut good holds. Belay bolts on top of the Pinnacle.

UK Trad	Fontainebleau colour (font grade)	Ticked

6a (5) Absent Friends (f 6a)   S   TR
Boulder problem.
Solo: 1990 Mike 'Spence' Spencer

6a (6) King Arthur (f 6a)   S   TR
Boulder problem.
Solo: 1980's

6b (7) Arthur's Little Problem (f 6b)   S   TR
Boulder problem.
Solo: 1987 John Sharratt or Paul Hayes

Access & Erosion: Most will boulder these routes with a crash pad. If you do want to top rope the problems, you will need a static rope, plus slings to hold the top karabiner in place and stop it rolling off the block.

Crag layout map - page 295
Graded tick list - page 296

UK Trad	Fontainebleau colour (font grade)		Ticked
4a	**(1) Milestone Arête (f 3a)**		S TR
	A fun little problem.		
4b	**(2) Milestone Stride (f 3b)**		S TR
	A fun route up the crack system.		
6a	**(3) Concentration Cut (f 6a)**		S TR
	A very awkward step up using the pocket.		
6b	**(4) Milestone Mantle (f 6b+)**		S TR
	Getting to the mantle is now the difficult part.		

Local chat: Two fun boulders. Milestone Boulder is on the high side but not too bad – tends to be tricky. Hippo Boulder is a lovely size and ideal for lower grade climbers getting used to Sandstone friction. Please always use a crash pad to protect the ground – and yourself obviously.

UK Trad	Fontainebleau colour (font grade)		Ticked
1a	**(1) Pleasure Dome (f 1a)**		S TR
	Doing the nose without hands is fun.		
2a	**(2) Step Up (f 2a)**		S TR
	Easy wall with pockets.		
2b	**(3) Bin the Trainers☆ (f 2a)**		S TR
	Delicate toe work required.		
3b	**(4) Grooving Away (f 3a)**		S TR
	Very awkwardly placed holds will spit you off.		
5a	**(5) Nobbly Knee (f 4a)**		S TR
	The clue is in the name.		
5a	**(6) Hairy Scary (f 4a)**		S TR
	Finishing this is awkward.		
5b	**(7) Jump Start (f 4b)**		S TR
	Direct up the front nose.		
5b	**(8) Font Blue (f 4c)**		S TR
	Classic short problem.		
6a	**(9) Backhander (f 5c)**		S TR
	A mantle to thwart wall climbers.		

Side tabs: HARRISON'S ROCKS · BOWLES ROCKS · HIGH ROCKS · HIGH ROCKS ANNEXE · HAPPY VALLEY · BULLS HOLLOW · ERIDGE GREEN · UNDER ROCKS · STONE FARM

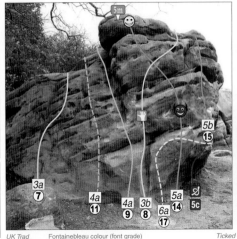

UK Trad	Fontainebleau colour (font grade)	Ticked
1b ①	Choo Choo Mama☆ (f 1c)	S TR
	The classic route to do with no hands allowed.	
2a ②	Zog the Dog☆ (f 1c)	S TR
	Straightforward.	
2b ③	Introductory Climb☆ (f 2a)	S TR
	The naturally easiest line.	
3a ④	Marmelade☆ (f 2a)	S TR
	Straightforward.	
3a ⑤	Tiger the Tiger☆ (f 2b)	S TR
	Fun up the centre.	
3a ⑥	Dynosaurs don't Dyno☆ (f 2b)	S TR
	The easy arête.	
3a ⑦	Thomas the Tank (f 2b)	S TR
	Short, delicate balance on green rock.	
3b ⑧	Bulging Corner (f 2c)	S TR
	Worn holds, not so easy for the short.	
4a ⑨	Open Chimney☆ (f 3a)	S TR
	More awkward than it looks.	
4a ⑩	Prelude☆ (f 3a)	S TR
	Worn holds make the start difficult.	
4a ⑪	Tiny Wall☆ (f 3a)	S TR
	Tricky.	

UK Trad	Fontainebleau colour (font grade)	Ticked
4b ⑫	Epitaph☆ (f 3b)	S TR
	Difficult move to leave the ground, wearing holds.	
4c ⑬	Ashdown Wall☆☆ (f 3c)	S TR
	Steep wall with good holds - but technical.	
5a ⑭	Transparent Accelerating Banana☆☆ (f 4a)	S TR
	Steep wall with a difficult finish, no cut holds allowed.	
5b ⑮	Bulging Wall☆ (f 4b)	S TR
	Steep wall with good holds - powerful.	
6a ⑯	Bulging Bastard☆ (f 5c)	S TR
	(f5c) Sit start and not using the right hand vertical crack.	
6a ⑰	Poohped☆ (f 6a)	S TR
	Low traverse with no hard moves, just stamina and negligable footholds.	

Local chat: Ashdown Wall is one of those perfectly sized bouldering walls with nice top outs. Plenty of holds to make up hundreds of variations and harder problems. A good selection of problems for anyone to warm up on.

Access & Erosion: Way up either left of right, insitu bolts on top - 2 slings needed. Please use a crash pad to protect the ground from wear, and only boulder with clean shoes.

[UK 5a] SOUTH WEST CORNER SCOOP (font 4a), Martin Randall ▷
Stone Farm Boulder

HARRISON'S ROCKS

BOWLES ROCKS

HIGH ROCKS

HIGH ROCKS ANNEXE

HAPPY VALLEY

BULLS HOLLOW

ERIDGE GREEN

UNDER ROCKS

STONE FARM

UK Trad	Fontainebleau colour (font grade)	Ticked		UK Trad	Fontainebleau colour (font grade)	Ticked
5a	**(1) SW Corner Scoop**★★★ ☠ (f 4a)	S TR		6a	**(4) Ducking Fesperate**★ ☠ (f 5c)	S TR

5a (1) SW Corner Scoop★★★ ☠ **(f 4a)**   S TR
Top part needs a steady head.
Solo: Pre 1950's

5a (2) Leaning Crack★★★ ☠ **(f 4a)**   S TR
A fierce start - with a delicate finish.
Solo: Pre 1950's

5b (3) Stepping Out★★ ☠ **(f 4b)**   S TR
Climbing the nose is pretty exposed.
Solo: Pre 1960's

6a (4) Ducking Fesperate★ ☠ **(f 5c)**   S TR
Sketchy in the top part.
Solo: 1980's   *TR:1970's*

6a (5) Hungry Heart★ ☠ **(f 6a)**   S TR
A very good excursion onto the upper in bulk wall.
TR: 1980 David Atchison-Jones

6c (6) Guy's Route★ ☠ **(f 7a+)**   S TR
Full on moves ascending the lower wall.
TR: 1980's Guy McLelland

Local chat: Stone Farm Boulder is one of the best climbing spots in the South East. There are great views and very clean rock which allow for some testing highballs & solos. Ideal for a picnic, sunbathing, etc. The exposed nature allows it to dry quickly. With water close by - the area will attract midges on a still summer's evening.

Top access & erosion beta: See East & North photo-topo. Climb up SE Corner Crack, the initial traverse being the crux. There are insitu bolts on the top, but you will need 3-4 slings for some of the routes, in order to keep the belay karabiner hanging clear over the edge.

HARRISON'S ROCKS

BOWLES ROCKS

HIGH ROCKS

HIGH ROCKS ANNEXE

HAPPY VALLEY

BULLS HOLLOW

ERIDGE GREEN

UNDER ROCKS

STONE FARM

UK Trad	Fontainebleau colour (font grade)	Ticked
4c	**(1) Primitive Groove**✮✮✮ 💀 (f **3c**)	S TR

A punchy start, then eases off happily.
Solo: Pre 1950's

| 5b | **(2) Stepping Out**✮✮ 💀 (f **4a**) | S TR |

Climbing the nose is pretty exposed.
Solo: Pre 1960's

| 5b | **(3) Time Warp**✮ 💀 (f **4c**) | S TR |

A full on highball for the grade.
Solo: 1982 David Atchison-Jones

| 5c | **(4) Mad as a Hatter**✮ 💀 (f **5b**) | S TR |

A dodgy high move.
Solo: 1980's

| 6a | **(5) Wind Me Up**✮ (f **5c**) | 🔒 S TR |

Lunge for the good holds then simply mantle.
Solo: 1980's Climbers various

UK Trad	Fontainebleau colour (font grade)	Ticked
6a	**(6) Boulder Wall**✮ 💀 (f **6a**)	S TR

A nasty highball.
Solo: 1980's

| 6a | **(7) Sticky Fingers**✮ (f **6a**) | S TR |

Toe in pocket, matching on the sloper & direct to top.
Solo: 1980's Climbers various

| 6b | **(8) Peter Pan**✮ (⚡f **6b+**) | S TR |

Direct up the wall, sit start from pocket.
Solo: 1990's Climbers various

| 6c | **(9) Stinging Nettle Variation**✮ (⚡f **7a**) | S TR |

Left hand in pocket with right underneath on sidepull.
Solo: 2002 Ian Stronghill

Crag layout map - page 295
Graded tick list - page 296

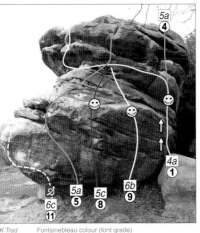
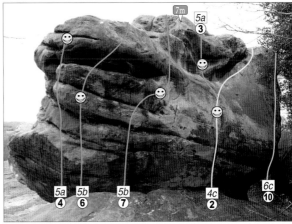

'K Trad	Fontainebleau colour (font grade)		Ticked

4a **(1)** SE Corner Crack ☆☆☆ (f 3a)   ☠   S TR

This is the easiest way up the boulder, but still hazardous.
Solo: Pre 1950's

4c **(2)** Green Wall ☆☆☆ (f 3c)   Slime S TR

The name is a clue to this north facing climb.
Solo: Pre 1950's

5a **(3)** Green Face ☆ (f 4a)   Slime S TR

The obvious direct finish - often greasy.
Solo: Pre 1960's

5a **(4)** North East Corner ☆ (f 4a)   S TR

Quite a nice delicate route - a bit highball.
Solo: Pre 1950's

5a **(5)** Balham Boot Boys ☆☆☆ (f 4a)   S TR

Quite good really, damn spiffing.
Solo: 1981 David Atchison-Jones

5b **(6)** Diagonal Route ☆☆ (f 4b)   Slime S TR

Usually greasy.
Solo: Pre 1950's

5b **(7)** Simpering Savage ☆ (f 4c)   S TR

A technical wall climb on greasy holds.
Solo: 1980's

5c **(8)** Clapham Common (f 5a)   ⚓ S TR

Obvious slots direct to mantle.
Solo: 1981 David Atchison-Jones

6b **(9)** Merton Mugger (f 6a+)   ⚓ S TR

Low start then struggle over the nose on the right.
Solo: 1980's

6c **(10)** Birdie Num Nums ☆ (f 7a)   Slime S TR

A boulder problem start to an easier finish.
TR: 1986 Ed Stone

6c **(11)** Stinging Nettle ☆ (∅ f 7a+)   S TR

Sit start right of the arête, with hands in the obvious break. Trend left and then left hand goes around arête to a tiny knobble, then finish straight up.
Solo: 2002 Ian Stronghill

Local chat: The north face of Stone Farm Boulder remains damp and slimey for most of the year. When dry it is fun, but don't hold your hopes up too much.

Top access & erosion beta: Climb up SE Corner Crack, the initial traverse being the crux. There are insitu bolts on the top, but you will need 3-4 slings for some of the routes, in order to keep the belay karabiner hanging clear over the edge. Note: Climbers are generally asked to climb down to minimise general wear on the rock. The top of SE Corner Crack is a bit tricky to reverse for the first time - so beginners should not solo down this.

Crag layout map - page 295
Graded tick list - page 296

◁ *[UK 6c] STINGING NETTLE (font 7a+), Ben Read*

HARRISON'S ROCKS · BOWLES ROCKS · HIGH ROCKS · HIGH ROCKS ANNEXE · HAPPY VALLEY · BULLS HOLLOW · ERIDGE GREEN · UNDER ROCKS · STONE FARM

HARRISON'S ROCKS
BOWLES ROCKS
HIGH ROCKS
HIGH ROCKS ANNEXE
HAPPY VALLEY
BULLS HOLLOW
ERIDGE GREEN
UNDER ROCKS
STONE FARM

HARRISON'S ROCKS
BOWLES ROCKS
HIGH ROCKS
HIGH ROCKS ANNEXE
HAPPY VALLEY
BULLS HOLLOW
ERIDGE GREEN
UNDER ROCKS
STONE FARM

HARRISON'S ROCKS

BOWLES ROCKS

HIGH ROCKS

HIGH ROCKS ANNEXE

HAPPY VALLEY

BULLS HOLLOW

ERIDGE GREEN

UNDER ROCKS

STONE FARM